About Island Press

Since 1984, the nonprofit organization Island Press has been stimulating, shaping, and communicating ideas that are essential for solving environmental problems worldwide. With more than 1,000 titles in print and some 30 new releases each year, we are the nation's leading publisher on environmental issues. We identify innovative thinkers and emerging trends in the environmental field. We work with world-renowned experts and authors to develop cross-disciplinary solutions to environmental challenges.

Island Press designs and executes educational campaigns, in conjunction with our authors, to communicate their critical messages in print, in person, and online using the latest technologies, innovative programs, and the media. Our goal is to reach targeted audiences—scientists, policy makers, environmental advocates, urban planners, the media, and concerned citizens—with information that can be used to create the framework for long-term ecological health and human well-being.

Island Press gratefully acknowledges major support from The Bobolink Foundation, Caldera Foundation, The Curtis and Edith Munson Foundation, The Forrest C. and Frances H. Lattner Foundation, The JPB Foundation, The Kresge Foundation, The Summit Charitable Foundation, Inc., and many other generous organizations and individuals.

The opinions expressed in this book are those of the author(s) and do not necessarily reflect the views of our supporters.

THE DIVIDED CITY

The Divided City

Poverty and Prosperity
in Urban America

Alan Mallach

Washington | Covelo | London

Island Press is a trademark of The Center for Resource Economics.

Library of Congress Control Number: 2017958895

All Island Press books are printed on environmentally responsible materials.

Manufactured in the United States of America
10 9 8 7 6 5 4 3 2

Keywords: affordable housing, Cleveland, Detroit, displacement, "eds and meds," gentrification, immigration, inclusion, industrial city, jobs, legacy city, millennials, mill towns, Philadelphia, Pittsburgh, poverty, public education, racism, real estate, small cities, St. Louis, transportation

Contents

Preface

The 1960s, the years when I went to college and entered the work world, were the era of the civil rights movement. They were also the era of urban renewal. The two came together for me when, as a Yale undergraduate, I joined the New Haven chapter of the Congress of Racial Equality and began to investigate the living conditions of people in neighborhoods undergoing urban renewal. I saw how the city was using federal dollars to buy up the homes of mostly poor people in mostly African American neighborhoods, and in the process had become the city's biggest slumlord. Hundreds of these people were living in squalor, neglected by the city, often without heat and other basic needs.

During those years, I also learned how pessimistic people in New Haven were about their city's future; I realized that for the city's politicians, urban renewal, even as it was undermining the city's neighborhoods, was a desperate roll of the dice in the hope that it might, somehow, alter what they saw as an otherwise inexorable path of decline. In those days, Yale was far from the economic powerhouse it is today. Officials saw no alternative other than to double down on what New Haven, in their eyes, had always been—an industrial city with a busy commercial downtown. Local officials convinced the city's two department stores to move to shiny new buildings, and persuaded some of the city's remaining factories to move to shiny new industrial parks, all on land cleared with federal dollars—but it didn't last. During the seventies and eighties the department stores closed, as did most of the factories.

When I think back to the sixties and seventies, I remember how daunting, even hopeless, the fate of the cities seemed. With riots seemingly a fixture of the urban landscape, whites fleeing the cities, and suburban shopping malls and office parks filling up with the stores and companies that had once been downtown, older cities all seemed to be on the same path of inexorable decline. As for myself, I spent much of my time during the seventies and eighties trying help poor people escape from the cities, by fighting suburban zoning barriers and trying to build affordable housing in the places to which those stores and companies had moved.

That changed in the nineties, when I went to work for the City of Trenton, New Jersey, as its director of housing and economic development. Despite being New Jersey's state capital, Trenton was basically an old factory town; in fact, it was much like New Haven without Yale. Once a manufacturing powerhouse, by 1990 it had lost most of its factories along with one-third of its population, and its downtown stores had gone out of business or decamped for suburban malls on Route One. I could no longer think of cities like Trenton as someone else's problem. Now they were my problem.

What I did and didn't do is not part of this story; I had some successes and some failures, got some things right and some things wrong. I also learned a lot about what was going on in Trenton and similar cities elsewhere in the United States, and I developed a fierce conviction that these places mattered. I left Trenton in 1999 after eight years on the job. Since then I've been spending most of my time visiting America's older once-industrial cities—as well as quite a few in Europe—listening to people, looking at a lot of data (I'm a numbers geek), and thinking and writing about them. It's been a great experience. I've seen a lot of interesting places, and made a lot of wonderful friends. From the beginning, though, I spent most of my time not in glamorous cities like New York or San Francisco, but in gritty cities like Detroit, Cleveland, Baltimore, and Flint. This book is about those cities, and it comes out of that experience.

I started my travels right at the turn of the millennium. At that point, there were a lot of signs that things might be picking up. More people were buying houses in cities like Newark and Cleveland. Property values were moving up. In 2000, I went to a forum in Washington, DC, held by the now-long-defunct Fannie Mae Foundation, where I heard one of the top housing market researchers in the county tell us that "the cities had the wind at their back" for the first time in recent memory. Only a few years later, though, it was becoming increasingly clear that a lot of that wind was coming from speculation and the subprime lending frenzy. Subprime mortgages grew rapidly as a part of the urban housing market starting around 2000, driving home prices in a lot of cities to levels that could not possibly be supported by the people living there. All of that came crashing to an end around 2006 or 2007.

At that point, with home prices plummeting and foreclosures rising exponentially, a lot of people wondered what would happen to the nascent urban boom. True, not everything I and others had observed during the previous years was fluff. Developers were rehabbing old factory buildings in Cleveland's Warehouse District and along Washington Avenue in St. Louis, putting up new houses in Chicago's Wicker Park, or constructing new apartment buildings in Center City Philadelphia. People, mostly young and childless, were moving into these places, and new stores and restaurants catering to their tastes were opening around them. Still, as foreclosures mounted, banks retrenched, and the nation fell into the Great Recession, I wasn't the only one wondering whether the first years of the new millennium would turn out to be just one more short-lived blip on the long downward urban trajectory that had begun after World War II.

Ten years later, as I write this, the answer is clear. It was not a blip, it was real. In many parts of the nation's older cities, in downtowns, around universities, and in neighborhoods like Shaw in St. Louis or Fells Point in Baltimore, demand came roaring back, led by young, well-educated millennials, a species for whom cities have become the natural habitat. Their habitat has steadily expanded; in Baltimore it has expanded beyond Fells Point, moving east along the inner harbor to Patterson Park and beyond, and west from the Johns Hopkins campus into Hampden and Woodbury. In Pittsburgh, it's moved up along the Allegheny River from downtown through the Strip District and into Lawrenceville. Million-dollar row houses and condos have become almost commonplace in Philadelphia, along with apartments where the monthly rent is higher than the monthly income of most Philadelphians. And people are moving to Philadelphia, buying those houses, and paying those rents.

Detroit, the largest American city ever to declare bankruptcy, is exuding new life. When I visited Detroit in 2003, and again in 2008, the city's downtown was all but deserted, as if people had turned the lights off and just walked away. I remember in 2003 standing in the middle of Grand Circus, a semi-circular downtown park ringed by handsome 1920s office towers, admiring the park's elegant landscaping; then, I looked upward, and realized that all the towers surrounding the park were empty shells. No longer. With a hefty assist from billionaire Dan Gilbert, downtown Detroit has begun to shine. One of the empty office buildings I saw on Grand Circus in 2003 is now the Aloft Detroit Hotel, where rooms go for close to $300 a night.

But something seemed badly off about this picture. By this point I was doing quite a bit of research on these cities, and one project powerfully brought what was going on home to me. A few years ago, I set out to map the extent of Milwaukee's gentrification. (I don't particularly like that word, because different people use it to mean so many different things, but I'll use it for now, and try to unpack its meanings in chapter 5.) When I looked at Milwaukee, I defined gentrifying census tracts as those that were low-income in 2000, and which showed above-average rates of increase in both household incomes and house prices from 2000 to 2012. Using that yardstick, I found a small cluster of tracts on the west bank of the Milwaukee River across from downtown that could be called "gentrifying." Not many. The entire area contained only about 1 percent of the city's population.

Then, I flipped the question. How many other areas had *declined*, I wondered, at the same rate that the gentrifying areas had improved, over the same period? The answer stunned me. At the same time that only a handful of the city's low-income census tracts were gentrifying, nearly half of the rest were getting poorer. It wasn't just that they weren't improving, but actually getting worse. People's incomes and the value of their homes, adjusted for inflation, were actually going down. The same was true in the city's middle-income neighborhoods, areas where people's incomes were roughly the same as the citywide average. Nearly half of them had lost significant ground since 2000; they too were getting poorer, and their homes were worth less. The only parts of Milwaukee—except for the gentrifying 1 percent—that had gained ground were the ones that were affluent to begin with.

I'm not picking on Milwaukee. The same pattern holds true in most of America's older industrial cities, to varying degrees. And yet, wherever I went in these cities, what people were talking about—shouting about, really—was gentrification. I had stumbled onto the cities' dirty secret, something a Detroit friend described to me as "the biggest problem nobody's talking about." Yes, the revival was real—all the hype was more or less true. But it was only touching small parts of these cities. Most of the rest were at best treading water, and a lot were going downhill. And a big part of it was about race. Cities were becoming more segregated, more polarized between poverty and prosperity, revival and decline, and black and white. For all the excitement and glitter of Baltimore's Harbor East, or Cleveland's University Circle, huge parts of these cities' people and neighborhoods were mired in poverty and despair, living surrounded by vacant lots and boarded-up houses, seeing little or nothing of their cities' newfound prosperity.

That's what I decided to write about. Not about New York and San Francisco, or the half-dozen or so hot coastal cities that get the headlines and dominate the blogosphere, but about the much larger number of cities in the American heartland, the former industrial cities that people are now calling "legacy cities," places like Buffalo or Cleveland, or the even larger number of smaller cities and factory towns, like Trenton, Youngstown, or Aliquippa, Pennsylvania.

This book is their story, not a flyover book about "cities" or "urbanism" but about real places and real people. I want to describe what is going on in these cities and explain why, but I also want to make the case that segregation and inequality are not baked into their future. There is a path, however difficult and demanding it may be, to more-inclusive future cities, where everyone has a shot at opportunity and a share in their community's prosperity. I hope this book can help bring this future a bit closer.

Acknowledgments

This book would have been impossible to write without the help of many, many friends, colleagues, and others from whom I have learned or who have inspired me with their work and commitment, as well as the organizations that have supported me, over the course of many years. I am particularly grateful to the Center for Community Progress, which has provided me with the ideal base for my activities over the past seven years, giving me a place where I could work on issues that deeply engage me along with the support and camaraderie of wonderful people sharing a common vision and mission. To all my present and former colleagues at the Center: you have my deepest gratitude and affection.

I want to thank Bruce Katz and his colleagues at the Brookings Institution, and Mac McCarthy and his colleagues at the Lincoln Institute of Land Policy, both of whom have supported my work for many years, for their support and friendship. My thanks also go to my city planning students at Pratt Institute, on whose critical minds I've tried out many of the ideas in this book as they evolved over the past few years.

Over those same years I have shared ideas with, argued with, and learned from many people, and have been inspired by the work others have done to build stronger neighborhoods and help people find the path to opportunity—two categories that often overlap. Among them are Frank Alexander, Heidi Alcock, Karen Beck Pooley, Ian Beniston, Karen Black, David Boehlke, Mike Brady, Lance Jay Brown, Nico Calavita, Don Carter, Joan Carty, Mike Clarke, Sean Closkey, Sabina Deitrick, Joe Della Fave, Margie Dewar, Frank Ford, Ben Forman, Yasuyuki Fujii, John Gallagher, Bill Gilchrist, Presley Gillespie, Ira Goldstein, Adam Gordon, Adam Gross, Annegret Haase, Nick Hamilton, Nicole Heyman, Dan Immergluck, Pete Kasabach, Dennis Keating, Jim Kelly, Congressman Dan Kildee, the late Joe King, Jen Leonard, Lisa Levy, Kermit Lind, Wayne Meyer, Hunter Morrison, Patrick Morrissy, Marcia Nedland, Ray Ocasio, Joel Ratner, Aaron Renn, Rick Sauer, Michael

Selden, Harold Simon, Joe Schilling, Michael Schubert, John Shapiro, Tamar Shapiro, Emily Silverman, Ken Steif, Tom Streitz, Brett Theodos, Steve Tobocman, Linda Warren, Bob Weissbourd, and Thorsten Wiechmann. I'd especially like to single out Lavea Brachman, Michael Braverman, Paul Brophy, Charles Buki, and Todd Swanstrom, five people with whom I've had the good fortune to speak often and who share clarity of mind, seriousness of purpose, and a deep commitment to cities and to social justice; and also Diane Sterner, who for many years has been my valued friend and colleague, sounding board, and critic. I apologize to the many other people who deserve to be on the list, but whom I have inadvertently and regrettably omitted.

I would like to thank Brad Garton and David Herrstrom, two friends who have no professional connection with my work, for reading and discussing with me initial drafts of much of this book; and my editor, Heather Boyer, whose engagement with this book has been a model of what the editor's role should be, but today so rarely is.

Finally, I'd like to thank two people whom, although they may not realize it, I have always thought of as mentors: George Sternlieb, who brought home the importance of looking facts in the face and following them wherever they might lead, and the late Paul Davidoff, who showed me what it meant to live a life devoted to the cause of social justice. I'd like to thank my parents, who taught me the lesson that a life without purpose is not much of a life; and finally, as always, my deepest appreciation and gratitude to Robin, my lifelong companion and partner, who has been with me every step of my journey.

Introduction: Revival and Inequality

Something very important and very exciting is happening in America's cities. It's no longer just happening in a few hot coastal cities like New York and Seattle, but has spread to a host of older industrial cities in the nation's heartland, to places like Baltimore, St. Louis, and Detroit. Well-educated young millennials are flocking to these cities in unprecedented numbers, and areas like Harbor East in Baltimore and Washington Avenue in St. Louis are throbbing with energy and excitement. In St. Louis, a new apartment building called the Orion has just opened in the city's Central West End, a neighborhood once on the shabby side but now tony. It has a Whole Foods on the ground floor, and the rent for the top-of-the-line apartments is over $5,000 per month, a lot more than what the average family in St. Louis makes in a month. Yet people are moving to St. Louis and paying those rents.

Downtowns are coming to life. Hundreds of one-time office buildings, warehouses, and factories have been converted into apartments and condominiums; new stores, restaurants, and night spots have opened up. Only a few years ago, Woodward Avenue, Detroit's main drag, was deserted after 5:00 p.m. Now it is bustling with life and activity well into the night. The factories are gone, but universities and medical centers are creating thousands of new jobs. Pittsburgh's Carnegie Mellon University and the University of Pittsburgh are spinning off tech start-ups and cutting-edge self-driving-car research. Pittsburgh, Philadelphia, and Baltimore have become global tourist destinations.

This isn't happening everywhere. Some of these cities are doing a lot better than others, and small cities like Flint or Dayton are still struggling. But for a lot of cities once all but given up for dead by politicians and pundits, the cities that people are starting to call America's "legacy cities," the last fifteen or twenty years have seen a remarkable transformation.

It adds up to a complex, exciting, yet deeply troubling picture. The revival is real. Across the United States, people no longer see cities as a problem but as places of opportunity and vitality. The mere idea that tens of thousands of talented young people, in many respects the best and brightest of their generation, would actively choose to live in cities like Baltimore, St. Louis, or Pittsburgh is exciting, particularly for those of us who can remember how city after city fell apart during the 1960s and 1970s as neighborhoods burned down and millions fled.

Yet that excitement is badly tarnished by the reality that in the process, these cities are turning into places of growing inequality, increasingly polarized between rich and poor, white and black, with unsettling implications for their present and future. Some areas have rebounded strongly from the mortgage bust and the Great Recession, but others are falling further behind. Some neighborhoods have been revived or gentrified, but others have become poorer and more dilapidated. In St. Louis, it's only a short walk north from the glittering Central West End to block after block of poverty, abandoned houses, and vacant lots. Cities have more rich people and neighborhoods, and more poor ones, but fewer in the middle. Thousands of new jobs have been created, but fewer and fewer of the cities' residents are working. Housing prices have risen faster than incomes, and tenants face crushing cost burdens. The median tenant in Baltimore spent 30 percent of her income for rent in 2000; by 2015, that had risen to nearly 40 percent. When mayoral candidate Bill de Blasio described New York City in 2013 as "a place that . . . has become a tale of two cities," he could have been speaking about any large city in the United States.[1]

From one legacy city to the next, as some areas gentrify, many other neighborhoods, including many that were pretty solid, relatively stable working-class or middle-class neighborhoods until fairly recently, are falling off a social and economic cliff. More often than not, the hardest-hit neighborhoods are disproportionately African American. Black neighborhoods saw more subprime lending and more foreclosures, are less likely to have recovered from the housing bust and the recession, and less likely to be seeing in-migration, whether through gentrification or otherwise. Thousands of African American homeowners are losing what little wealth they had and are seeing their neighborhoods fall apart around them. If you rely on the media, you might think that gentrification is the big story of American cities in the twenty-first century, but that has more to do with the fact that most of our information comes out of a handful of coastal cities where it really *is* the big story, places like Washington, DC, or Seattle. Gentrification may be happening in a few corners of Detroit, but the big story in that city—even if it doesn't get the attention it deserves—is the persistence of concentrated, debilitating poverty and the decline of once-healthy, vital neighborhoods.

Some of this reflects national trends—the shift from manufacturing, with the loss of solid working-class jobs and the decline of the industrial unions—all factors that have led the middle class, in economist Robert Samuelson's words, to be "hollowed out, as more Americans find themselves in either upper- or lower-income households. The extremes grow at the expense of the center."[2] A parallel phenomenon is known as "economic sorting," in which neighborhoods have tended to become either richer or poorer, with fewer left in the middle. Yet broad national trends tend to be magnified in the older cities, where poverty and wealth confront one another in the next block, across the street, or on the sidewalk.

American cities have always had rich and poor. In 1890, reformer Jacob Riis wrote, with his anger and indignation vividly coming through, that "three-fourths of [New York's] people live in the tenements . . . the hot-beds of the epidemics that carry death to rich and poor alike; the nurseries of pauperism and crime that fill our jails and police courts; that throw off a scum of forty thousand human wrecks to the island asylums and workhouses year by year; that turned out in the last eight years a round half million beggars to prey upon our charities; that maintain a standing army of ten thousand tramps with all that that implies; because, above all, they touch the family life with deadly moral contagion."[3]

That was a reality, although to be fair, far more people were able to live decent lives and raise healthy children in those tenements than Riis ever gave them credit for, while conditions in most other industrial cities, where most people lived in their own houses, perhaps with a roomer or two, were rarely as bad as in New York. At the same time, though, others flaunted their wealth to such an extent that the era has come to be known as the "Gilded Age"—an age of excess and corruption, lavish banquets at Delmonico's and pretentious seafront "cottages" in Newport.

While inequality grew worse in the 1920s and persisted through the Great Depression, after World War II the United States moved toward greater equality as we became a nation in which more and more people were fundamentally middle-class, and fewer either particularly wealthy or poor. Experts estimate that when Jacob Riis was writing, as many as two out of three Americans lived in poverty.[4] By the end of World War II, it was one of three, and by 1973, that number had been cut by two-thirds, to 11 percent. This is a remarkable transformation. Since 1980, though, as Thomas Piketty and others have taught us, we have steadily moved back to the inequality of the Gilded Age, nowhere more than in the nation's older cities.

There are three dimensions to inequality in American cities—spatial, economic, and racial—all closely related. Baltimore shows this starkly. In 2015, the median house sales price in Baltimore was about $75,000. In twenty-nine census tracts, about one out of seven, the median price was over $200,000, as shown in the map on the left (fig. 0-1).[5] In the national picture, $200,000 isn't that much for a house. In 2015, it was about 10 percent less than the national median sales price for existing homes, which, according to the National Association of Realtors, was $222,400. But it's a lot for Baltimore. These areas are tightly concentrated: about half wrap around the Inner Harbor, while the other half include a cluster around Johns Hopkins University and historically upscale Roland Park and Mount Washington to the north. This small area, where 15 percent of the city's population lives, contains almost half of the total residential real estate value in the city.

Sales price over $200,000 in 2015   African American population share
under 25 percent

Figure 0-1 Sales Price and Race in Baltimore. (Source: PolicyMap)

As the map on the right shows, though, these areas are not only the most expensive and most affluent areas in the city, they are also, with few exceptions, the whitest. In a city that is nearly two-thirds African American, the population of the high-value, high-income census tracts is almost 90 percent white. None of them are majority black, and only two tracts are over one-third African American. One local blogger calls it the "white L" surrounded by the "Black Butterfly."[6]

Baltimore is typical. In some respects, these cities are increasingly integrated. Black faces are prominent in the most modest and the most upscale restaurants and boutiques. More than one hundred African American families live in Roland Park, Baltimore's ritziest neighborhood. At the same time, in Baltimore and elsewhere, most areas tend to be either predominately white or predominately black. The ones that are more mixed tend to form a penumbra around the edges of largely African American neighborhoods; there are fewer of them, and they are often in transition from one form of racial preponderance to the other.

Why is this happening? Why is the revival of America's industrial cities leading to such an increase in racial, economic, and spatial polarization? There are so many different reasons, as to suggest that this outcome was all but inevitable. Some of these are baked into larger trends, such as demographic shifts in the American population or global economic trends, while some reflect what's been taking place in the cities themselves, like the outward flow of the African American middle class. At the same time, still others reflect political and economic *choices*; in other words, the outcomes might have been different if the people with the power to make decisions and control the resources had made those decisions and spent those resources differently.

Demographic change has both helped and harmed in different ways. The influx of single, childless, college-educated people in their twenties and thirties, whom I call Young Grads, eager to be part of a diverse, vital urban scene and increasingly inclined to defer marriage and childrearing, is the fuel that has revived downtowns and selected neighborhoods in city after city. At the same time, the erosion of the middle class, particularly the traditional childrearing married-couple family that was historically the norm in American urban neighborhoods, has all but undone the neighborhoods that make up much of the rest of the city. The number of children in the cities, particularly those from middle- and upper-income families, has continued to decline. Not unreasonably, urban commentator Joel Kotkin has called the twenty-first-century city a "post-familial city," a city that is "increasingly childless and focused on the individual."[7]

The erosion of the middle class, although a national phenomenon, has had a far greater impact on older cities than on the rest of the country. For decades, poor schools, aging housing, fear of crime, and deteriorating public services have driven families who could afford it to move from the cities to the suburbs. And even as Young Grads have begun to fill up empty buildings in downtown neighborhoods, families continue to move to the suburbs. In recent decades, despite an often powerful emotional commitment to their cities, more and more African American families have decided to make that move.

One-time industrial powerhouses have seen their local economies go through wrenching change. Cities like Pittsburgh, Detroit, and Buffalo were icons of America's industrial might, manufacturing cities above everything else. Factories sustained the local economy, and, after the union battles of the 1930s, the Wagner Act and postwar prosperity, the jobs they offered ensured that working-class men with little formal education could earn enough to support a family with dignity and become part of the middle class. Those jobs are all but gone, and most of the people who hold the few good factory jobs that still exist in places like Detroit or Cleveland today live in the suburbs.

That story is partly about globalization and the changing nature of manufacturing, but it's mainly about the cities themselves. Manufacturing is alive and well in the United States, but not in the cities that were the cradle of America's industrial might. Companies walked away from obsolete plants in congested urban areas for modern plants where they could operate more efficiently and hire a cheaper nonunion workforce to replace the well-paid workers they left behind. A lot of new factories have opened since the 1980s in the United States, but they aren't in the older cities, or for the most part in Northeastern or Midwestern states. They are in the South and West, in Texas, California, and South Carolina. While automation has reduced the number of factory jobs, manufacturing is still going strong in the United States—but not in Detroit, Buffalo, or Flint.

In the more fortunate cities, like Baltimore and Pittsburgh, burgeoning global universities and medical centers have substituted in some ways for their lost factories, but as they've done so, they've drawn from an increasingly suburban, well-educated workforce. Factory workers, who were proud of their work and were part of a rich, multilayered culture built around the factory, the union, and the neighborhood, have found themselves adrift in a new and alien environment. City residents who lack specialized skills and college degrees have found themselves out in the cold, often quite literally in the case of those who now commute long hours to poorly paying jobs in suburban Walmarts, shopping malls, and nursing homes.

America's legacy cities are old places in a country where many people have always preferred things to be new and shiny. Age and history may be a draw in walkable downtowns and historic districts with Victorian houses, but those areas are only a small part of each city. Houses in cities outside the reviving, gentrifying core are also old—even in the newest areas they tend to be over fifty years old—and usually suffer from deferred maintenance, or they need substantial repairs. Most are ordinary, and often have only one bathroom. They have postage-stamp yards and are far smaller than what most of today's homeowners are looking for.

Even where the houses themselves might appeal to middle-class families, the neighborhoods they are part of may be less appealing, with struggling schools, endemic crime and disorder, crumbling streets and sidewalks, neglected parks, and public services that are erratic at best. Meanwhile, just around the corner from every legacy city are one or more inner-ring suburbs that, while not without their own problems, are at least somewhat safer, with schools that are (or are perceived to be) better, and where houses are affordable to almost any family earning at least $30,000 or so, the minimum that makes one a credible candidate for homeownership, whatever the price of the house.

Powerful as these changes have been, this transformation was far from simply a matter of inevitable social and economic change. All of the changes were paralleled by public policies that led to disinvestment in the cities, razed vital black neighborhoods in the name of urban renewal or the interstate highway system, and promoted suburbanization for white people through racial covenants and FHA restrictions—while locking African Americans and poor people in central cities, and starving those cities of the resources they need to provide the services their residents and workers need. While much of this is in the past, its legacy still haunts the cities; even today, state legislatures still roll back even modest efforts by cities like Cleveland or St. Louis to improve conditions for their workers by raising minimum wages or requiring local hiring on construction projects.

All of this adds up to a complicated, seemingly contradictory picture. In the 1970s and 1980s, neighborhood decline was seen not unreasonably as part and parcel of the overall economic decline of the nation's older cities. Now these cities are seeing levels of investment and activity beyond the wildest hopes of those decades, yet at the same time large segregated, poverty-stricken ghettoes house thousands of people for whom revival has brought little new hope or opportunity, and once-healthy neighborhoods of modest, well-tended homes are turning into the slums of tomorrow. The tide is rising, but it's not lifting many boats.

It's not that people in these cities don't know what's going on. In contrast to the national media and some urban pundits, who have difficulty grappling with complexity, and tend to look at cities either as dystopian settings for *Robocop* movies or as feel-good comeback stories, plenty of local people get it. And thousands of them have brought amazing energy and determination to their efforts to make their cities better places not just for upscale millennials but for everyone. Yet for all of their hard work and small wins, it's just not working. We need to admire their efforts and celebrate their achievements, but we also need to drill down to understand why, for all their hard work over many decades, things are not getting better, and even the cities where revitalization efforts *are* working continue to become more and more polarized places with more rich people and more poor people and fewer in the middle, more upscale neighborhoods but also more poor, struggling, or neglected ones.

And we have to ask, if all our efforts are barely making a dent, what that means for the future of America's older, once-industrial cities. Because these cities matter. Not only do millions of people live in America's legacy cities, and even more millions in suburbs that are inextricably linked to those cities and their future, but also, because as America becomes more urban, cities are increasingly regaining their historic role as the economic engines of their states and their regions. As the United States grapples with the difficult challenges of the twenty-first century, to paraphrase Eldridge Cleaver, our cities can be part of the solution to those challenges—or part of the problem itself.

Today, America's once industrial and now postindustrial cities appear to be on a trajectory to a future in which they become more and more polarized places where bustling, glittering enclaves of prosperity are ringed by declining or largely abandoned areas, and where millions are relegated to lives of poverty and hopelessness. These cities are at a crossroads. There is no inherent reason why today's trends could not continue to the point where American cities may resemble the Jakarta that David Smith describes: where behind "the veneer of great commercial activity, prosperity, and growth, . . . in the less visible parts of the city—in slums off the main avenues and sprawling squatter settlements and shanty-towns on the outskirts of the metropolitan area—the masses of Jakartans live starkly different lives."[8]

This is not a future that we should aspire to, either for our cities or as a nation. In the heyday of these cities' industrial prosperity at the beginning of the twentieth century, these cities were also economically polarized places, where the rich lived in mansions and the poor in tiny row houses and tenements. But for all their dirt, grime, and poverty, they were first and foremost places of opportunity, places that propelled the mass of Americans into the middle class and created a standard of living for our nation that became the model for the rest of the world.

The problem is not that today's American cities have poor people living in them. The problem is that the cities have largely stopped being places of opportunity where poor people come to change their lives, and that today's poor and their children remain poor, locked out of the opportunities the cities offer. The most pressing question facing the cities is whether that can change, and whether, as they continue to revive, they can once again become the places of hope and opportunity they once were.

This is what this book is about. It is the story of what has really been going on in America's older industrial cities since the turn of the millennium, why it is happening, what that means for their future, and how, I believe, the path they are on can be changed. That story begins with the large economic, social, and demographic changes that are driving the transformation of these cities, but it doesn't end there. It is about how those changes relate to the complexities of race, poverty, and power, and how those complexities translate into the changing reality on the ground. It is about how real cities like Detroit and Baltimore, and real neighborhoods in those cities, have become very different places from what they were only a short while ago, and how that in turn has changed the lives of the people who live in those cities and neighborhoods.

In chapter 1 of the book I set the stage, describing how America's industrial cities became such potent centers of prosperity and opportunity, and then how, after World War II, they fell into the long decline from which they have only begun to revive. The next two chapters look at the broad changes in American society and the economy that have most powerfully driven the change in the cities. In chapter 2, I show how changing demographics and consumer preferences, including the rise of the millennial generation, the decline in the traditional married-couple family, and the rise of immigration have fundamentally changed the character of the cities and their neighborhoods, while in chapter 3, I show how, as the factories closed, new economic sectors, most prominently health care and higher education, came to dominate these cities' economies.

The next three chapters might be summed up as "space and race"; they look at the shifting neighborhood dynamics of legacy cities. Chapter 4 begins where any serious discussion of the American city needs to begin—with the persistent significance of race, as seen not least in the persistence and spread of urban ghettos (racially defined areas of concentrated, multigenerational poverty) in the midst of the urban revival, and how the pernicious legacy of racial discrimination and segregation is still a powerful force, just below the surface. As William Faulkner famously said, "The past is never dead. It's not even past."[9] Chapter 5 is about gentrification. I look at what is actually happening, how it is affecting neighborhoods and their residents, and at the critical subtext underlying why it has become such an intense, polarizing controversy. Chapter 6, then, looks at the opposite side of the coin, which is the widespread decline of neighborhoods that were until recently vital places, and the many forces working to undermine their vitality.

Chapter 7 changes the focus to ask a very different but also difficult question. I look at why the hundreds of smaller once-industrial cities, factory towns, and aging suburbs are falling so badly behind their bigger-city counterparts, and I try to explain why size matters so much more in today's economy than in these places' heyday. In the next chapters, I move on to look at how people have tried to tackle the critical challenges faced by the older industrial cities. In chapter 8, I look at how cities, community development corporations, and others are trying to reverse neighborhood decline and breathe new life into disinvested, struggling neighborhoods, and I grapple with some of the reasons why their efforts have largely been unsuccessful, while in chapter 9, I look at the reasons for the opportunity gap and the persistence of poverty, and the efforts, often remarkably successful, that people have made to bridge the gap through education and training, as well as some of the reasons why those efforts haven't spread further than they have.

The last two chapters turn back to the big issues that I've laid out in these pages. Chapter 10 explores how each city's course is driven by local policies and decisions, how those decisions in turn reflect the power dynamics of the city, what that means in terms of how we should think about equity and opportunity, and why all successful strategies must, in the final analysis, be local strategies. Finally, in chapter 11, I offer a body of broad, far-reaching, and in a few cases perhaps controversial recommendations aimed at bringing about greater equity and opportunity, while simultaneously sustaining the legacy cities' revival. Their revival, although real, is still fragile; yet, unless that revival is sustained, few of the opportunities of which people dream can ever become a reality.

I believe that far greater equity and inclusion are achievable, and that cities can once again be places of hope and opportunity for the many, not just the few. It will be a far more complicated task, though, than either the liberal mantra of more programs and more money—although that can help—or the conservative mantra of unleashing the unbridled power of the market—although the market is an important part of the picture—would have us believe. I do not want to join the crowd of people offering laundry lists of federal programs or simplistic invocations of the market, nor do I want to offer utopian solutions no more plausible than the rise of Atlantis from the bottom of the sea. Instead, I ask what must happen to change a trajectory that is both driven by powerful social, economic, and demographic forces, and tied to equally powerful realities of power and politics.

Those realities are national and global, but also intensely, powerfully local. America's cities are actors, not merely passive bystanders or victims. The federal government can help in myriad ways, but ultimately, the decisions that determine whether people are included or excluded, and whether opportunity becomes a reality for those who have been left behind by revival, will be made locally by local actors. What that means, in turn, is that any successful movement for equity and opportunity must be above all a local movement—or rather, hundreds of separate local movements. It will be a long, hard slog, city by city and metro by metro. It will be a struggle, but one well worth the effort. It is part of the struggle for the soul of our country.

Chapter 1

The Rise and Fall of the American Industrial City

The Founding Fathers' United States was a narrow strip of land along the Atlantic Ocean, an agrarian country whose cities were centers of trade, not industry. While that began to change soon after the end of the Revolution, as the Northwest Ordinance opened up vast tracts of the Midwest to settlement, for years western places like Pittsburgh, Detroit, or Cincinnati were small villages, barely more than fortified outposts, situated along rivers and surrounded by forests still largely populated by long-established Native American peoples. As late as 1820, more people lived on the island of Nantucket than in the city of Pittsburgh.

These Midwestern towns were small, but not sleepy. They bustled with an entrepreneurial energy that in some ways was greater, and certainly more single-minded, than in cities back East; Frances Trollope, visiting Cincinnati in 1828, noted with disdain that "every bee in the hive is actively employed in search of that honey . . . vulgarly called money."[1] At the time, Cincinnati was by far the largest town west of the Alleghenies, a status it retained until the Civil War. Over the next few decades, as millions of migrants moved westward, one city after another emerged along the region's rivers and lakes, linked first by canals and then by railroads. In 1837, a different, more generous English visitor could describe Detroit "with its towers and spires and animated population, with villas and handsome houses stretching along the shore, and a hundred vessels or more, gigantic steamers, brigs, schooners, crowding the port, loading and unloading; all the bustle, in short, of prosperity and commerce."[2] By the eve of the Civil War, Cincinnati, St. Louis, Chicago, and Buffalo were all among the ten largest cities in the United States.

Most manufacturing in the early years of the nineteenth century was still taking place on the East Coast, in large cities like New York and Philadelphia as well as in dozens of smaller cities around them. Lowell, Massachusetts, and Paterson, New Jersey, were founded as mill towns and grew into cities; the first potteries making tableware were founded in Trenton early in the nineteenth century, while Peter Cooper and Abram Hewitt opened their first iron mill in that city in 1845.[3] By the middle of the century, Philadelphia was calling itself the "workshop of the world."[4] These East Coast cities were soon rivaled, though, and in many industries overtaken by the growing cities of the Midwest.

Midwestern cities were hives of industrial activity from the beginning; an 1819 directory of Cincinnati listed two foundries, six tinsmiths, four coppersmiths, and nine silversmiths; a nail factory, a fire engine maker, fifteen cabinet shops, sixteen coopers (barrel makers), and many more.[5] Detroit's shipyards started out as repair yards, soon branched into manufacturing marine engines, and by the 1840s were making steamships for the growing Great Lakes trade. All this activity was fueled by a growing regional market as the population of Northwest Territories exploded. From an 1810 population of 12,282, Illinois's population reached 1.7 million by 1860, second in the Midwest to Ohio, which by then had over 2.3 million residents. This population explosion was driven not only by continued migration from the East, but also by the arrival of the nation's first mass immigration, from Germany and Ireland, just before mid-century.

While long-settled cities like Boston and Philadelphia had dignity if not grandeur, Midwestern cities, for all their ambition, were still modest affairs. A late-nineteenth-century description of 1860 Detroit noted that "only a few leading thoroughfares were paved. There were neither street railways nor omnibus lines. Old-fashioned drays did the hauling.

There were no public street lamps except in the central part of the city. [...] There were but three stone business fronts."[6] Still, there were intimations of greater things to come; pictures of Cleveland from the 1850s, when it was still a small city of only 17,000, show an impressive row of four-story masonry buildings along Superior Avenue leading to the lavishly landscaped Public Square, then and now the heart of the city (fig. 1-1).

Figure 1-1 A city in the making: downtown Cleveland in the 1850s. (Source: Western Reserve Historical Society)

For all the bustle and activity of its cities, though, the United States on the eve of the Civil War was still an agrarian nation. Only one out of six Americans lived in towns of more than 2,500 population. Fewer than 19,000 of Indiana's 1.3 million people lived in Indianapolis, the state's largest town; of Illinois's 1.7 million people, only 112,000 lived in Chicago, the state's only city of any size, whose economy was still heavily based on meatpacking and other agricultural products, which were shipped back East. Except for a handful of Northeastern mill towns, no American city could be characterized as an "industrial city"; most factories other than textile mills were small in scale, more like workshops than the vast factories that emerged after the Civil War.

That changed quickly. By the late 1880s, the United States had become the world's leading industrial nation, while in the thirty years following the Civil War, places like Cleveland and Detroit had gone from overgrown towns to become major urban centers. Historians and economists have singled out many different reasons for the simultaneous explosion of industrialization and urbanism in late-nineteenth-century America—so many that one is led to believe that America's industrial supremacy was meant to be. America had everything: rich lodes of natural resources such as coal and iron; ample and inexpensive energy sources; a far-flung, efficient transportation infrastructure; a growing and increasingly affluent domestic market; transformative technological innovations, such as the Kelly-Bessemer process that turned steelmaking from an artisanal to an industrial process; a flourishing entrepreneurial culture operating with few restraints curbing its activities; seemingly inexhaustible sources of inexpensive immigrant labor; and, of course, the leadership of a powerful band of inventors, financiers, and industrial barons, whose names, whether acclaimed or reviled, still resonate as giants in the American saga: Carnegie, Rockefeller, Morgan, Vanderbilt or Edison.

It wasn't pretty. Workers worked long hours, under grueling and often dangerous conditions; "you don't notice any old men here," said a laborer in Carnegie's Homestead Mill in 1894. "The long hours, the strain, and the sudden changes of temperature use a man up."[7] In contrast to the small workshops of the past, the new steel mills were vast, impersonal places employing thousands of people. In Carnegie's mills workers worked twelve-hour days, seven days a week, with only the Fourth of July off. Death and dismemberment were routine daily events. Safety regulations and limits on working hours or child labor were all still in the future.

Living conditions outside the factories were often not much better. With the social safety net also still in the future, poverty and destitution were widespread. Thousands of immigrant families were crammed into tiny houses, often sharing them with one or more other families. While tenements were rare outside New York City, conditions in Baltimore's alley houses or Newark's triple-deckers were often only marginally better. In 1900, two or more families doubled up in over half of all the houses and apartments in Worcester, Massachusetts, and Paterson, New Jersey.

Yet that was not the entire story. As the century neared its end, remarkable transformations took place in city after city, particularly in the great Midwestern cities that were at the heart of the nation's industrial expansion. As these cities' prosperity grew along with their middle-class populations, they became true cities, not merely in the sense of large agglomerations of people and business activity but, following as best they could the models of ancient Athens or renaissance Florence, as centers of civic, cultural, and intellectual life. While their achievements may have fallen short of those ideals, they were nonetheless notable.

Much of the cities' efforts were devoted to beautification, often emulating the boulevards and palaces of the great cities of Europe. After Frederick Law Olmsted completed Central Park in Manhattan and Prospect Park in Brooklyn, the next city to commission work from him was Buffalo, followed by Chicago and Detroit. Buffalo, indeed, hired Olmsted to design not only a park, but an entire network of parks and landscaped parkways forming a green ring around this gritty industrial city. Following on the heels of the 1893 Columbian Exposition in Chicago, Daniel Burnham and his colleagues created an elaborate Beaux Arts plan for downtown Cleveland featuring a three-block landscaped mall 400 feet wide, flanked by the city's principal civic buildings, including the county courthouse, city hall, public library, and public auditorium. During the same years, the great downtown department stores came into being, as did the first wave of skyscrapers, led by the "father of skyscrapers," Chicago's Louis Sullivan.

Physical embellishment was matched by cultural embellishment, taking the form of universities, symphony orchestras, and museums, but even more by civic improvement. Reform movements sought to clean up hitherto corrupt municipal governments, ameliorate the living conditions of the poor, introduce proper sanitation, electrify the streets, modernize public transportation, and provide universal public education, introducing all of these features into what had become increasingly polluted and crowded utilitarian places. Lincoln Steffens hailed Cleveland's Mayor Tom Johnson in 1905 as "the best mayor of the best-governed city in the United States."[8] There was no doubt that the civic leaders of these cities saw them as great cities; as the governor of Illinois said at the 1889 dedication of Chicago's Auditorium Building, it was "proof that the diamond of Chicago's civilization has not been lost in the dust of the warehouse, or trampled beneath the mire of the slaughter pen."[9]

Beaux Arts schemes like the Cleveland mall may have existed at least in part to burnish the self-image of the cities' leadership, but the transformation of the industrial city was not merely for the benefit of the elite. Despite—or perhaps because of—sustained labor and civic unrest, the nature of the urban working class was changing. Trade unions were organized, while immigrants became Americanized and their children steadily moved into the middle class. And move they did; as research studies have shown, intergenerational mobility in the United States was at its height from the end of the Civil War to the 1920s, and far greater than in Western Europe at the same time.[10] Although it may have become rare for skilled workingmen to open small factories and modestly prosper, the transformation of the American economy had opened up millions of new middle-class jobs for armies of industrial and retail clerks, salesmen and saleswomen, government officials, and the growing ranks of professionals, while factory jobs themselves were increasingly propelling people into the middle class. By 1900, nearly two out of every five families in Cleveland, Detroit, and Toledo owned their own homes, and in contrast to crowded New York City, only one out of eight Detroit families, and one out of fourteen in Toledo, shared their home with another family.

The great industrial cities of the Midwest were only the most visible parts of the nation's industrial archipelago. During the latter part of the century, manufacturing grew by leaps and bounds, with 2.5 million factory jobs added between 1880 and 1900. In cities as varied as Philadelphia, Pittsburgh, Cincinnati, and Newark, two out of every five workers worked in factories. By 1900, manufacturing had come to dominate the economies of one-time merchant cities like New York, Philadelphia, and Baltimore, while hundreds of smaller cities like Trenton, New Jersey, Reading, Pennsylvania, or Lima, Ohio, each had its factories, its immigrant neighborhoods, and its trappings of prosperity in the form of parks, concert halls, and pillared city halls.

Trenton is an archetypal small industrial city. Famous for its role in the American Revolution, its industrial history began in the 1840s with small pottery manufactories, as they were called, and an early iron mill that made rails for the region's growing number of railroads. As the century progressed, both industries grew. The presence of Peter Cooper's ironworks brought a German immigrant named John Roebling to Trenton, where he established his own factory for the construction of steel cables; by late in the nineteenth century, over seventy ceramics factories and workshops had been established, from Lenox, makers of fine china, to the predecessors of the Crane and American Standard makers of sanitary porcelain. Other industrial products of the city included rubber tires, canned foods, and one of the sportiest of the early automobiles, the Mercer Runabout. The city's population grew from 6,000 in 1850 to 73,000 by the turn of the century and nearly 120,000 by 1920, including thousands of immigrants, mostly from Italy and Poland.

As was true of far larger cities, as Trenton grew, it took on the trappings of prosperity. In 1891, Frederick Olmsted's Cadwalader Park opened to the public, while in 1907, a new Beaux Arts city hall with an imposing marble-pillared façade was dedicated. The city's sense of itself as first and foremost an industrial city was reflected in the decoration of the new council chambers, which featured a large mural by Everett Shinn, a prominent member of the Ashcan School of American artists. In two vivid panels, it depicts the fiery interiors of the city's iconic industries, the Maddock ceramics factory on the right, and the Roebling steel cable plant on the left, both all but dripping with the sweat and the exertion of Shinn's muscular workingmen. About the same time, the local Chamber of Commerce held a competition to coin a new slogan to epitomize the city; the winning entry, "Trenton Makes—the World Takes," was mounted in 1911 on a bridge across the Delaware River. The same sign, albeit in a new digital version, still heralds one's arrival in Trenton by train from Philadelphia and Washington.

As Robert Beauregard writes, "the first two decades of the twentieth century, and the latter decades of the nineteenth occupy a privileged position in American urban history."[11] It was not to last. Although it is customary to think of the decline of American cities as beginning after the end of World War II, the first signs of decline were visible as early as the 1920s. One intimation was the growth of the suburbs, as the nation's transportation systems began to shift from rails and water to a new system based on the car and the truck, the road and the highway. The number of private cars in the United States more than doubled between 1920 and 1925; by 1925, there were over 17 million cars and 2.5 million trucks on the country's increasingly congested roads, and half of all American households owned a car.

With little fanfare, suburbs began to grow. Earlier streetcar suburbs had remained small, limited to chains of villages along the spokes established by commuter railroads and streetcar lines; now, suburbs could be built anywhere, and they began to fill in the spaces between the spokes, ringing the now largely built-up city with what gradually became a wall of separate towns, villages, and cities locking central cities into their pre-1920s boundaries. While most cities continued to grow during the 1920s, their growth rates were slowing, especially after the drastic restrictions on immigration that went into effect after 1924.

Industry was beginning to disperse as well. St. Louis was the nation's leading shoe manufacturer, but during the course of the 1920s, as Teaford explains, "St. Louis shoe moguls were shifting much of their production to plants in impoverished small towns scattered through southern Illinois, Missouri, Kentucky, Tennessee, and Arkansas. [...] Corporate headquarters would remain in St. Louis and the other heartland hubs, but the corporations' factories would depart."[12] With water power no longer needed to fuel industry, many of Lowell's famous textile mills decamped to the South during the 1920s. The city saw its population shrink by over 10 percent during the decade. Although Lowell has been growing again since the 1980s, it has yet to completely regain the population it had in 1920.

The increasingly footloose nature of American industry reflected changes in the structure of the urban economy in ways that marked the beginning of the end for what historian John Cumbler has called "civic capitalism," or the interconnected network of locally based entrepreneurs and capitalists who were part of the fabric of each industrial city, and who saw their fortunes intertwined with those of their communities.[13] As Douglas Rae writes about New Haven, "Beginning even before 1920, a great many local firms, including the largest and most productive, would be drawn out of the local fabric by increasingly muscular and invasive national corporations, . . . headquartered far from the city, and thus escap[ing] the control of locally rooted managers and owners."[14] While civic capitalism was paternalistic, and often exploitative, it was also linked to the community, not only through companies' contributions to their city's physical and social well-being, but also in their economic calculus, which balanced hard economics with local loyalty. Hard economics was on the rise, and local loyalty less and less relevant.

Although these changes were noticed by acute observers in the 1920s, they did not prompt widespread concern. Lowell was an exception. Most cities were still growing, and most had yet to see any significant industrial exodus. Although more and more people were living in the suburbs, their numbers were modest compared to what was to come later, and the great majority of each region's population still lived in the central city. Suburbanites may have lived outside the city, but they still came downtown to work, to shop, or go to the movies. With automobiles now crowding the streets and new skyscrapers like Cleveland's iconic Terminal Tower going up, cities seemed livelier and more dynamic than ever.

The next fifteen years, though, were a roller-coaster ride for America's industrial cities. The Great Depression devastated the cities. As early as July 1930, one-third of Detroit's auto jobs had disappeared, leaving 150,000 workers idle. Factories were closed, banks collapsed, and homebuilding nearly ground to a halt. By 1933, half of Cleveland's total workforce was unemployed; as a local newspaperman wrote, "Threadbare citizens daily trooped into newspaper offices, without a dime to buy a sandwich, looking for handouts. The welfare offices were swamped, and unable to furnish emergency relief."[15] As late as 1936, 143,960 people, or one out of every four Buffalo residents, lived on relief or make-work.[16]

While New Deal programs had begun to alleviate the effects of the Depression by the late 1930s, it was World War II that reversed the downward spiral, though just briefly. Factories that had been idled came back to life. Detroit's auto industry was retooled to make tanks and airplanes, and the city came to be known as the "arsenal of democracy"; author Hal Borland wrote in 1941 that "this mammoth mass-production machine has a wholly new tempo, a grim new purpose. Smoke rises from a thousand stacks. [...] Detroit is busier than it has been for years, and the wheels are speeding up."[17] Hundreds of thousands of whites from

Appalachia and African Americans from the Deep South flocked to the city; with little new housing being built, they crowded into existing houses and apartments, built shantytowns, and camped out in city parks.

The thirties and forties were also years of extraordinary turmoil and social change in America's industrial cities. The 1930s saw the rise of the industrial union through a wave of strikes that often prompted violent responses; the 1937 sit-down strike against General Motors turned the city of Flint, Michigan, into an armed camp, "with more than 4,000 national guards . . . including cavalry and machine-gun corps."[18] After many such labor battles, unions like the Steelworkers and the United Automobile Workers had firmly inserted themselves into the American economy. By 1943, the UAW had become the largest union in the United States, and by 1949 its membership exceeded 1 million workers.

Violent conflict often also marked the mass migration of African Americans, drawn by the work to be found in the cities and the decline of traditional Southern agriculture. Racial conflict had been a recurrent theme ever since large-scale black migration began during the years of World War I and immediately after, when the Ku Klux Klan found fertile soil in many Northern cities. Tensions simmered in many cities during the 1930s and 1940s, overflowing in Detroit in 1943, when a fight that began in the city's Olmsted-designed Belle Isle Park triggered three days of violence, leaving thirty-four dead and hundreds injured. It was both the culmination of decades of conflict and a harbinger of what was to come in the 1960s.

As World War II ended and the troops came home, it was not unusual to expect that life and work in the cities would return to normal, which for many people meant life as it had been during the years before the war and the Depression. And so it appeared, at least for a while. Even though, in hindsight, the evidence of urban decline was visible almost from the end of the war, the late 1940s and the 1950s were not bad years for most industrial cities. Factories quickly retooled for domestic markets, and by 1948, America's carmakers produced over 5 million vehicles, nearly 4 million of them passenger cars. Steelmaking in Pittsburgh was bigger than ever. The Jones & Laughlin Company embarked on a massive expansion of their flagship plant to meet postwar demand, while conversion of plants from coal to natural gas was making the city's air cleaner than it had been for a long time. Pittsburgh's notorious pea-soup fogs were becoming a thing of the past. While the number of factory jobs in cities like Pittsburgh and Cleveland fell off from their World War II levels, there were still more people working in those cities' factories in 1958 than in 1939. And for the most part, they were doing well; as Ray Suarez puts it, "after World War II, the bosses were making so much money that even the workers were in for a taste. Everybody was working, in folk memory and in fact."[19]

Housing production picked back up. From the end of the war to 1960, nearly 100,000 new homes and apartments were built in Detroit and even more in Philadelphia. Home ownership took off in the central cities, not just the suburbs. From 1940 to 1960, the homeownership rate in Detroit went from 39 to 58 percent, in Philadelphia from 39 to 62 percent, and in Akron from 49 to 67 percent. In 1960, nearly three out of four families in Flint, mostly headed by men working in the GM plants, owned their own homes, 15,000 of which were newly built in the 1950s.

Neighborhoods seemed largely unchanged from prewar days, and if different, often for the better. In 1960, almost half of all the households in Dayton and Youngstown were married couples raising children (compared to 8 percent today), and most of the rest were married couples who had either not yet had their first child, or just seen their youngest leave the nest. To hear from Suarez again, "the teeming ethnic ghettos of the early century had given way to a more comfortable life, with religious and ethnicity, race and class still used as organizing principles for the neighborhood. The rough edges of the immigrant 'greenhorns' were worn smooth, and a confident younger generation now entered a fuller, richer American life."[20]

It is easy to romanticize the cities of the 1950s, and Suarez, along with some others who have written about those years, sometimes fall into that trap despite their best efforts. Large parts of the cities were shabby places that had been starved of investment since the 1920s. Most cities were still segregated like St. Louis, where the "Delmar divide," the unwritten law that no African American could live south of Delmar Boulevard, was violated at peril to life and limb. Yet a strong case can be made that, taken as a whole, the 1950s were the best years America's industrial cities had ever seen. If the era lacked the raw energy and dynamism of the turn of the century years, it more than made up for it in the far greater quality of life it offered the majority of its residents. Working conditions were far better, and thanks in large part to the growth of unions, wages were higher. Most families now owned their own homes, and doubling up, or taking in boarders to make ends meet, were things of the past.

Yet these thriving cities were dancing on the edge of the abyss, and the signs were there for those who looked closely. The prosperity of the cities reflected the growing prosperity of the nation, masking the reality that their share of the pie had begun to shrink. For all the new houses being built, the cities were drawing few new residents. The 1950 Census marked the population high-water mark for most of America's industrial cities. While some cities continued to grow or, like Chicago and Cleveland, experienced only modest losses during the 1950s, others saw their population plummet. Milwaukee lost 130,000 people, or 15 percent of its 1950 population, while Pittsburgh and St. Louis each saw their population drop by more than 10 percent.

The nation's energy had begun to shift irrevocably from the cities to the suburbs and from the old Northeast/Midwest to the Sunbelt. During the 1950s, Houston added 340,000 people, San Diego 240,000, and Phoenix quadrupled its population, with 33,000 new arrivals each year. The 1950s also saw suburban populations begin to outstrip central cities. Up to 1920, central cities typically contained three-quarters or more of their immediate region's population. The ratio began to shift gradually downward during the 1920s and 1930s, as landlocked cities started to run out of room to grow, but they continued to hold the majority of their regions' populations. The 1950s, though, were the watershed. For the first time, suburbanites outnumbered central-city residents.

Once the shift had begun, it accelerated. By 1970, cities like Detroit or Trenton each contained little more than one-third of their regions' populations. Oakland and Macomb counties, the Detroit area's two outlying counties, had a combined population of less than 130,000 in 1920. That number grew to 580,000 by 1950, but nearly tripled again to over 1.5 million by 1970. Central cities were becoming less and less central.

Many people were aware of what was going on. With New Deal models in mind, the federal urban renewal program, Title I of the 1949 Housing Act, was created to help older cities not only remove slum conditions, but sustain their competitive position as more and more jobs and businesses moved to their growing suburbs. The urban renewal program awarded large federal grants to cities to acquire and demolish properties; reconfigure blocks, entire neighborhoods, or downtowns; and market the land to developers to put up new homes, office buildings, and commercial centers. While the initial impetus for urban renewal may have been to eliminate blighted areas and improve housing conditions, in the course of the 1950s the thrust of the program shifted, and became increasingly aimed at helping cities hold on to their middle-class populations and arrest the decline of their downtowns.

While the principle behind urban renewal reflected a mélange of influences, from the Radiant City ideas of Le Corbusier to the vision of an automobile-oriented future famously presented by General Motors at the 1939 World's Fair, it was a straightforward one: cities were obsolete. Despite the occasional grand boulevard and the clusters of ornate 1920s skyscrapers, the typical urban downtown was still a crowded collection of smaller buildings, mostly with ground-floor stores and offices above, sitting cheek by jowl on small lots and mostly on narrow streets. In a future where everyone would drive their cars to and from large, freestanding buildings, those crowded cities, with their antiquated infrastructure, needed to modernize to survive. Lots had to be assembled and consolidated into "buildable" development parcels, streets needed to be widened and realigned to allow traffic to move faster, parking garages needed to be built, and above all, the disorder of cities that had grown through accretion since the mid-nineteenth century needed to be replaced with an urban form deemed more appropriate for the modern world.

It was a plausible theory, but it turned out to be a bad one. The fundamental premise that assembly and clearance of large development sites was the key to urban revitalization was fatally flawed; as Jon Teaford wrote, "it taught America what *not* to do in the future."[21] It was an expensive and painful lesson. Over 600,000 families, mostly poor and many African American, were displaced, often disrupting or destroying neighborhoods that had existed for decades, even centuries, and leaving a lasting residue of anger and resentment.[22] Less heralded, but perhaps even more destructive, was the simultaneous construction of hundreds of miles of interstate highways cutting through the hearts of America's older cities; in contrast to urban renewal, which at least left some historic buildings standing, highway construction destroyed everything in its path, leaving a legacy of fragmented, crippled neighborhoods and downtowns, and new barriers between the survivors.

While the allure of urban renewal had begun to wane by the mid-1960s, the riots that erupted in city after city during those years prompted greater awareness of the intensity of the urban crisis, which led to a host of new federal initiatives. Between 1965 and 1977, the cities were the beneficiaries of more separate federal urban initiatives—the war on poverty, revenue sharing, the Model Cities program, Urban Development Action Grants (UDAG), and Community Development Block Grants (CDBG), along with housing programs such as Section 235, Section 236, and Section 8—than before or since. In addition to initiatives that explicitly targeted urban conditions, these years saw a vast expansion of other programs, most notably increases in health and welfare benefits, but also rising federal spending for job training, transportation, community health centers, and education, all directly or indirectly affecting urban America. The mid-1970s were the high-water mark in federal urban spending.

They may also have been the low point in American urban history. These were the years when the phrase "the urban crisis" became part of the American vocabulary. When one thinks about the excitement that people today feel about American cities, it may be difficult to believe how gloomy, even despairing, most people's feelings about cities were forty or fifty years ago, when a "pervasive sense" existed, as one writer put it, "that cities in America were no longer vital places,"[23] and prominent urban advocate Paul Ylvisaker could comment ruefully that "you don't rate as an expert on the city unless you foresee its doom."[24] In 1971, social critic Stewart Alsop, in a *Newsweek* column with the foreboding title "The Cities Are Finished," informed his readers that "the cities may be finished because they have become unlivable; that the net population of cities will continue to fall, . . . and that the cities will come to resemble reservations for the poor and the blacks surrounded by heavily guarded middle-class suburbs,"[25] quoting New Orleans Mayor Moon Landrieu that ". . . the cities are going down the tubes."[26]

Older industrial city populations continued to hemorrhage as more and more families fled for the suburbs or the Sunbelt. In the wake of the riots, white flight became a flood. Detroit's population dropped by 169,000, St. Louis's by 128,000, and Cleveland's by 126,000 during the 1970s. For the first time in the nation's history, thousands of homes and apartment buildings were abandoned in the hearts of American cities, from the burning tenements of the South Bronx that prompted Howard Cosell's famous although perhaps apocryphal cry from Yankee Stadium during the 1977 World Series, "Ladies and gentlemen, the Bronx is burning!"[27] to the row houses of North Philadelphia and the workers' bungalows of Detroit.

Smaller cities were particularly hard-hit. East St. Louis, Illinois, across the Mississippi from St. Louis, Missouri, lost 20 percent of its population during the 1970s; in 1981, a reporter could describe "streets steeped in dilapidation, the abandonment distorted and magnified by open lots where houses have been demolished or are burnt-out shells." By 1985, all five of Gary, Indiana's, department stores had closed; four were boarded-up hulks, while the fifth had been converted into the county's department of public welfare.[28]

The 1970s were also the decade when the factories closed. In Youngstown, September 19, 1977 is still remembered as "black Monday," the day Youngstown Sheet & Tube abruptly shut down its plant and furloughed 5,000 workers. Youngstown civic leaders put an ad in the *Washington Post* begging for President Carter's help to "keep self-help alive there and in the rest of Ohio," while others looked for scapegoats, one worker saying "the dirty Japs . . . killed my father in World War II, and are now taking food from my kid's table."[29] It was to no avail. Of the 25,000 factory jobs in Youngstown in 1954, only 5,000 were left by 1982. The heartland's industries—steel, cars, heavy machinery, tires, and more—were cutting back or disappearing in the face of obsolescence and global competition. By the end of the decade, most of the major industrial cities had lost nine out of ten of their factory jobs, as we can see in figure 1-2. Although jobs in retail trade and services were growing, it was not the same thing. The jobs that were gone were those that had defined these cities and created not only a strong blue-collar middle class but an entire culture. Their loss is still felt over forty years later.

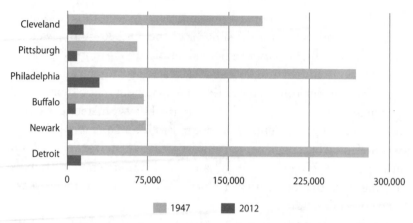

Figure 1-2 Vanishing factories: manufacturing jobs in major cities in 1947 and 2012. (Source: US Census of Manufacturers)

The 1980s and 1990s saw a dramatic shift in thinking in America's increasingly postindustrial cities. As reflected in Youngstown's civic leaders' futile appeal, throughout the 1970s cities continued to look to the federal government for help, although as the decade went on, the first rumblings of federal disengagement could be heard. Even before the Reagan Administration had begun to disassemble the nation's urban programs, the federal government under Jimmy Carter had signaled a reappraisal of the federal role; reflecting their loss of hope for the cities' future, the President's Commission on a National Agenda for the Eighties in 1979 called for "a long-term reorientation of federal urban policy" away from "place-oriented, spatially sensitive national *urban* policies" to "more people-oriented, spatially neutral, national social and *economic* policies" (emphasis added), admitting that this could have "traumatic consequences for a score of our struggling largest and oldest cities." In the 1980s, the federal government largely abandoned any pretense of pursuing urban policies, or showing any particular concern for the continued distress of the nation's older cities. Cities started to realize that they were on their own.

As both the message from Washington and the loss of their flagship industries sank home, cities began to rethink their prospects and the implications of an overtly postindustrial future in which they would be increasingly at the mercy of a shifting marketplace. As often as not, the response was to rebrand the city as an entertainment destination, and, as Kevin Gotham writes, devote "enormous public resources to the construction of large entertainment projects, including professional sports stadiums, convention centers, museums, redeveloped riverfronts, festival malls, and casinos and other gaming facilities."[30] Along with this grew a proliferation of public incentives for private firms and developers, including tax abatements, tax increment financing, industrial revenue bonds, and business improvement districts. All of this activity, coupled with the availability of inexpensive capital and favorable depreciation schedules, fostered something of a building boom in urban downtowns in the 1980s, belying the reality that little had fundamentally changed to justify the boom in either social or economic terms.

While the overall trajectory of the industrial cities continued to be downward, there were a few hopeful signs. While populations continued to decline, the rate of decline was slowing down, and a handful of cities, most notably Boston, even began to regain lost population. Here and there, a major public–private investment took off and began to spin off economic activity, as happened at Baltimore's Inner Harbor. The Harborplace "festival marketplace," as its developer James Rouse called it, opened its doors in 1980, and in 1981 attracted more visitors than Walt Disney World.[31] It was followed by a Hyatt Hotel, the beneficiary of public financing, and the National Aquarium, funded with a complicated package of federal, state, and philanthropic dollars.

At the same time, small numbers of so-called urban pioneers began to transform dilapidated urban neighborhoods like Baltimore's Otterbein or Philadelphia's Spring Garden into enclaves of beautifully restored row houses. Elsewhere in these same cities, newly minted community development corporations took on the daunting project of reviving struggling low-income neighborhoods, not through an influx of urban pioneers but with and through the people who already lived there.

The proliferation of high-profile public–private projects during the 1980s, along with a handful of widely publicized success stories, obscured the reality of continued decline. The failures of Rouse's other "festival marketplaces," such as Toledo's Portside, got less attention than Baltimore's success. Heralded upon its opening in 1984 as the savior of

Toledo's downtown, by 1990 Portside's "main entrance . . . reek[ed] of urine . . . and the decorative water fountains [were] dry and filled with trash."[32] Later that year, it closed its doors for good.

The cities' decline was exacerbated by the arrival of the crack cocaine epidemic. Crime continued to rise through the 1980s, peaking in most cities in the mid-nineties, and only then beginning to decline to today's low levels. Despite the pockets of revival, and scattered cases of "the return to the cities," throughout the 1990s central-city populations continued to become poorer relative to their suburbs and to the nation as a whole.

Even though revival in America's postindustrial cities during the 1980s and 1990s was modest and was far outweighed by continuing decline, the trends that were to lead to dramatic change in the new millennium were starting to emerge. When Richard Florida published his influential *The Rise of the Creative Class* in 2002, talented young people were already flocking to cities like Austin, Seattle, and San Francisco. Florida describes how one gifted Pitt graduate responded to his question about why he was leaving Pittsburgh for Austin: "There are lots of young people, he explained, and a tremendous amount to do, a thriving music scene, ethnic and cultural diversity, fabulous outdoor recreation, and great night life."[33] In 2000, that graduate did not see staying in Pittsburgh as an option comparable to Austin; today that may no longer be the case.

The transformation of America's industrial cities is not just about what has been aptly called the "March of the Millennials." Over the past two decades, the United States has seen dramatic changes in demographic patterns, consumer preferences, immigration, and the economy, all of which have affected cities in different ways. Cities like Pittsburgh, Baltimore, and St. Louis are very different places today—for good or for ill—than they were only fifteen or twenty years ago. In certain respects, one can reasonably say that these cities have risen from the ashes of decades of neglect, disinvestment, abandonment, and impoverishment. In others, though, they continue to struggle. Poverty, distress, and abandonment remain very much part of today's urban reality.

Two fundamental transformations, though, have taken place in America's once-industrial cities: a demographic transformation, largely driven by millennial in-migration; and an economic transformation from manufacturing to a new economy based on higher education and health care, the so-called eds and meds sector. In the next two chapters we will see how both are fueled by a unique juxtaposition of national change and embedded local assets, which, at least in some cities, had been there all along.

Chapter 2

Millennials, Immigrants, and the Shrinking Middle Class

Max's Taphouse on South Broadway in Baltimore's Fells Point neighborhood is a local landmark. It claims "Maryland's largest selection of draught beers, 103 rotating taps, five cask beer engines, more than 1,200 bottled beers, as well as amazing food."[1] It is only one of over a hundred restaurants, taverns, and nightspots in this historic neighborhood east of Baltimore's Inner Harbor to which thousands of people throng nightly, eating, drinking, and simply hanging out on the cobblestoned streets and along the nearby waterfront. Off Broadway and Thames Street, the neighborhood's two principal streets, the side streets glisten with beautifully restored row houses, where a tiny two-bedroom row house with a postage-stamp backyard on a narrow, treeless alley was recently listed for $375,000.[2] Not long before writing this, I was talking to a friend, now in her sixties, who'd been born in Fells Point. When she was a little girl in the 1960s, the family moved out because "it had become too dangerous," her father told her. Today, almost half of Fells Point's population is between twenty-five and thirty-four years old.

Every large city in America can tell a similar story. At the dawn of the twentieth century, Washington Avenue was St. Louis's garment district, lined with block after block of majestic five- and six-story buildings where people made clothing, shoes, and hats for the entire Midwest. After World War II, these factories began to close, and by the 1980s the avenue was all but deserted. Today, much like Fells Point, it is packed with bars, cantinas, hookah parlors, and more, drawing not only the thousands who live in the lofts and apartments that have been carved out of the old garment factories but still more thousands from all over the city and the region. Some call it St. Louis's loft district, others its entertainment district, but either way, it has come vividly back to life.

Areas like Fells Point and Washington Avenue are just the most visible face of the astonishing transformations that are taking place in America's cities. Neighborhoods are changing—often faster than their residents, neighborhood associations, or city governments can deal with. While Fells Point may be a playground for affluent millennials, only a little more than a mile east lies Highlandtown, a neighborhood being remade by Latino immigrants. Much the same thing is happening in Southwest Detroit in an area known as Mexicantown, where Mexican immigrants have transformed a stretch of that gritty city's landscape to a place where thousands come from throughout the region for the neighborhood's restaurants and stores. A community leader I spoke to had a simple explanation: "We're all from Jalisco," he said, "and people from Jalisco are Mexico's entrepreneurs."

This is not the whole story, of course. The neighborhoods that are being transformed in this way are only part, and often a small part, of Detroit, Baltimore, or St. Louis. Walk not too many blocks north of Washington Avenue, and you find yourself in an utterly different world, a lunar landscape of scattered houses, many of them empty, acres of vacant land where houses, long-since demolished, once stood, including the site of the infamous Pruitt-Igoe housing project, now gradually reverting to woodlands like those that covered the site before the first French settlers arrived in 1765. Other neighborhoods in St. Louis or Baltimore that still look and feel like respectable neighborhoods are falling apart, hit by foreclosures, poverty, and rising crime, as vacant, abandoned houses—once unthinkable—start to appear on streets with well-maintained homes and front yards.

The transformation of America's urban neighborhoods, like any major social phenomenon, is being driven by many different forces. Perhaps the most significant, though, are the changes to the makeup of America's population and where and how people want to live. We are a very different country from what we were in the 1960s, when the decline of the cities became part of the national consciousness; we are even a very different country from what we were as recently as the end of the last millennium. To understand what is happening in our cities, we need to understand how we have changed as a nation over these years.

It is hard to believe how different the United States was in 1960 compared to what it is today. Two-thirds of all the houses and apartments in the country had a married couple living in them, and most of those couples were raising children. If you were a child, you were almost certain to be living with both of your parents; over 90 percent of all the households with children in the United States were headed by married couples. If you weren't in a married couple, you were probably a single person living by yourself in an apartment, a rental room, or a single-room-occupancy hotel. Eighty-nine percent of the population were classified as "white," and barely 5 percent of the country's population had been born outside the United States. There were so few Latino immigrants from countries other than Mexico that the Census Bureau didn't even bother to distinguish them by country, lumping them into a single "Other Americas" category.

As figure 2-1 shows, the picture today is very different. Although the number of households in the United States has doubled since 1960, the number of married couples with children has actually gone down; there are 2.4 million fewer such families in the United States today than in 1990, and they make up only 19 percent of American households, and a much, much smaller share of urban households—only 9 percent of Pittsburgh's and 7 percent of Cleveland's households. One-third of childrearing families are single-parent families, mostly headed by women. The number of people living by themselves has increased by nearly 20 million, and there are 7.5 million "non-family households," which includes people sharing homes, straight and gay unmarried couples, and the like, a category that didn't even exist in the 1960 Census. Our foreign-born population has gone from less than 10 million to 42 million people, of

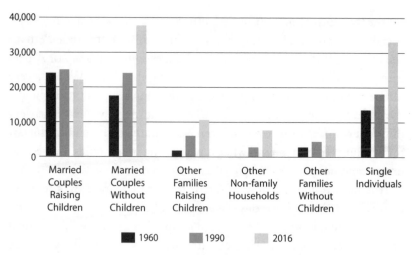

Figure 2-1 Change in the number of households by household type 1960 to 2015. (Source: US Census Bureau)

whom half are from Latin America. The "non-Latino white" population share has steadily declined, and today makes up only 64 percent of the nation's population.

In 1960, despite the G.I. Bill and the growth of higher education, there were only 2.5 million people aged twenty-five to thirty-four with four years of college under their belts, or about 1.5 percent of the population. By 2014, their numbers—members of the millennial generation, born between 1980 and 1990—had increased to 14.5 million, or about 4.5 percent of the United States population.

At the same time, the middle class has steadily shrunk, or, as some writers have put it, has been "hollowed out." If we define middle-income households as those earning between 75 percent and 150 percent of the national median income—which translates roughly to $40,000 to $80,000 today—their share of all American households has dropped from 43 percent in 1970 to 25 percent in 2014. We have many more affluent households, most of them headed by people with college degrees, and far more struggling, lower-income households, most with less formal education. While, fifty years ago, having a college degree gave young people a modest 24 percent boost in income compared to their high-school-graduate peers, the gap has widened to 72 percent today, as more and more of the good, well-paying jobs for people without college degrees have dried up.[3] Even though some people may not think so, having a college degree matters a lot in twenty-first-century America. Having a college degree may not be a ticket to success, but success is almost impossible today without one.

Paralleling the loss of millions of middle-class households is a related phenomenon which researchers have dubbed "economic sorting" or the growing tendency of people to sort themselves economically. In other words, there used to be a lot more neighborhoods where low-, middle-, and upper-income families were mixed together; today there are a lot fewer of those, and more and more that are either mainly poor or mainly affluent. Scholars Sean Reardon and Kendra Bischoff have studied this trend in detail; looking at 117 large and medium-sized metropolitan areas, they found that between 1970 and 2009, the percentage of families living in "middle-income" neighborhoods, where the neighborhood median income was 80 to 125 percent of the metro median, dropped from 65 percent to 44 percent. The number of families living in "poor" neighborhoods, where the neighborhood median income was two-thirds or less of the metro median, more than doubled, growing from 8 to 17 percent.[4]

All of this is very interesting, to be sure, especially for numbers wonks like me, but what does it mean for the cities? Each of the factors I've mentioned has a major impact on the trends in American cities. Let's start with the people who fill Max's Taphouse and its equivalents in other American cities every weekend.

It's become something of a cliché to say that the millennial generation is flocking to the cities, but it's true just the same. It's been written about enough that some writers have tried to debunk the idea, but they miss the point; it's not *all* millennials that are drawn to cities, just the roughly one-third of them with the college degrees, the tech skills, the earning power, and the yen for an urban environment—or a really cool taproom. They are changing the cities in ways small and large. I call them the Young Grads.

It's not as if young people haven't been drawn to cities before; the story of the young person who leaves his village to seek fame and fortune in the big city goes back hundreds if not thousands of years. Even as American cities declined after World War II, there has always been some contrary motion. A book entitled *Back to the City*, published in 1980, described the 1970s trend of "young, middle-class professionals . . . buying homes in those lower-income urban neighborhoods that contain structurally sound or attractive housing."[5] I know a lot about this trend because I was part of it, a newly remarried thirty-something professional who bought a barely habitable row house in Philadelphia's then-borderline Fairmount neighborhood in the late 1970s.

We were "urban pioneers," a term that suggests both how exciting the phenomenon was in some respects, but also how marginal it was in others. We plugged into a network of like-minded pioneers, through whom we found out which plumbers were reliable and which were not, learned about the man who refinished floors and made a paste out of the sawdust to fill the cracks, and met the man who rebuilt our marble fireplaces so beautifully that one would never guess that, when we bought the house, we found the smashed fragments in a cardboard box. We had to drive five miles to the suburbs to buy groceries, but we had Fairmount Park on our doorstep, and lots of hot new restaurants in Center City like the Commissary and Astral Plane.

In retrospect, though, the effects of the "back to the city" movement of the 1970s and 1980s were quite modest; outside of a handful of outlier cities like Boston, it had little effect on American cities' overall trajectory. Here and there an urban neighborhood was dramatically transformed or gentrified—a term that came into vogue during the 1970s—and stayed that way. Spring Garden, which was closer to Center City than Fairmount, and had truly magnificent houses, became an upscale neighborhood during those years, and has never looked back. Many more, including Fairmount, languished for decades.

For most cities, the urban pioneering of the 1970s was a blip, not a trend. The house we bought in the late seventies steadily lost value relative to inflation over the next twenty years. By then we'd moved and rented the house out. Around 2000, Fairmount started to change rapidly; the value of our house more than doubled from 2000 to 2003, and we sold, to a young single lawyer. By that point, moving to the city was no longer a quirk of a small atypical minority. It had become a normal thing, a pattern that began in magnet cities like Seattle or Washington,

DC, and then spread to the legacy cities. Every year since 2010, 4,000 or more Young Grads have moved into Baltimore, and 3,000 or more into Pittsburgh. By 2014, more than one in nine Pittsburghers were Young Grads, nearly three times the national average. As figure 2-2 shows, this is a growing trend—little or nothing in the 1990s, a lot more in the 2000s, and still more since 2010.

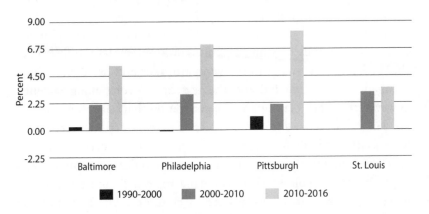

Figure 2-2 The Young Grads move to the cities: average annual increase in college-educated population, ages 25–34. (Source: US Census Bureau)

What is going on? In a nutshell, the pull of urban living for today's educated young people is far greater than at any time in the recent past. To understand why, we must look both at the cities and at the Young Grads themselves. America's legacy cities have changed a lot since they were gritty centers of industry. As urban economies have shifted from manu-facturing toward health care and higher education, they have also become, in sociologist Terry Nichols Clark's phrase, "entertainment machines."[6] We will discuss this phenomenon in detail in the next chapter.

Another important factor is that cities in the last twenty years have become much safer places. Most of America's older cities were fairly dangerous places in the 1990s, only to see crime drop sharply over the ensuing decades. New York City's story is famous, but many other cities saw similar trends; between 1995 and 2005, the FBI crime index—a composite of the most serious violent and property crimes—dropped by a quarter in St. Louis and Philadelphia, and by over 50 percent in Baltimore and Washington. Not only are cities, or at least those parts where Young Grads gather, safer, but the word has gotten out: people with no particular sensitivity to the nuances of urban life feel safer in cities. While in the 1990s many people were wary of walking through Washington's DuPont Circle after dark, ten years later it had become a millennial playground, thronged with young people comfortably hanging out well into the night.

When we look at the recent Young Grad in-migration, it is impossible to tell precisely how much credit is due to the ways the cities have changed, and how much to the ways attitudes and preferences have changed from one generation to the next. There's compelling evidence, however, that both play a part. The generation that has reached adulthood in the last ten or fifteen years does seem to have a different attitude toward cities and urban living than its predecessors. A host of recent surveys have found that people in their twenties and thirties are more likely to prefer cities as a place to live, would like to do without a car, and tend to seek out places with diverse people and cultures; as one 2016 study put it: "'Location, location, location' for this generation means being close to an urban core so that millennials can easily get to work, amenities, and transit. Studies show a new fondness for living near service amenities like music venues, theaters, bars, gyms, etc."[7] Not only are there far more Young Grads than ever before, but they are deferring marriage and childrearing longer than previous generations, which means that more of them are single or in the sort of informal relationships that go well with being part of a lively urban social scene.

Some media pundits would have one believe that the urban revival is just as much about empty-nesters and retiring baby boomers as it is about millennials, but the numbers don't bear them out. It's not completely untrue. The number of well-educated, affluent empty-nesters and baby boomers living in the cities is growing. But that growth has to be seen in proportion. Their numbers are growing less because boomers and empty-nesters are flocking to the cities, than because their numbers are increasing so fast overall—their numbers are rising almost everywhere.

Starting in the 1960s, a lot more people in the United States began going to college. As a result, between 2000 and 2014, the number of people over sixty-five with college degrees in the United States more than doubled, as the big cohort of 1960s and 1970s college graduates moved through their life cycle. Their numbers increased almost everywhere. The fact is, though, that *relative to that age group's growth in the population as a whole*, older American cities—even the most successful in terms of drawing Young Grads—are still lagging.

Washington, DC, is seeing an influx of college graduates in their late thirties and early forties along with the younger people who have changed the character of that city. So is Baltimore, although to a lesser extent. Both cases may be in part an echo effect from the migration of Young Grads in the previous decade, but may also reflect a greater readiness of some affluent, well-educated people to stay and raise their family in the city. Neither of these cities, though, are seeing as much growth among older adults. Yes, there *are* empty-nesters and baby boomers who are moving to the cities, but their numbers are still modest compared to those who are moving elsewhere, or simply staying put. They are contributing to urban revival, but not driving it.

The second big demographic change in cities, though, is not about growth, but about decline—specifically, the loss of the population that historically defined the American middle class and the American urban neighborhood: the childrearing married couple. In our postmodern era of fluid roles and personal reinvention, such families, with their *Leave It to Beaver* overtones of husbands off to work in the morning toting lunch pails or briefcases and wives staying home to raise the children and cook hearty, filling family dinners, seem uncomfortably anachronistic.

That way of life may be gone forever, and many people may see that as a good thing, yet as is often the case with major social changes, the unintended consequences, particularly for America's industrial cities, are far from benign. In this case, the consequences have had to do with the kinds of places the neighborhoods of legacy cities actually are. Rather than being made up of blocks of tenements familiar from images of Manhattan, the traditional, early-twentieth-century urban neighborhood in the United States was a neighborhood of single-family homes, designed and built for the sole purpose of accommodating married couples, those raising children, those planning to do so, or those who had finally seen the last of their brood leave the home. These neighborhoods still exist as physical spaces, but as I will discuss in detail in chapter 6, as the pool of childrearing married couples has declined—and as we'll see, all but disappeared in many cities—they have lost the function for which they were built, with, at least so far, nothing comparable to take its place.

Let's look at two of Ohio's smaller industrial cities, Akron and Youngstown. These were hard-core industrial cities. Akron was called "the rubber capital of the world," and in the early twentieth century was the home of Goodrich, Goodyear, Firestone, and General Tire. Steel-making was to Youngstown what rubber tires were to Akron. In 1960, nearly half of the workers in each city worked in the factories, and most of the rest supplied groceries, health care, and government services to the factory workers. More than two-thirds of all the households and 90 percent of all the families in both cities were married couples. Over half of those couples were raising children under eighteen.

Today, most of the factories in both cities have closed, and most of the manufacturing jobs have disappeared. Instead of 24,000 factory workers as in 1960, only 2,800 live in Youngstown today. But the number of married couples raising children has dropped even faster. Less than a quarter of the households in Youngstown are married couples—a bit more in Akron—and only a quarter of them, or less than 5 percent of all households, have children in the home. From 21,000 married couples with children in 1960, there are only 1,000 today. More than two out of every five households in both cities is a single person living alone. Even though Youngstown has only half as many households today than it had in 1960, it has the same number of single people as it did then.

There are many reasons why childrearing married couples, of all races and ethnicities, who are the epitome of the American middle class, continue to leave the cities. The racially driven white flight of the 1960s and 1970s may be a thing of the past, but middle-class flight, made up of as many if not more black than white families today, continues. They are frustrated by the continuing challenge of ensuring that their children can get a good education, and by the pervasive presence of crime in their lives—not so much the murderous violence that continues to devastate the cities' most distressed neighborhoods, but what one might call the constant pinpricks of urban life: the break-ins, the petty vandalism, the graffiti on the walls. They are worn down by the high property taxes and the poor public services, and the fact that it may take hours for the police to show up and the streets are potholed and many of the streetlights broken. As Ray Suarez writes, fatigue sets in: "The strain of having eyes in the back of your head, higher insurance, rotten local services, and the day-upon-day-upon-day of bad news finally carries you across a line. . . ."[8] Above all, they leave because they can. With two wage earners in most married-couple families today, they have lots of options in the city's suburbs.

The upshot is that the number of kids in cities has steadily dropped, and the number of kids in married-couple families has dropped even faster. There is no evidence that the long-term trends have begun to shift. While I hear stories in my travels about how a particular charter school has drawn families with school-age children back to urban neighborhoods here or there, as with the City Garden Montessori school in St. Louis, the data tells me that these situations are outliers in a larger trend of continued decline. As figure 2-3 shows, while a few cities have seen an increase in the number of *preschool* children in married-couple families since 2000, they have all seen precipitous declines in the number of *school-age* children in married-couple families, beginning at the age of six. St. Louis and Philadelphia are seeing more infants and toddlers, and

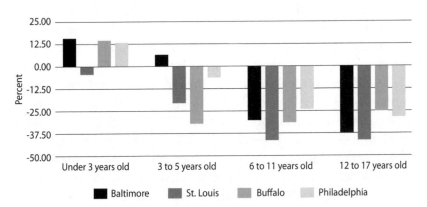

Figure 2-3 Change in the number of children in married-couple families by age group, 2000–2015. (Source: US Census Bureau)

in Baltimore, the number of three- to five-year-old children is also on the increase, but at that point the drop-off begins. Moreover, in none of these cities is there much difference between the trends for the elementary and those for middle- / high-school age groups.

As these families leave, the demand for the cities' single-family neighborhoods declines. The aspiring Young Grads want to live in downtowns and high-density neighborhoods around universities, and few want to buy tired, turn-of-the-century, frame houses or small fifties bungalows in outlying areas far from the scene and the action. As the number of married couples with children has declined, the number of single women raising children has gone up—although by a far smaller number—but with few exceptions they are far poorer than the families they replaced, and have a far harder time making ends meet, let alone maintaining the old houses that are wearing out around them. They are far less likely to be able to buy their home, and except for the fortunate few who win the housing voucher lottery and obtain a rent subsidy, chronic income insecurity puts them constantly at the mercy of their landlords.

As we'll see in chapter 6, there are a lot of other reasons why many urban single-family neighborhoods are declining, while the same city's downtown and other areas populated by Young Grads are booming. But it all starts with the demographic changes taking place in the United States, and particularly in the country's older industrial cities.

There's another demographic story, though, that offers an important and hopeful counter-trend and is increasingly being seen in America's legacy cities. That story is immigration. Detroit's Conant Street is a long, gritty street that starts just north of General Motors' Detroit-Hamtramck Assembly plant, and runs north by northwest to the Detroit city line at Eight Mile Road. As you drive north on Conant, first through Hamtramck—a small city completely surrounded by Detroit—and then through Detroit itself, you see store signs first in Arabic and then more and more in Bengali, the language spoken in Bangladesh. A little north of Caniff Street, where one side of Conant is in Detroit and the other in Hamtramck, the stores cluster more closely together. Al-Hishaam Islamic Gifts and Indian Fashion is quickly followed by Amar Pizza, Islamic Bargain ("Clothing, Oils, Jewelry, and

More"), Universal Multiservices (tax, travel, and immigration services), Bengal Spices, Aladdin Sweets & Café, Al-Amin Supermarket, Zamzam Bangladeshi, Indian and Pakistani Cuisine, Shah Puran Grocery & Halal Meat, and on and on.

You are in Banglatown, a neighborhood half in Hamtramck and half in Detroit. Steve Tobocman, founder of Global Detroit, tells me that half of the residents are foreign-born; half of those are from Bangladesh, and about half of the rest are from Yemen. Global Detroit has partnered with the Bangladeshi American Public Affairs Committee to help build the business community and ultimately make it a regional visitor destination. As Ehsan Taqbeem, founder of the Committee, says, "[in Detroit] we have Mexicantown, we have Greektown"—citing the city's better-known immigrant neighborhoods and restaurant destinations. "So, let's have Banglatown."[9]

Banglatown may or may not ever become a visitor destination. It isn't pretty or picturesque. Conant Street will never be a historic district. The buildings that house the stores are basic, undistinguished, and often tired properties. They are interspersed with parking lots, used-car dealers, and gas stations on a street where the only greenery in sight are the weeds coming up through the cracks in the curbs and sidewalks. But it is vibrant and full of life, and the housing vacancy rate in the blocks of neatly tended bungalows on either side of Conant Street is only 2 percent, compared to over 22 percent in the rest of Detroit.

Banglatown is not unique. Across the city, Mexican immigrants have revived much of the Southwest Detroit neighborhood. Cambodians and Vietnamese have brought new life into fraying parts of South Philadelphia. Cherokee Street west of Jefferson Street in St. Louis has become a vibrant Latino shopping street. Newark's Ironbound neighborhood, its name supposedly coming from the railroad tracks that once ringed the neighborhood, became a heavily Portuguese immigrant neighborhood in the 1950s. Although many of the children of those immigrants have since moved to the suburbs, they created a Portuguese-language infrastructure of stores, sports clubs, restaurants, cafes, doctors, and lawyers that not only draws visitors from all over the New York metropolitan area, but has also drawn a second wave of Portuguese-speaking immigrants from Brazil and the Cape Verde Islands, along with other Latin

American immigrants. The Ironbound is Newark's most vital neighborhood, and Ferry Street, its main thoroughfare, Newark's liveliest
shopping street.

In many respects, this is nothing new. Ethnic neighborhoods are the
matrix from which much of modern American society emerged. A hundred years ago, the neighborhoods of America's industrial cities were
largely ethnic enclaves, often dominated by a single ethnic group. A 1911
ethnic map of Newark delineated the "areas where different nationali-
ties predominate," showing large zones of German, Italian, and Jewish
concentration, along with smaller pockets of Irish, Negroes, Greeks,
Slavs, and Chinese (fig. 2-4). While the Newark map shows the heavi-
est concentrations of Germans, Italians, and Jews (and simply refers to
"Slavs" generically, reflecting their modest role in the city's ethnic jigsaw
puzzle), a Cleveland map from the same era distinguishes among Polish,
Czech, Ukrainian, Slovak, Slovenian, Serbian, and Croatian ethnicities,
large communities in their own neighborhoods, and smaller ones in
multiethnic clusters.[10]

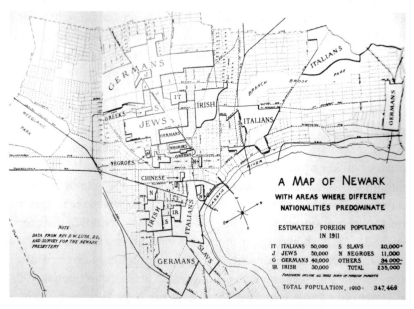

Figure 2-4 Mapping ethnicity: Newark in 1911. (Source: Littman Architecture and Design Library, New Jersey Institute of Technology)

Although a handful of exceptions like The Hill, an Italian neighborhood in St. Louis, or the still largely Jewish neighborhood of Squirrel Hill in Pittsburgh hang on, the European ethnic enclaves of the cities' industrial heyday have almost entirely disappeared, done in by assimilation, prosperity, generational change, suburban flight, and in particular by the lack of new immigrants from those countries to replace those passing away or fleeing to the suburbs. Places like Banglatown, Mexicantown, or the Cambodian pocket in South Philadelphia are in many respects the twenty-first-century counterpart of the early twentieth-century ethnic enclave, places where new immigrants can find a community of people who share their language and culture while figuring out how to fit into a new, often daunting country.

Will the new ethnic neighborhoods last? Cities are constantly in flux, and neighborhoods constantly change. Detroit had a flourishing Chaldean Town made up of Christian immigrants from Iraq in the 1970s, but it disappeared, victim of the push of rising crime and the pull of suburbanization.[11] The Ironbound, on the other hand, is going strong well into its third generation as a largely Portuguese-speaking but increasingly also Spanish-speaking enclave. One can never tell about any one neighborhood, but as long as the United States continues to welcome large numbers of immigrants, immigrant communities are likely to form in places where the opportunity exists to settle, find affordable housing, and find a job or open a business. Some will disappear as their residents blend into the American mainstream, but new ones will emerge. Some will struggle, but others may thrive.

Up to now, though, America's legacy cities have lagged as immigrant destinations. No older industrial city has the rich mosaic of ethnic immigrant neighborhoods that give New York City or Los Angeles, or for that matter Houston, so much of their propulsive energy. None of the older industrial cities has a foreign-born population share equal to the national level, and immigrant enclaves like Banglatown or Cambodian South Philadelphia are still only small pockets within their city's larger fabric.

This may be changing, though. Between 2000 and 2015, the foreign-born population nearly doubled in Baltimore, and grew by nearly 50 percent in Philadelphia and in Pittsburgh. This is still a far cry from a hundred years ago, when nearly two-thirds of Pittsburgh's population and fully three-quarters of Cleveland's were either foreign-born or the children of immigrants. Still, it is another sign that things are changing in America's older industrial cities.

Chapter 3

From Factories to "Eds and Meds"

T alking about New Haven, real estate broker John Keogh says, "this is a company town, simply put."[1] New Haven is indeed the epitome of the twenty-first-century company town. The company, though, is not a steel mill or an automobile plant, but a university. Yale University, along with its affiliate Yale New Haven Hospital, dominates this small Connecticut city. The university and the hospital employ nearly 25,000 people, or roughly one out of every three people who work in New Haven, while the university's 12,000-strong student body accounts for one out of every eleven New Haven residents. When one factors in the effects of the university's spending, the dollars spent by its workers and its student body, and the thousands of jobs and hundreds of businesses that this spending supports, it is probably not an overstatement that Yale is responsible for three-quarters of the city's economy.

While Yale has been part of New Haven for over 300 years, its role in the city's economy for most of its history was far more modest than it is today. Well into the 1960s, as reporter Fred Powledge wrote at the time, "beyond frequent scrapes between the students and the townspeople, Yale had little to do with the city around it."[2] Sitting quietly on the north side of the picturesque colonial-era New Haven Green, Yale was in but not of New Haven, subtly exerting such influence as it felt necessary to protect its interests through the interlocking relationships between its trustees, its top administrators, and the rest of New Haven's civic and business elite, cemented through golf matches at the New Haven Country Club and lunches at the Graduate Club.

New Haven itself, into the 1960s or 1970s, was a typical small industrial city of immigrants, factories, and workshops. In 1910, when its population of nearly 134,000 was larger than it is today, more than two-thirds of its residents were immigrants or the children of immigrants, with Italians, followed by Irish and then Russian Jews, predominating. The city boasted over 500 manufacturing plants, of which the largest— Sargent Hardware, Winchester Repeating Arms, and New Haven Clock—in Douglas Rae's words, "operated almost as cities unto themselves."[3] Not much changed over the next forty years. The city's population leveled off in the 1920s at around 160,000, and remained there through the 1950s. In 1947, there were still over 400 factories in New Haven employing 28,000 production workers and another 5,000 clerks, guards, janitors, and managers—half of the city's workforce.

As with of the nation's other older industrial cities, that changed. By 1987, the number of factory workers had dropped to 5,700, and by 2012 to a mere 1,500 in seventy establishments, most of them more like workshops or studios than factories. New Haven Clock closed in the 1960s; Winchester, after struggling for decades, in 2006. Only Sargent survives, in a diminished state as a division of the Swedish conglomerate Assa Abloy. As the factories disappeared, Yale grew. Over the years it transformed itself from a regional to a national and then a global institution. Today, New Haven's industrial heyday is no more than a distant memory.

Although New Haven, a small city with a single big institution, may be something of an extreme case, its story is the opposite of unusual. It encapsulates a trend that has refashioned city after city around the country, the transformation of the urban economy from one dependent on manufacturing to one equally if not more dependent on higher education and health care—the "eds and meds" sector.

The story of Pittsburgh, the iconic steelmaking city of the United States, closely resembles that of New Haven. Few cities better epitomized America's industrial history; in Herbert Casson's 1907 panegyric to the steel industry and its titans, he wrote that "Pittsburgh is more than a city. It is the acme of activity: it is an industrial cyclone. To its steel mills and furnaces there is no intermission—no rest—no sleep. [...] No other American city works so hard, with both muscle and brain, to make an honest living."[4] In 1958, nearly 100,000 people worked in the city's 1,000 factories.

Today, there are only 7,300 manufacturing jobs left in Pittsburgh, but 90,000 in the city's new leading industries—education and health care. Most of the rest are in finance, information technology, and hospitality, reflecting the city's secondary role as a center of tourism and entertainment. The "heat map" of Pittsburgh jobs in figure 3-1 shows the picture clearly. The large blob on the left is downtown, and the one on the right is Oakland, less than two miles away, home to Carnegie Mellon University and the University of Pittsburgh (known as "Pitt").

Over 50,000 students attend Carnegie Mellon, Pitt, and their smaller neighbor, Duquesne University, or one out of every six residents of Pittsburgh. The Pitt-affiliated University of Pittsburgh Medical Center—locally known as UPMC—is the largest nongovernmental employer in the state of Pennsylvania, employing over 50,000 people. In 2007, the medical center moved its corporate offices to the sixty-four-story US Steel Building in downtown Pittsburgh, which had been built in 1971 to serve both as that company's headquarters and as a symbol of its industrial might. In a dramatic gesture exemplifying the city's transformation, the medical center erected giant illuminated steel letters spelling out "UPMC," at the top of the city's tallest building, which loom over the Pittsburgh skyline (fig. 3-2).

In 1907, Casson wrote,

> The United States Steel Corporation owns as much land as is contained in the three states of Massachusetts, Vermont, and Rhode Island. It employs one hundred and eighty thousand workers. [...] More than a million of the American people ... depend on it for their livelihood. [...] It has nineteen ports and owns a fleet of one hundred large ore-ships. [...] It makes more steel than either Great Britain or Germany and one-quarter of the total amount made in all the countries of the world.[5]

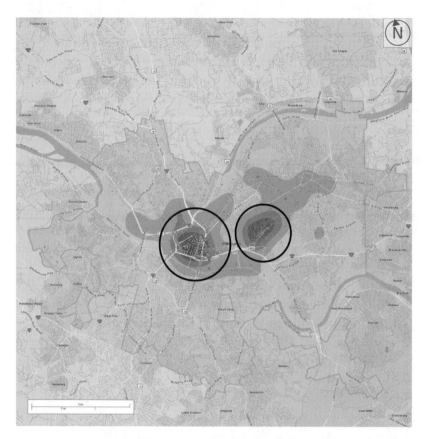

Figure 3-1 Where the jobs are: employment "heat map" of Pittsburgh, 2014. (Source: US Census Bureau, On-the-Map)

The US Steel Corporation still exists, a shadow of its former self. It occupies a much smaller suite in the same building as UPMC.

The transformation in these once-industrial cities' economies has been profound and, for such a fundamental change, sudden. It raises many questions: why did urban manufacturing collapse to such an extent, and why did eds and meds grow large enough to take their place? Were either of these changes simply the product of forces beyond any city's control, or was either part of a deliberate strategy for change? And finally, what do these changes mean for these cities' future? While an entire book could be written on any one of these questions, I will try to

Figure 3-2 US Steel Building with UPMC logo in downtown Pittsburgh. (Source: Matt Robinson/PittsburghSkyline.com)

address them in brief, because they are critical to understanding what is going on in America's cities.

Manufacturing in the United States is down, but far from dead. Contrary to what one might believe from some accounts, we still make a lot of things. Manufacturing generated $2.1 trillion in Gross Domestic Product (GDP) in 2013, about 12.5 percent of total US GDP. This is only about half of what its share of the economy was in the 1960s, but manufacturing is still the nation's largest single economic sector. It has changed, though. We make different things, and it takes far fewer workers to make them than were required in the past. In 1960, roughly one out of every four jobs in the United States was a factory job; today, barely one out of twelve. Tellingly, in 1980 it took twenty-five workers to create $1 million in manufacturing output—today it takes only six and a half workers to get the same results.[6]

What's happened in the older industrial cities, however, is far more than simply a reflection of national change. Whatever we make today, we make far less of it in the older industrial cities and towns of the

American heartland than we once did. The communities that have borne the brunt of these losses are the nation's older industrial cities; as Berkeley economist Enrico Moretti writes, "Manufacturing is no longer the engine of prosperity for local communities. If anything, the opposite is true. The big manufacturing centers of America, once proud and wealthy, have been humbled and are now struggling with shrinking populations and difficult economic prospects."[7]

In many respects, American industry in the 1950s and 1960s was living in a fool's paradise. Not only was the nation's economy surging, but with most of Europe and Japan still digging out of the rubble of World War II, American manufacturers faced little competition. But, as Vaclav Smil points out, the seeds of future decline were already there: "it was a producer's market, and an era of abundant and inexpensive energy." With the economy running at high speed, he adds, "US manufacturers could sell almost anything they made. Product durability, functionality, and design quality were of secondary (and sometimes, it seems, of hardly any) importance compared to the quest for quantity, a quick profit, and built-in obsolescence."[8]

The first manufacturing crisis, in the 1970s, brought together three global shifts that ended the charmed life of US industry: the growth in manufacturing elsewhere, first in Europe and Japan, and then spreading to other parts of the world; the sudden hike in energy costs with the rise of OPEC and the oil crisis of 1973; and the global slowdown in demand, particularly demand for steel, that followed. These shifts led to two striking changes in US manufacturing, each of which disproportionately undermined the nation's older industrial cities.

First, with the most dramatic impact on the cities, was the crisis in steelmaking, an industry that had been concentrated in cities like Pittsburgh, Youngstown, and Gary. US steel production, which had been steadily growing since the mid-1950s, peaked at over 130 million metric tons in 1973, only to plummet to less than 70 million metric tons a decade later. Hundreds of plants closed their doors. Between 1976 and 1986, 300,000 steelworkers lost their jobs.

September 19, 1977, is still known in Youngstown and Ohio's Mahoning Valley as Black Monday, the day the Youngstown Sheet & Tube Company announced that it would shut down their Campbell

Works. Over the next four years, they shuttered their Brier Hill Works, while US Steel and Republic Steel also closed their plants. According to one source, the Youngstown area lost 40,000 manufacturing jobs in the wake of the steel closings.[9] The city has never recovered from Black Monday.

The second change was even more far-reaching. After the dust settled, US manufacturers found themselves in a world where it was more expensive to do business, where unlimited demand was no longer a given, and which was far more globally competitive than the world they were accustomed to. Their reaction was to embark on a massive restructuring in order to increase the efficiency and reduce the cost of their operations. By this time, many of the manufacturers that had their roots in cities like Cleveland, Pittsburgh, and Trenton had long since become national or even global firms. The Trenton Iron Works, founded by famed ironworker Peter Cooper in the 1830s, had been part of US Steel since the 1950s, while the Trenton Potteries were now part of the Crane Company. As historian John Cumbler points out, "When decisions are made at national headquarters removed from traditional production sites, there are few constraints. Decisions are likely to be made on the narrowest of economic grounds, and these affect all segments of the society."[10]

Manufacturing did not disappear, nor did manufacturing jobs. Nationally, manufacturing jobs dropped modestly from 19 to 17 million, and stabilized there until the end of the century. That seeming stability hides two huge shifts, one geographic and one economic. As executives looked at their urban plants, they saw two things. First, with few exceptions, their plants were old, inefficient, and often obsolete, particularly by comparison to the new plants coming on line in Europe and Japan. Second, their heavily unionized workforce, although hard-working and productive, was also expensive, again by comparison to workers elsewhere. Concern for the cities in which these plants were located, or for the people, often the third or fourth generation of the families who worked in these plants, was at best secondary, and more often nonexistent.

The bloodletting that began in those years hollowed out the economy of city after city. Buffalo's Lackawanna works, which employed over 20,000 in its heyday, closed its doors in 1982. Milwaukee lost

Allis-Chalmers, Delco, AC Spark Plug, Pabst, Louis Allis, Kearney & Trecker, and Outboard Marine. During the 1980s, General Motors closed eleven plants, and announced closings of twenty-one more in 1991. A young writer coming home to the Monongahela Valley near Pittsburgh in 1982 wrote that "When I got there and drove up the valley to my hometown, [I] was amazed by how fast the valley had gone downhill in just a few months. [...] The valley seemed weirdly quiet. None of the banging and crashing sounds. No smoke in the sky, of course. I was just startled."[11]

In many cases, the shift was less abrupt and more protracted over time. Massive complexes like the US Steel works on the south side of Chicago, the flagship Bethlehem Steel plant in Bethlehem, Pennsylvania, or Bethlehem Steel's Sparrow Point plant in Baltimore did not close suddenly, but gradually declined, cutting production and workers, often lingering for many years before finally closing in the 1990s or early 2000s. Still others, like US Steel's Gary works, remain open, but with 5,000 workers rather than the 30,000 who once worked there.

It was not just antiquated, inefficient plants, many of which had seen little investment since the end of World War II, that the companies were trying to shed, as I know from my own experience. In 1996, when I was the director of housing and economic development in Trenton, our last large-scale manufacturer from our industrial heyday, Hill Refrigeration, announced that it would close its plant and move to Virginia, laying off over 800 workers. It was a big blow to a small, struggling city.

Recognizing that their Trenton plant, a congeries of pieces built between the 1880s and the 1960s, was woefully inefficient, the city, county, and state all approached Hill hoping to keep them, if not in the city of Trenton—where finding a suitable site for a new plant that size would be all but impossible—then at least in the area, so the workers could keep their jobs. The firm's response implied some amusement at our naïveté. "You don't understand," I remember hearing more or less in these words. "The building isn't the big issue. The big issue is how much we're paying our workforce. None of our competitors are union, and to be competitive we need to start over with a nonunion workforce." Tellingly, Hill did not offer any of its Trenton workers jobs in its new plant.

Manufacturing jobs shifted massively to the Sunbelt. While New York State lost two-thirds of its manufacturing jobs and Pennsylvania half between 1967 and 2002, the number of factory jobs stayed roughly the same in North Carolina, Tennessee, and California, while Texas gained nearly 200,000 jobs.

Corporate America's attitude toward trade unions, which had gradually turned into one of grudging acquiescence and at times even a sort of implicit partnership during the 1940s and 1950s but which had already become more adversarial during the 1960s, became increasingly hostile as the manufacturing environment changed. Companies moved out of the cities, and out of the heavily union-oriented Northeast and Midwest altogether, moving to the South and Southwest, where they could start over in places where unions were weak, and where state "right to work" laws gave them the upper hand. The numbers tell the story. In 1950, nearly 36 percent of all American private-sector workers were union members. By 1991, after the first wave of plant closings and relocations, that number was down to 16 percent. Today, fewer than 7 percent of private-sector workers are union members.

People did not sit passively by as the plant closings were taking place, but tried to take action on many fronts. As Owen Bieber, the UAW president, said, "The proper answer to the insatiable demands of the Ebenezer Scrooge types who run Wall Street is not a snappy 'Yes, sir!' salute."[12] Bills were proposed in Congress and state legislatures to require advance notice of plant closings, reimbursement of public incentives, and compensation for displaced workers. Demonstrations were held, and petitions were sent to Washington. Workers in some cities, often led by veterans of the New Left of the 1960s, made direct efforts to take control of the closed facilities. Religious and civic leaders in Youngstown, guided by radical scholar-activist Staughton Lynd, tried without success to acquire, modernize, and reopen the Campbell Works under community–worker ownership. Activists in Pittsburgh mounted direct-action campaigns against the companies they saw as leading the deindustrialization effort, including "depositing dead fish in [Mellon Bank] safe deposit boxes and spraying skunk oil in bank lobbies."[13]

Other than a few largely symbolic notification laws, and some modest federal retraining funds for displaced workers, these efforts bore little fruit. While his administration imposed some restrictions on steel imports, President Jimmy Carter showed no interest in either supporting federal legislation to restrict plant closings or providing federal funds for community–worker coalitions to buy and reopen steel mills. Under President Ronald Reagan, this largely hands-off policy hardened. In the end, the only steel mill that reopened under worker ownership was in the small industrial city of Weirton, West Virginia, where workers were able to buy and reopen the former National Steel works in 1984. The plant made money for a few years but ran into increasing difficulties in the 1990s. The workers lost their majority control in 1994, and the new owners filed for bankruptcy in 2003.

It is doubtful that any forms of federal financing or other intervention, or changes of heart by corporate executives, at least in the steel industry, would have made much difference beyond perhaps cushioning some of the short-term social and economic distress that the affected cities were going through. In Western Europe, which was undergoing a similar crisis at the same time, the nations of the European Union (EU) were far more actively involved, putting up billions to keep plants open, maintain jobs, and preserve social stability. Their efforts merely slowed down the process. By the end of the 1970s, the EU was forced to admit defeat. Steel production plummeted. Between 1977 and 1990, the steel-making workforce in the EU shrank by 48 percent.

The effect of losing their industrial base on cities already reeling from suburbanization, white flight, and the aftermath of the riots of the 1960s was traumatic, going well beyond the pain and suffering of the thousands of workers who found themselves without the jobs that had all but defined their existence. Working for Youngstown Sheet & Tube or General Motors was more than a job—it was an identity. Buttressing that identity, an entire urban culture had grown up since the late nineteenth century around the plants and the neighborhoods that surrounded them, a culture of churches, union halls, taverns, softball leagues, and neighborhood, ethnic, and civic organizations. For cities like Youngstown and Cleveland, manufacturing was not just *an* economic engine, it was *the* economic engine. It paid the wages that enabled its workers to patronize the city's department stores, jewelers, and bakeries. The health benefits its workers had won through their union contracts supported the city's hospitals and doctors. With the loss of the factories, the very fabric of these cities began to unravel.

Elsewhere in the United States, after the first wave of plant closings and job losses things more or less stabilized for a while. New jobs in emerging industries like computers replaced the ones that were lost, and between the early 1980s and the end of the millennium, the number of manufacturing jobs in the United States as a whole stayed about the same. That was not true in the Rust Belt states, particularly their older industrial cities. Almost like an epidemic, job losses and plant closings seemed contagious; in city after city, manufacturing jobs continued to disappear. As figure 3-3 shows, cities lost about half of their 1967 jobs by 1982, half of those remaining in 1982 were gone by 1997, and half of those remaining in 1997 were gone by 2012. The big difference, though, wasn't that the cities were losing all that many more factory jobs than elsewhere—it was that, unlike places like Texas or California, they weren't creating any new ones.

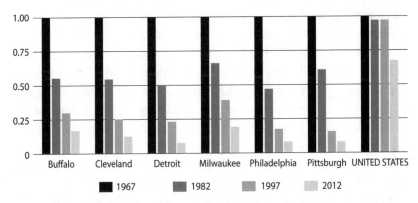

Figure 3-3 Lost manufacturing jobs in the United States and selected cities, 1967 to 2012. (Source: US Census of Manufacturers)

By 2012, Philadelphia had only 23,000 manufacturing jobs left of the 264,000 it had had in 1967. Pittsburgh had barely 7,000. By this point, two things had happened. First, the relative stability that had characterized American industry for over a decade came to an end. Starting around 1999 or 2000, the cumulative impact of global competition, offshoring, and technological change sent manufacturing jobs into a tailspin; the nation lost 6 million factory jobs before things bottomed out in 2010 at the end of the Great Recession. By then, though, cities like Philadelphia and Pittsburgh were very different places from what they had been in the 1970s and 1980s, with the ruins of their industrial history now visible alongside vital new economies built around eds and meds and, secondarily, entertainment, culture, and tourism. Rather than *industrial* cities, people were now calling them *postindustrial* cities. While for some, that term has an almost visionary, or Brave New World quality, I think of it as a simple reflection of reality. They were industrial cities once, but no longer.

What has fueled the eds-and-meds explosion in the now postindustrial cities? Again, we need to look at both the larger national trends and the particular features of the cities. In both respects, they form almost the mirror image of the picture we have painted of the trends driving manufacturing during the same years.

The most powerful factor driving change has nothing to do with the cities as such. Spending in the United States on higher education and medicine, particularly the latter, has exploded since the 1950s. In 1950, the United States spent $12 billion on health care, which translates to $117 billion in 2014 dollars adjusted for inflation. In 2014, with a national population slightly more than twice what it was in 1950, we spent just over $3 *trillion* as a nation for health care, more than twenty-five times what we spent in 1950. Of that total, nearly $1 trillion went for hospital care. Over the same period, spending on medical research, although a small part of the total, went from under $1 billion (again, adjusted for inflation) in 1950 to $46 billion in 2014, almost fifty times what it was in 1950!

Furthermore, the growth in health care expenditures has not been the same over that entire period; instead, it has sharply accelerated in recent decades. Between 1950 and 1975, health care expenditures increased at an average of $17 billion per year, from 1975 to 1990 at an average of $51 billion per year, and since 1990, at an average of $72 billion per year.

The growth of higher education has not been quite as spectacular as that of health care, but it's still dramatic. On the eve of World War II, only 5 percent of US adults had graduated from a four-year college, and a college degree was more a token of membership in a privileged social class than a ticket into one. By 1965, the total had grown, but only to 9 percent. Today it is 32 percent. Total higher education enrollment went from just under 6 million in 1965 to over 20 million in 2014, as the college degree has gradually become an all-but-mandatory requirement for anyone aspiring to mobility, opportunity, and a stable middle-class life in today's America. In 1970, even after the spurt in community college and public university growth of the 1960s, total higher education expenditures were $23.4 billion, or $142.8 billion in today's dollars. By 2014, the annual total had grown to $532 billion, almost four times as much.

The point of this long string of numbers is straightforward: *health care and higher education make up a vastly larger part of the American economy than they did fifty or even twenty-five years ago.* Moreover, today's major medical center or university is a very different place than what it was fifty years ago. James Wagner, president of Atlanta's Emory University from 2003 to 2016, wrote in 2007 that "forty years ago Emory's research enterprise was small, its community impact marginal, and its mode of operation very similar to [when it was] planted in Druid Hills in 1915—more like a family than a business."[14]

In 1963, Clark Kerr, then president of the University of California, coined the term *multiversity* to describe where American higher education was heading.[15] Somewhat ruefully, Wagner wrote in 2007 that "the 'multiversity' is exactly what Emory has sought to become—a major research institution to which policy wonks turn for expertise, industrialists turn for research, government agencies turn for funding proposals, and donors turn for leveraging their philanthropy into the greatest impact on America and the world."[16] Not every college or university is a multiversity; thousands of community colleges as well as small private and public colleges, not to mention the burgeoning ranks of for-profit universities, do not fit that mold. But major universities today are multi-billion-dollar businesses, vast machines for raising and spending money and turning out not only graduates but also research projects and profitable business spin-offs.

The same is even more true for the nation's major medical centers. Johns Hopkins Medicine is an $8-billion a year "integrated global health enterprise," to quote their website, including a medical school, six academic and community hospitals, four suburban health care and surgery

)

centers, and 39 primary and specialty care outpatient sites.[17] In 2014, Johns Hopkins received $593 million worth of research grants from the National Institutes of Health.[18] The symbolism of the UPMC letters on top of the US Steel Building resonates beyond Pittsburgh. In many respects, institutions like UPMC, Johns Hopkins, Yale New Haven Hospital, or Barnes-Jewish Medical Center in St. Louis have taken the place of the vast manufacturing companies as the mega-businesses of twenty-first-century urban America.

While legacy cities were at a disadvantage when it came to keeping their factories, decisions made long ago put them in a strong position to take advantage of the explosion in higher education and health care. The roots of the institutions that turned into today's mega-institutions go back to these cities' industrial heyday or even earlier. It is those roots, and the rich connections they have spawned between cities and institutions, that have led these universities and medical centers to be known today as "anchor institutions." While some university presidents may have dreamed of starting over elsewhere during the darkest days of the 1970s or 1980s, reality dictated that there was no way a Yale or a Johns Hopkins could ever have left New Haven or Baltimore and replicated their magnificent campuses elsewhere. Today, the question has become meaningless, as their relationship to their host cities has become thoroughly symbiotic.

Anchor institutions tend to cluster together. Cleveland's University Circle district, four miles east of downtown Cleveland, is a good example. The area's history goes back to the 1880s, when two small colleges— later to merge into Case Western Reserve University—moved there from cramped downtown quarters. They were followed by University Hospital in 1916 and by the Cleveland Clinic in 1921. The Cleveland Institute of Art opened in 1905, followed by the Cleveland Museum of Art, the Cleveland Natural History Museum, and Severance Hall, home of the Cleveland Orchestra. Some 50,000 people work in University Circle. Over the past decade, that number has grown by nearly 20,000, while the same number of jobs have disappeared in the rest of the city. During that decade, University Circle has seen an explosion of new restaurants, stores, upscale apartments, and a Montessori high school, which opened its doors in 2008.

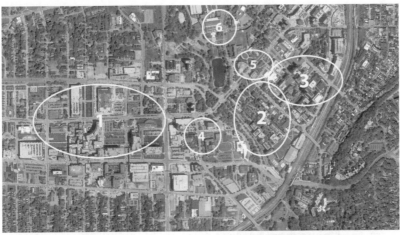

1	Cleveland Clinic	4	Cleveland Institute of Art
2	Case Western Reserve University	5	Severance Hall
3	University Hospital	6	Cleveland Museum of Art

Figure 3-4 The cluster of anchor institutions in Cleveland's University Circle. (Source: base map from Google Earth, overlay by author)

Major universities and medical centers are economic powerhouses. They employ tens of thousands of people and buy billions of dollars' worth of goods and services each year. But their power in an urban economy is not limited to what happens inside their doors. They generate billions more indirectly, through spin-offs and through the spending of their employees and—increasingly—their student bodies.

Universities like Stanford and MIT have spotlighted the role of universities and medical centers as hubs of innovation, generating hundreds of businesses, thousands of jobs, and millions of dollars in licensing fees and spin-off businesses. While Silicon Valley and the Boston/Cambridge area remain the nation's principal magnets for tech investment, legacy cities like Pittsburgh, New Haven, Baltimore, and St. Louis have begun to draw their share.

Carnegie Mellon University (CMU) in Pittsburgh has become famous for its role in autonomous vehicle—read "self-driving car"—technology. They got headlines in the business press when Uber stole forty of their key people in 2015 and set up its own research shop in Pittsburgh. Ottomatika, a firm created in 2013 by CMU professor Raj

Rajkumar to produce self-driving vehicle software, was bought by Delphi Automotive in 2015 but stayed in Pittsburgh. Since 2011, CMU faculty and students have created 148 spin-off companies and executed 871 licensing agreements, while Pitt students and faculty created another 70 companies and signed 674 licensing agreements.[19] These companies and agreements generate money for the universities and economic activity in the city.

Of Connecticut's fifty-two biotech firms, twenty are located in New Haven, and another nineteen in the city's immediate environs, drawn by proximity to Yale University.[20] Working with the city, Yale has taken over a large part of the old Winchester works site and converted it into Science Park, a center for technology and innovation. In Baltimore, the University of Maryland has established BioPark, on twelve acres in distressed West Baltimore adjacent to the University, "to create a university-associated research park that accelerates biotechnology commercialization and economic development in the surrounding community and throughout the region." In addition to creating 800 jobs so far, BioPark focuses on community benefits, including creating a Life Sciences Institute of the Baltimore City Community College to train community residents for jobs in bioscience fields.

One of the most ambitious of these efforts is the Cortex Innovation Community in St. Louis, a joint venture of the city's major universities and medical centers. Founded in 2002, Cortex bills itself as "the Midwest's premier innovation hub of bioscience and technology research, development, and commercialization, serving as the anchor of St. Louis' growing ecosystem for innovative startup programs and established companies." Covering 200 acres in the heart of the city adjacent to St. Louis's iconic Forest Park, it has already brought over 4,000 jobs to the city and, when complete, expects to contain 4.5 million square feet of mixed-use space and 15,000 permanent technology-related jobs. Cortex works closely with the St. Louis Public School District's new Collegiate Medical and Bioscience High School, located adjacent to the district, to create career paths for potential future Cortex employees and entrepreneurs.[21]

Cortex is a prime example of what Brookings's Bruce Katz has dubbed an "innovation district"; as he describes them, they are "geographic areas where leading-edge anchor institutions and companies cluster and connect with start-ups, business incubators, and accelerators. They are also physically compact, transit-accessible, and technically wired and offer mixed-use housing, office, and retail." Katz stresses that they are more than just places, but "the manifestation of mega-trends altering the location preferences of people and firms and, in the process, reconceiving the very link between economy shaping, place making, and social networking."[22]

Many of these projects have struggled; Yale's Science Park was established in the 1980s but did not take off meaningfully until the past ten years. Moreover, they raise questions about how they may or may not contribute to the growing trends toward polarization and inequality that plague America's legacy cities. That said, they make up an increasingly important part of these cities' economic scene, a direct outgrowth of the new eds-and-meds-based urban economy.

As urban economies have been remolded by eds and meds, a second transformation of the older industrial city has been taking place—its reinvention as a center of consumption. Cities have increasingly become, in sociologist Terry Nichols Clark's phrase, "entertainment machines," or, as Michael Sorkin puts it more pejoratively, "theme parks." To the visitor who heads to Baltimore's Inner Harbor or samples the nightlife along St. Louis's Washington Avenue, this is the most visible part of the new postindustrial city. As Clark puts it, "entertainment, consumption, and amenities" have begun to drive urban policy and migration.[24]

This is a total reversal of the way economists, planners, and others in the United States have thought of cities. Traditionally, and to a distressingly large extent even today, they saw the economy of cities, and the relationship between the economy and urban amenities, as looking roughly as shown in figure 3-5:

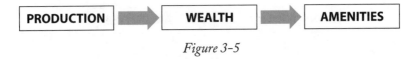

Figure 3-5

Factories made money for a class of wealthy people, who spent much of it in the city where they made it, often using it to create amenities such as parks, concert halls, or museums. Those amenities were enjoyed by the city's population, but had little or no effect otherwise on the city's economy. No factory ever moved to a city because it had a great art museum. This is a simplified but not inaccurate way of looking at what was going on a hundred years ago.

The picture is very different today, and more complicated. America still produces wealth in a lot of different ways, but much less of it is created in its legacy cities. Cities, instead, are places where wealth is more often spent than produced. The spending includes a lot of what are generally seen as necessities, such as education and health care, which supports the pivotal eds-and-meds sector; but there is also a lot of spending on things that more people might see as luxuries, such as Starbucks lattes and tickets to basketball games. Spending may come directly from people's wealth, or as in the case of most health care spending, from taxes or insurance payments that are a by-product of the wealth created elsewhere. Either way, the city can be seen even more as a "consumption machine" than as Clark's "entertainment machine." The ability to maximize consumption by providing the amenities that consumers are looking for becomes critical; as Harvard economist Edward Glaeser and his co-authors in a prescient 2000 paper summed it up, "Attractive cities will thrive; unpleasant cities will decay."[25]

The actual picture is even more complicated, because there's a feedback system among wealth, consumption, and amenities. Amenities, which can be anything from a scenic waterfront to a cluster of theaters and restaurants like Cleveland's Playhouse Square, are not merely the product of consumption demand but are themselves generators and multipliers of demand, by drawing people with money to spend and with potential wealth-creating skills to cities. Thus, the picture starts to look more like figure 3-6:

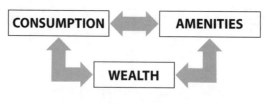

Figure 3-6

A critical part of this is what Clark calls the "scene." When enough amenities cluster in one area to form a critical mass, they create scenes. Scenes draw people together to share activities, to participate in a distinctive shared atmosphere, and define themselves by sharing the scene with other like-minded people. Scenes also offer young, unattached people the greatest opportunity to make friends and identify potential romantic partners. It was Austin's scene, more than anything else, that convinced the young tech wizard we met in chapter 1 to leave Pittsburgh; as he summed it up, "I can have a life in Austin, not merely a job."[26]

That appears to have been Richard Florida's "aha" moment. People were no longer moving for jobs, as the classic economic thesis would have it; people's decisions were now more about place, and about what that place offered talented, creative people in terms of its scene. Jobs were not irrelevant; but, as Florida writes, "I have come across many people who have moved somewhere for the lifestyle and only *then* set out to look for employment there" (his emphasis).[27] Austin, Texas, still has a justly celebrated entertainment scene, but the competition is getting stiffer. Pittsburgh, Philadelphia, Baltimore, and St. Louis have scenes. Cleveland, Detroit, and Buffalo are moving in that direction. Today, that same young man might have stayed in Pittsburgh.

The millennials who set the pace for urban revival cluster closely in areas that offer the amenities that most resonate with their interests and lifestyles. These are the areas that not only have the restaurants, cafes, and music venues, but also have high density and lively mixtures of different activities on the same block, or even in the same building. Most of these areas also share a special visual or aesthetic quality. That quality can come from distinctive old buildings, like the one-time warehouses on St. Louis's Washington Avenue or the nineteenth-century row houses in Baltimore's Fells Point. It can come from being on a riverbank or lakeshore, or, for the more artistically inclined, it can even be a sort of reverse aesthetic, as in the pockets of artists that have sprung up in gritty, grimy industrial areas.

The virtuous cycle driven by consumption and amenities may be an oversimplification, but it's not that far from reality. And it has another important dimension. When the mix of consumption and amenities gets strong enough, it starts generating production, not just more consumption. The more talent (and money) that a city can draw with its amenities, the more likely it is that more of that talent and money will be directed to production, rather than solely to consumption. A research-oriented university or medical center doesn't just enroll students or admit patients; it starts generating inventions and spin-offs. Young people who come to the city because of its amenities start creating businesses and hiring people to work for them. As a result, you now get two feedback loops that look like figure 3-7:

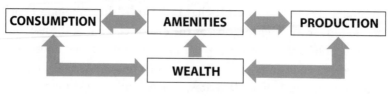

Figure 3-7

The decision by Ottomatika to stay in Pittsburgh rather than move to Silicon Valley reflects this second feedback loop. Ottomatika doesn't *need* to be close to Carnegie Mellon, or anything else Pittsburgh offers. It *chooses* to be in Pittsburgh, not only because that's where they started and it's hard to pick up and move, but because Pittsburgh offers the amenities that its owners and its workforce are looking for, and that make it possible for them to attract new, highly skilled workers. If it didn't, they'd be in Austin or San Francisco. Amenities help cities retain the new businesses that start there, and eventually, they start drawing other businesses.

None of this would be possible, of course, were it not for the economic underpinning provided in the first place by the eds-and-meds institutions, something that observers overlook at their peril. At the same time, the leaders of those institutions know that the quality of their city's amenities have everything to do with whether they can continue to recruit the talented students, faculty, and researchers they need to maintain their competitive position in the national or global market.

Yale has spent millions over the past decade buying properties and recruiting a carefully curated mix of restaurants and retailers into areas adjacent to the Yale campus, transforming two scruffy but lively urban shopping streets into The Shops at Yale, an upscale shopping and dining mecca. Yale has methodically assembled a collection of nearly one hundred retail tenants designed to add amenities desired not only by the university community, but by present and anticipated affluent New Haven residents, and not incidentally, further the Yale "brand." Attracting the Apple store, according to Yale vice president Bruce Alexander, "was a major effort. It took us three years to put the Apple deal together." In an interview with local reporter Ed Stannard, Alexander described how they recruited KIKO, a hip Italian cosmetics firm: "When KIKO's representative was in town," he said, "we found three women at Yale who were undergraduates who were Italian—not Italian-American, but Italian. They all started speaking Italian to each other. [...] [We're] convinced to this day that it was those three undergraduates from Italy who made this deal."[28]

The Yale story, and others like it, raise complicated but also disturbing questions. In an amenity-driven age, Yale is doing what it not unreasonably sees as necessary to maintain its position as an elite global institution. The university's ability to maintain its competitive edge, not to mention the money that students, faculty, and visitors spend daily in The Shops at Yale, is critical to New Haven's present and future economic vitality. And yet it raises the question that keeps coming up as one looks at the postindustrial American city: vitality for whom?

Tellingly, Win Davis, head of New Haven's downtown business improvement district, told the same reporter that "something that Yale has helped us to overcome is . . . getting [retailers] to come to town despite the Census data."[29] New Haven, as Davis knows well, is still a poor city. I remember Chapel Street and Broadway from my long-past years as a Yale undergraduate. Both were somewhat run-down but lively shopping streets, lined with inexpensive and sometimes funky stores patronized by Yale students and residents of nearby low-income neighborhoods alike, usually albeit sometimes warily coexisting. These areas have now been redefined as the turf, not only of the university, but of a privileged social and economic class, as clearly as if one had built a wall with checkpoints around them. In microcosm, The Shops at Yale are a mirror of the way in which social and economic polarization is embedded in the new urban economy. Then again, one must ask: is that polarization being driven by urban economic transformations, or does it simply mirror the polarization that is increasingly part of the national economic and social picture? And also, to what extent is it a *choice*, driven by the preferences and priorities of those with the power and resources to mold the urban economy?

While The Shops at Yale are still about consumption, the same needs to be said about the way in which a city's amenities may be helping to restore at least some of its productive capacity. In many respects, that capacity is far from what existed during these cities' industrial era. Most of the companies that are emerging are small, and most of the people they hire are engineers, coders, and others with advanced degrees and specialized skills, many of whom live in the cities' suburbs. As I discuss in chapter 9, while these businesses and jobs are important for their cities' economic vitality, they leave most of the people who live in these cities behind. At the same time, that may not be inevitable; in that same chapter, I explore some promising efforts people are making to make the new economy work for more than just the favored few.

Finally, amenities are the engine for another economic sector that has become important to postindustrial cities: visitors, tourists, and conventions. Mega-events like Superbowl weekends and national political party conventions tend to be hyped well beyond their real value to a city's economy, but just the same, tourism should not be underestimated. Tourists and visitors are *all* about amenities, though, along with the facilities they need, like hotels, airports, and parking garages.

Up to a point, tourism leverages the same amenities that fuel the city's internal economy. The same restaurants, nightlife, and arts scene that appeal to resident millennials also add to a city's tourist and visitor appeal. Adding tourism to a city's economy, however, can be costly; in recent years, the competition for visitor dollars among cities has taken on the character of an increasingly expensive arms race. Most notorious are convention centers, routinely financed by taxpayers to the tune of hundreds of millions of dollars, often through backdoor financing arrangements that would most probably be rejected by voters if they had the choice. Between 1989 and 2011, 34 million square feet in convention-center space was added in the United States, nearly doubling the amount available, while the convention business barely grew.

No wonder Heywood Sanders, one of the few scholars who has systematically studied the industry, could write in 2014, "After the public promises of new spending, economic impact, job creation, and development, often comes a reality that is rather different. City after city builds a big new center, only to realize little or no new convention activity, and see no real job creation . . . yet that apparent failure . . . invariably yields a call for more space, an adjacent hotel, or an 'entertainment district' that will propel the city into the front rank of convention destinations."[30]

That does not mean that tourism does not make a significant economic contribution. It's not clear exactly what contribution the $1.5 billion Pennsylvania Convention Center makes to Philadelphia's tourism industry, but that industry appears to be burgeoning. According to an economic impact study commissioned by Visit Philadelphia, one of two organizations that promote tourism to that city, the total regional economic impact of tourism in 2015 was over $10 billion, of which $6 billion was in the city of Philadelphia. Even granting a certain generosity in what was included in order to reach that figure, it's a lot. Philadelphia has been adding an average of almost 500 hotel rooms each year since 2010—a major source of jobs, albeit largely poorly paying ones. As the report points out, in percentage terms the "leisure and hospitality" sector of the regional economy has been the fastest-growing of any economic sector, although its overall numbers are still much smaller than those of the education and health sectors.

None of this comes cheap. The competition among cities for tourists, and even more for conventions, is fierce, particularly among cities like Cleveland or Philadelphia that are far from international brands. Visit Philadelphia spends $11 million per year promoting the city, while its crosstown rival the Philadelphia Convention & Visitors Bureau spends an additional $17 million doing many of the same things. Not only do cities, counties, and states subsidize the construction of convention centers, which at least remain in public ownership, but they also subsidize the construction of nearby privately owned hotels. To build the Marriott Marquis hotel at the Washington, DC, convention center in 2010, the city's Convention Center Authority issued $175 million in bonds through what is known as Tax Increment Financing, or TIF, where the hotel's future property tax payments go to pay off the bonds, rather than to the District of Columbia's treasury. As a result, the city will receive no property tax revenues from the project until the bonds are paid off.

In the hopes of gaining more convention business, the city of Kansas City agreed to cover half of the cost of renovating the Marriott Downtown hotel. About 60 percent of the $16.5-million tab would be covered by city convention and visitor sales tax revenues, and about 40 percent would be covered by a one-cent community improvement district sales tax surcharge collected on sales and room rentals at the hotel.[32] Steep hotel taxes have become commonplace, as cities find it relatively easy to levy high taxes on out-of-town visitors who don't vote in local elections or show up at city council meetings. St. Louis tacks an 18 percent tax onto hotel bills, while Indianapolis hits visitors with a 17 percent tax.

Ever since Rouse's Harborplace development at Baltimore's Inner Harbor showed its value as an amenity that drew both residents and visitors, cities have put billions of dollars into financing or supporting similar projects. While the transformation of Washington Avenue in St. Louis was driven by private entrepreneurs, the public sector soon jumped in. The city provided financing for some of the pioneering developers, and in 1998 the state of Missouri enacted a historic-preservation tax credit that gave developers a powerful incentive to turn the street's old factory buildings into apartments. Two years later, the city chipped in $17 million to install "custom lights, unique trash cans, expanded sidewalks, and a zipper-and-stitch-like paving pattern with LED-lit button 'runway lights' striped down the center," the last feature being a subtle homage to the street's days as the city's garment center. Sadly, by 2015 the elaborate improvements were starting to crumble, a testimony to the painful reality that it is often easier to find money to make improvements than to maintain them.[33]

Spending on amenities that are clearly designed to attract what Ed Glaeser calls "high human capital" residents, even as large parts of the same cities continue to decline, clearly raises difficult equity issues; Glaeser argues, though, that "traditional cities will only succeed when they provide amenities that are attractive to high-human-capital residents."[34] This may be true to a point, but the question remains whether this spending leads to enough benefits to a city's lower-income residents, whether through more jobs, higher wages, or improved quality of life, to offset the higher costs that follow in the wake of the in-migration of more affluent people. When we look at the big-ticket items, the convention centers, football stadiums, and the like, the relationship between costs and benefits seems particularly out of balance.

There is some evidence that a rising tide lifts some, if not all, boats. Berkeley economist Enrico Moretti found that the salaries of high school graduates correlate highly with the percentage of workers in the area with a college degree, a good indicator of the area's economic strength; as he puts it, "a worker with a high school education who moves from a city like Miami . . . where 30 percent of the population are college graduates, to a city like Denver, where 40 percent of residents are college graduates, can expect a raise of $8,250 just for moving."[35] Of course, that worker may find herself spending that much or more in increased housing costs.

For many urban residents, though, the answer is that the benefits are not substantial; that little of the economic growth triggered by either public or private action filters down, particularly to the people who need it most—the poor and near-poor families and individuals who typically make up anywhere from one-third to more than half of the population of the cities I'm writing about. When we get to chapter 9, we'll explore that question in more detail, and we'll try to understand why that is so, why in the midst of growth and increasing prosperity, the ranks of the poor and near-poor are often growing, rather than shrinking.

Chapter 4

Race, Poverty, and Real Estate

The multidimensional, conflicted, and stressful relationship between white and black in America is the inescapable presence, the unavoidable elephant in the room of American society. It is nowhere more so than in the nation's legacy cities. Over fifty years ago, in his powerful book *Crisis in Black and White*, Charles Silberman wrote that "solving the problem of race is not only the most urgent piece of public business facing the United States today; it is also the most difficult."[1] Soon thereafter, in the wake of the riots that convulsed American cities in the 1960s, the Commission on Civil Disorders appointed by President Johnson began its 600-page report with the warning that "our nation is moving toward two societies, one white, one black—separate and unequal."[2] The commission concluded that the present course of action "would lead to the permanent establishment of two societies, one predominately white and located in the suburbs, in smaller cities, and in outlying areas, and one largely Negro located in central cities."[3] Although their prediction that the line would run neatly between cities and suburbs has not stood the test of time, their underlying conclusion is no less true today than it was fifty years ago.

To understand how race, real estate, and revitalization are so intertwined, though, one has to go much further back. As small numbers of African Americans trickled into northern industrial cities toward the end of the nineteenth century and early in the twentieth, they were not welcomed warmly. While efforts to keep blacks out of large parts of the cities, or to keep them from competing for valued factory jobs, were informal, they were often enforced with violence. In 1910, after local black lawyer George McMechen and his wife moved into a row house at 1834 McCulloh Street in what was then a white neighborhood, Baltimore decided it was time to give racial segregation the force of law. The city enacted an ordinance specifying that "no negro may take up his residence in a block within the city limits of Baltimore wherein more than half the residents are white."[4] In the grand tradition of forbidding rich as well as poor from sleeping under bridges, the ordinance also barred whites from living in predominately black blocks.

Baltimore's mayor justified this step, arguing that "Blacks should be quarantined in isolated slums in order to reduce the incidents of civil disturbance, to prevent the spread of communicable disease into the nearby White neighborhoods, and to protect property values among the White majority."[5] In a decision unusual for its time, the Supreme Court struck down Baltimore's ordinance in 1917; hostility to black families looking for better housing, however, grew along with the rapid growth in urban black populations during and after the First World War.

During the 1920s, conflicts erupted in many cities, including Detroit. Legal scholar Douglas Linder describes the events there in 1925:

> In April, 5,000 people crowded in front of a home on Northfield Avenue, throwing rocks and threatening to burn the house down. "The house is being rented by blacks," someone in the crowd explained to police arriving at the scene. [...] The next month, John Fletcher and his family were the targets of mob violence. The Fletchers had just sat down to a meal in their new home on Stoepel Avenue when they were spotted through a window by a passing white woman. The woman began to yell, "Niggers live there! Niggers live there!" Soon a crowd of 4,000 had gathered. Some in the crowd yelled, "Lynch them!" Chunks of coke smashed through windows.[6]

The Fletchers moved out the next day. That fall, though, a black doctor named Ossian Sweet moved with his family into a house on Garland Street, in a then-white neighborhood of the city. Although the first night passed without event, the next night a mob gathered around the house, shouting, "Niggers, niggers, get the damn niggers!" A fusillade of rocks hit the house, smashing windows. Fearing that the mob would soon invade the house and lynch them, someone inside fired into the crowd from the second-floor window, killing one man and wounding another. Sweet and his family members, all of whom had been arrested after the shooting, were tried and found not guilty, thanks to a brilliant defense by Clarence Darrow. A historic marker commemorating the episode stands alongside the house today (fig. 4-1).

Figure 4-1 Dr. Ossian Sweet's house on Garland Street. (Note historical marker at left.) (Source: Google Earth)

Although Dr. Sweet moved back into the Garland Street house not long after the trial and lived there until 1948, his story and others like it, rather than opening doors for others, led to redoubled efforts to maintain segregation in northern cities. With local ordinances no longer permitting overt segregation, the preferred tool became the racial covenant, a legal provision in the deed of sale typically barring the buyer from selling or renting the house to "any person or persons not of the white or Caucasian race," often barring Jews or other ethnic groups as well. The use of such covenants grew through the 1920s and 1930s until they were struck down by the Supreme Court in 1948. Between 1921 and 1935, 67 out of 101 new subdivisions filed in the city of Columbus, Ohio, included racial covenants.[7] Even the University of Chicago's famously liberal president of the time, Robert Maynard Hutchins, defended the local use of racial covenants "to stabilize its neighborhood as an area in which its students and faculty will be content to live."[8]

The effect of racial covenants was compounded by redlining, which emerged in the 1930s with the creation of "residential security" maps of each city's more or less desirable neighborhoods, most famously by the federal government's Home Owner's Loan Corporation to demarcate the areas where the HOLC would provide federally backed loans to refinance mortgages on homes threatened with foreclosure. While the extent to which the maps affected the HOLC's activities is still debated, with some arguing that they did little more than ratify existing practices, they firmly put the federal government's stamp on racial discrimination by rating most black neighborhoods with a D, or unsuitable for lending.

Whether or not the Federal Housing Administration, which was created in the New Deal to open up home-buying to working- and middle-class American families, actually used the HOLC maps is unclear; what is clear is that the FHA's lending practices strongly encouraged racial segregation long after the Supreme Court had voided racial covenants and well into the 1960s, even after President Kennedy's 1962 executive order calling for "the abandonment of discriminatory practices with respect to residential property and related facilities heretofore provided with federal financial assistance."

What makes the intensity with which whites defended the color line in the 1920s and 1930s even more striking is that the black populations of most cities were still quite small compared to what they would become after World War II. In 1925, when Ossian Sweet and his family went on trial, African Americans made up only 6 percent of Detroit's population; in 1940, less than 10 percent of Cleveland's residents were African American. The growth of these cities' black population during the first Great Migration of the 1910s and 1920s, however, had been rapid; the black population of Detroit went from 6,000 in 1910 to 41,000 in 1920 and 120,000 by the eve of the Great Depression. Detroit's white population was also growing rapidly during the same years, though, going from less than half a million in 1910 to nearly 1.5 million by 1930.

As African Americans moved to the cities in search of better living conditions and greater opportunity, they encountered many barriers to achieving either goal. Black workers seeking factory jobs came up against intense resistance from white workers; even as World War II raged, thousands of white workers walked off the job at the Detroit Packard plant, which made engines for PT boats and bombers, when the management promoted three African American workmen. White clerical workers at Hudson's, Detroit's flagship downtown department store, walked off the job when the company began to hire black women to work alongside them.[9] With few neighborhoods open to them, blacks moving to Detroit mostly squeezed into the Black Bottom area east of downtown, along with a few smaller pockets elsewhere in the city.

Black Bottom, which was named after its rich black soil long before the first African Americans arrived, had been an immigrant neighborhood since the mid-nineteenth century, where Germans, Poles, Jews, and Italians had each lived briefly and moved on. Discrimination, however, prevented the African Americans who began to move into Black Bottom in the early twentieth century from similarly moving on. By mid-century, this small area was home to over 140,000 people. It had become increasingly a dilapidated, dangerously overcrowded neighborhood made up of rickety wooden structures, most built before 1900. Many lacked indoor plumbing, and their residents depended on the 3,500 latrines that dotted the neighborhood.[10] Few owned their own homes, and nearly all were at the mercy of the landlords who owned all but a handful of the neighborhood's houses and apartments.

At the same time, it was a dynamic, vibrant community with a strong commercial core along Hastings Street and a thriving music scene, particularly in the northern part of the area known as Paradise Valley. As Detroiter Elaine Moon wrote, "It was the black downtown, Broadway, Las Vegas. A place of fun, brotherhood, and games of chance. A place known from here to Europe. In the 1930s and early '40s in Detroit, a night on the town, for Black or White, was not complete without a stop at Paradise Valley."[11]

Bad as things were by the end of World War II, though, in many respects they were to get worse. The fifties and sixties not only saw millions of African Americans flock to the nation's industrial cities, but they were also the era of urban renewal and the Interstate Highway program. While neighborhoods of all descriptions, along with large parts of most cities' downtowns, fell to the wrecking ball, black neighborhoods, particularly those strategically close to downtown, were often singled out for removal. Black Bottom was quite literally obliterated. Most of it, including Hastings Street, was buried under the Chrysler Freeway (I-75), while much of the rest was razed to build the upscale Lafayette Park development, three apartment towers and 186 townhouses in a landscaped, self-contained nineteen-acre "superblock" designed by famed Bauhaus architect Mies van der Rohe. While Lafayette Park is now on the National Register of Historic Places, its construction was made possible by the displacement of some 7,000 African Americans, most of whom moved elsewhere into homes little better than the ones they had been forced to leave.[12]

City after city tells a similar story. In Pittsburgh, much of the Lower Hill district, immortalized in August Wilson's great cycle of plays, was razed to construct the Civic Arena, built in 1967 and demolished in 2011. As many as 8,000 residents were displaced and dispersed, some to public housing, some to other parts of the Hill, and others across the city of Pittsburgh and nearby mill towns. Mill Creek Valley, a run-down African American neighborhood in the shadow of downtown St. Louis, was demolished in 1959, displacing 20,000 residents; as one account put it, "The bulldozers swiftly transformed the city's 'No. 1 Eyesore' into an area derided as 'Hiroshima Flats.'"[13] By 1960, only twenty original families still called Mill Creek home. Of the million or more American families displaced by both the interstate highway program and urban renewal, perhaps as many as half were black.

Part of this was driven by the same perverse logic that led engineers to route other highways through parks and along waterfronts. Land occupied by poor people cost less to acquire, and poor people had less ability to fight back. Unlike Jane Jacobs and her Greenwich Village neighbors, who successfully organized to block Robert Moses' plan to run a highway through the area, few black communities had the political clout or organizational strength to keep the bulldozers out. But there was a darker side to the planners' thinking, a pervasive association of slums with disease, not only in the narrow sense of their being seen as breeding grounds for diseases like tuberculosis or typhus, but as a disease in themselves; as noted Finnish-American architect Eliel Saarinen wrote in his influential 1943 book *The City*, "large areas in the heart of the city have become the centers of a contagious disease which threatens the whole organism." After describing this in detail, he came to his point, printed in bold in the book for emphasis: "Urban conditions cannot be cured in [a] superficial manner. [The planner] must unearth the roots of the evil. He must amputate slums by a decisive surgery."[14] Over the next decades, the word *slum* was gradually replaced by *ghetto*, and the disease metaphor took on an increasingly racial character. That, too, must be seen as part of the climate that allowed local governments, corporations, and institutions to obliterate long-established black neighborhoods with such seeming indifference to the effect on their residents and businesses.

Meanwhile, the Second Great Migration of African Americans from the nation's South to the North and West that began during World War II, an exodus that dwarfed the earlier migration, was well under way. Between 1941 and 1970, 5 million African Americans left the South for other parts of the country, with large numbers heading for northern industrial cities. From 1940 to 1970, Chicago's black population went from 277,000 to 1.1 million, and that of Detroit from 149,000 to 660,000. By 1980, fully half of the black residents of both cities had been born in the South.

The response they received, though, although no warmer, was radically different from that which had greeted the first migration, and which had brought the neighborhood toughs out to throw stones at Dr. Sweet's house. If the white response in the 1920s was to fight, in the 1950s and 1960s it was flight. Millions—over a million and a half from Chicago alone—fled the cities for their burgeoning suburbs or the booming cities of the Sunbelt, their flight often accelerated by the blockbusting and other unsavory tactics practiced by local realtors and speculators.

Many different factors contributed to white flight after World War II, but even after taking account of the enticements of affordable suburban houses and inexpensive mortgages, the new highways, and the shabby postwar condition of many cities after years of disinvestment, race stands out as the most powerful; UCLA economist Leah Boustan has calculated that "each black arrival was associated with 2.3 to 2.7 white departures,"[15] as figure 4-2 shows. With white departures substantially outnumbering black arrivals, America's older cities began to shrink.

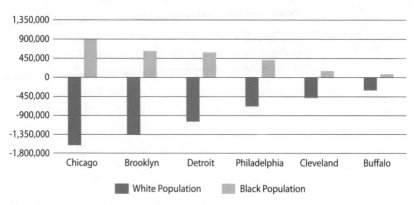

Figure 4-2 Change in white and African American populations of selected cities, 1940–1980. (Source: US Census)

White flight, coupled with the gradual effects of civil rights and fair housing laws, meant that thousands of African Americans were now able to move out of the crowded areas where they had largely been confined up to that point. From the 1960s through the 1980s, black families moved into large parts of American cities that were being abandoned by their longtime white residents.

This created new opportunities for many African Americans, but it also meant the end of the traditional black neighborhood. Created by segregation and rife with poverty, overcrowding, and substandard housing, they were neighborhoods with a vital energy, with their own stores, their own doctors and lawyers, where rich, poor, and middle-class lived side by side and mingled daily in the streets, the stores, and the churches. Looking back at the 1960s, African American columnist Eugene Robinson wrote in 2010, "no one quite realized it at the time, but Black America was being split."

Those who could, moved; those who could not, stayed. Robinson sums up the change:

> Some moved out—to neighborhoods unscarred by the riots, to the suburbs . . . and moved up, taking advantage of new opportunities. They moved up the ladder at work, purchased homes and built equity, sent their children to college, demanded and earned most of their rightful share of America's bounty. They became the Mainstream majority. Some didn't make it. They saw the row houses and apartment buildings where they lived sag from neglect; they hunkered down as big public housing projects . . . became increasingly dysfunctional and dangerous. They sent their children to low-performing schools that had already been forsaken by the brightest students and the pushiest parents. They remained while jobs left the neighborhood, as did capital, as did ambition, as did public order. They became the Abandoned.[16]

In 1970, the average African American lived in a neighborhood that was more economically mixed, with the well-to-do, middle-class, and poor living side by side, than the neighborhoods where most white people lived. Only a decade later, that was no longer true. As Bischoff and Reardon write, "segregation by income among black families . . . grew four times as much [as among white families] between 1970 and 2009."[17] They add that "although income segregation among blacks grew substantially in the 1970s and 1980s, it grew at an even faster rate from 2000 to 2009." (We will look at the factors driving that change later in this chapter.)

The transformation Robinson describes could be subtitled "The Making of the Ghetto," not only as a reality, but as a term that came into common use in the 1960s and 1970s to describe the distressed, poor African American neighborhoods that now seemed to be a fixture of every older city in America. How the word *ghetto*, a word coined in sixteenth-century Venice, became the code word for these neighborhoods is itself a useful object lesson in how words become racialized, and what that comes to mean.[18]

When the Venetian authorities forced the city's Jews to move into a small walled compound in Cannaregio in 1516, that area came to be known as the Ghetto, a name whose origins are still obscure. The word caught on, appearing in the papal bull that created the Rome ghetto in 1562. During the sixteenth and seventeenth centuries, in city after city Jews across Western Europe were confined to ghettos, most famously perhaps in Rome, where in addition to being segregated, Jews were regularly herded into churches to be forced to listen to sermons exhorting them to convert to Christianity and taxed to pay for the priests giving the sermons.

With the coming of the Enlightenment in the eighteenth century, the ghettos were gradually abolished. The last one to be dismantled was in Rome, with the end of papal rule in 1870. The ghetto was revived in far more horrific fashion in the twentieth century by Nazi Germany, which herded Jews into closed zones in Eastern European cities, either to exploit their labor or to confine them to interim holding camps pending their murder by the Nazi killing machine.

During the first half of the twentieth century, before the word *ghetto* took on its association with the Holocaust, it was applied loosely in the United States to racial and ethnic enclaves of all sorts, but particularly to Jewish immigrant communities. A popular book of 1902, Hutchins Hapgood's *The Spirit of the Ghetto*, about the Jewish Lower East Side of Manhattan, described the "intense and varied life [of] the colony of Russian and Galician Jews who live on the east side and form the largest Jewish city in the world."[19] During World War II, though, spurred by the awareness of what was going on in Eastern Europe, people in the United States began to focus on the black or "Negro" ghetto, making the point that—in contrast to the white ethnic "ghettos"—urban blacks who tried to move out "hit the invisible barbed-wire fence of restrictive covenants."[20]

Whether or not St. Clair Drake and Horace Clayton, the two black sociologists who wrote those lines in their magisterial work *Black Metropolis* in 1945, were deliberately drawing an analogy with the barbed wire the Nazis used to build their ghettos is unclear, although it is hard to imagine that it was not on their minds. As with Kenneth Clark, who published *Dark Ghetto* twenty years later, it was largely African

Americans, both scholars and advocates, who used the term *ghetto* to call attention to the fact that, unlike white ethnic groups that initially clustered together for mutual support and cultural solidarity and for the most part moved onward as they assimilated and prospered, black people were kept hemmed in by the outside white world.

As Robinson's "Mainstream majority" began to move out of the traditional black neighborhoods in the 1960s and 1970s, the idea of what a ghetto meant was transformed once again. Now, it was no longer an area defined by race, but by race *and class*. It was no longer clearly hemmed in by explicit, formal barriers, but by more subtle, if equally powerful, barriers of social pressure and poverty; as Dutch scholar Talja Blokland puts it, it became the "spatial expression of social processes."[21] The term *inner city*, which came into use in the 1960s and 1970s, came to be seen as almost a synonym. Despite its literal meaning, though, *inner city* is not a geographic term; as Brooklyn blogger Justin Charity writes, it can be anywhere: *inner city* "is a uniquely American term. In its common usage, it signifies poor, black, urban neighborhoods. The term somehow applies regardless of whether [or not] such neighborhoods are downtown or central to the city grid."[22]

Both terms, especially as used by the larger society to stigmatize the people it has left behind, are sometimes resented, but they have also become a trademark for many young African Americans who have come to use *ghetto* and *inner city* to stand for a distinct, oppositional strand of African American culture that challenges white mainstream culture. Leaving culture aside, though, the terms reflect a physical reality: the presence of large areas of concentrated, persistent, and largely African American poverty in almost every older city in the United States. These areas are as distinct and important a type of urban neighborhood as the gentrifying areas or the middle neighborhoods we will explore in the following chapters. Whatever one's feelings toward these terms, whether used by white politicians or black rappers, these are the places people are thinking about when they say *ghetto* or *inner city*. They are real.

Putting the words *concentrated poverty* and *African American* together in the same sentence is not accidental. While there are many poor white families in the United States, many of whom live in urban areas, few live in urban areas of concentrated poverty. In Baltimore, half of all poor

African Americans live in areas of concentrated poverty, compared to only one out of five poor whites. In Milwaukee, over 70 percent of poor blacks live in high-poverty areas.

In contrast to the bustling, vibrant streets of the mid-century African American neighborhoods depicted by so many writers, though, the most powerful visual impression many longtime ghetto areas make today is one of sheer emptiness. Walking down Market Street in North City St. Louis, shown in figure 4-3, one sees block after block of vacant, derelict houses and vacant lots, mixed with scattered still-occupied homes and churches, occasionally interspersed with a low-income housing project or two. It hardly comes as a surprise to learn that this part of St. Louis, where nearly 37,000 people lived in 1970, houses only a little more than 6,000 today.[23]

Figure 4-3 North Market Street in North City St. Louis. (Source: Google Earth)

North City may be extreme, but it is not unique. The Kettering section of Detroit's East Side housed 45,000 people in 1970, but only 9,000 today. Not surprisingly, a 2013 survey found that over half of the area's houses have been torn down, with vacant lots left in their place, while over a quarter of the remaining houses are vacant and abandoned.

Detroit's East Side and North City St. Louis may be further down the path of abandonment than equally distressed areas in some other cities, but the story is the same—a steady progression of decline that has gone on for decade after decade. As we showed earlier, far more white people fled the cities than African Americans came to take their place. Some American cities, like St. Louis and Pittsburgh, started to lose population in the 1950s, while the exodus turned into a flood in the 1960s and 1970s. As Robinson's Mainstream majority moved out of the ghetto, the poor stayed behind.

Gradually, a vicious cycle emerged. As areas became increasingly poor and run-down, fewer and fewer people who could afford to live somewhere else wanted to stay. With more areas open to African American families, ghetto residents who got a promotion, a college degree, or a new, better, job, moved out. As fewer and fewer people wanted the houses, just as the law of supply and demand would predict, they were worth less and less, to the point where a house cost less than a good used car. Owners made fewer and fewer repairs—why bother when you'd never get your money back?—and the houses started to fall apart. A lot of owners stopped paying property taxes, and their properties started to wind up in the hands of city governments, which took them over even though they didn't really want them and usually didn't know what to do with them. Here and there, a developer or a nonprofit organization got federal money and put up a low-income housing project. That meant that a few poor people had better housing, but it did nothing to change the area's downward spiral.

Soon, the only people buying houses in these areas were absentee owners, usually short-term speculators, who rented them out to people who couldn't afford anything better. Eventually, when the cost of maintaining the house got too much, they walked away. Gradually no one wanted to own the houses anymore. In the entire census tract shown in the picture of St. Louis's North Market Street, only one house was sold during 2015. The price was $9,900.

When an area gets to that point, as families move out, or elderly homeowners pass away, the houses stay empty, and are sooner or later vandalized for the copper in the pipes, trashed by squatters or gangs, or set on fire. Eventually, the city may get around to knocking them down, usually to the relief of the remaining neighbors. Cleveland activist Frank Ford told me about how an elderly homeowner once buttonholed him about the empty house next door: "I don't care if they fix it up or tear it down," she said. "Just *do* something!"

Despite the robust urban revival, areas of concentrated poverty are growing in America's cities and metropolitan areas. Urban Observatory's Joe Cortright has studied the long-term trends in the nation's larger cities and metro areas. He concludes: "A few places have gentrified, experienced a reduction in poverty, and generated net population growth. But those areas that don't rebound don't remain stable: they deteriorate, lose population, and overwhelmingly remain high-poverty neighborhoods. Meanwhile, we are continually creating new high-poverty neighborhoods."[24] While poverty itself is debilitating to body and spirit, decades of research since Kenneth Clark's *Dark Ghetto* has shown how much more destructive it becomes when concentrated in areas of persistent, concentrated poverty.

Cortright found that out of 1,100 high-poverty neighborhoods in the fifty-one cities he studied in 1970, fewer than one in ten had "rebounded," in that their poverty rates had declined from over 30 percent to below 15 percent, which was still at or below the national average. More than two-thirds of those areas still had poverty rates over 30 percent in 2010. Meanwhile, over 1,200 neighborhoods that had been low-poverty in 1970 had become high-poverty areas by 2010. All told, there were nearly three times as many high-poverty areas in these fifty-one cities in 2010 as in 1970.

Cortright didn't factor race into his study, but when we compare the location of areas in many cities that are both majority black and high-poverty in 2000 and in 2015, we find the same pattern: a few areas may no longer be majority black, high-poverty areas, but many more areas have been added. While a handful of areas in Milwaukee are no longer majority black, high-poverty areas, large parts of the city's North Side have been added; all in all, the number of Milwaukee's African American residents living in areas of concentrated poverty grew by 36,000 between 2000 and 2015, while the percentage of all African Americans living in those areas grew from 46 percent in 2000 to 58 percent, or well over half, by 2015. In the map of Detroit shown in figure

4-4, the areas outlined in black were ghetto areas in 2000, while the gray areas were ghetto areas in 2015. Detroit's ghetto has spread from the central parts of the east and west side across the city, today including many of the city's one-time middle-class neighborhoods to the northwest and to the east.

Figure 4-4 The spread of Detroit's ghetto, 2000–2015. (Source: PolicyMap)

Tracking one small area, the black circle on the map of Detroit, over the past nearly fifty years sheds light on how urban neighborhoods change. This area, a small neighborhood known as Crary-St. Mary's after its public school and its Catholic church, was built from the 1930s through the 1950s, a time mostly of prosperity and rapid growth in Detroit. From the beginning it was a middle-class neighborhood, with smallish but solid brick houses set back from the street by generous front yards; in fact, it was a modest, miniature version of nearby Palmer Park, where the Big Three executives lived in brick and stone mansions. It was a neighborhood of married couples and homeowners. As late as 1970, it was still entirely white. That changed almost overnight in the 1970s, though, as Detroit's white middle-class families fled the city for the burgeoning suburbs. By 1980, the area was 84 percent black.

The skin color of the people living in the houses may have changed, but little else did. The great majority of the black newcomers were middle-class strivers themselves. They earned about the same as the people they replaced, and they owned their own homes, where they raised their families. The number of married couples with children in the area actually went up from 1970 to 1980. Things stayed pretty much the same through the 1980s. While there were subtle signs of change during the nineties, as the number of homeowners dropped slightly and incomes started to tail off, the area was still in fairly decent shape as the millennium ended. Few residents were poor, and few houses were empty.

Then Crary-St. Mary's fell off an economic cliff. By 2015, the neighborhood's population had dropped by a quarter. The number of poor residents more than doubled. The neighborhood became a concentrated poverty area, where nearly two out of five residents lived below the poverty level. At the same time, the number of "middle-class" people in the area, defined as people whose family income is more than double the poverty rate, fell by over half. That's a low bar, less than $50,000 per year for a family of four. The number of homeowners dropped by more than 300, over a quarter of all the homeowners in this small neighborhood. By 2009, houses were selling for barely more than $10,000. The number of empty houses tripled, and people started to get used to living next door to boarded-up houses, as seen in figure 4-5. As the city became increasingly aggressive about knocking down empty houses, more and more vacant lots started to pop up in the neighborhood.

Whether Crary-St. Mary's can be restored to its one-time vitality, and what that would take, is a complicated question. Here, though, the question is why it collapsed the way it did. It's a complicated story, but an important one. It's partly about what was going on in the United States, and partly about what was happening in Detroit, and how, when the United States caught cold, Detroit caught pneumonia. It's also about race.

The story of how America went on a home-buying spree around the turn of the millennium, and its disastrous aftermath, has been told often. Without going into the sordid details, a toxic mix of subprime loans and predatory lenders; greedy, ignorant, or duped borrowers; and a public sector dominated by a combination of free-market fundamentalists like

Figure 4-5 Empty houses on Biltmore Street in Crary-St. Mary's, Detroit. (Source: Google Earth)

Alan Greenspan and heedless cheerleaders for an ever-rising homeown-ership rate all combined to set off a speculative frenzy of homebuilding and home-buying that sent house prices soaring through most of the United States.

Subprime lending began as what seemed, at least to lenders, to be a good idea. Traditionally, lenders offered a single set of financial products to "prime" borrowers. Based on a loan officer's review of your credit, your work history, and so forth, you either made the cut or you didn't. If you made the cut, you got a loan, and if you didn't, you didn't. As automated underwriting gradually took the place of loan officers' judgment during the 1990s, people in the industry had a new idea. If we can predict risk from credit scores, they figured, instead of simply disqualifying "sub-prime" borrowers why don't we adjust the interest rates on our loans to reflect the higher risk of making loans to them, so we can lend to subprime borrowers as well?

That makes sense, up to a point, although the "quants" who did the research badly overestimated their ability to predict future risk. But, as economists Randall Dodd and Paul Mills point out, for this kind of lending to work, "lenders must control the risks by more closely evaluating the borrower, setting higher standards for collateral, and charging rates commensurate with the greater risks." That didn't happen; instead, fueled by vast amounts of money from all over the world looking for a place to land, and the ease of turning mortgages into securities that could be sold to unsuspecting investors, a feeding frenzy ensued. By the early 2000s, as one lender at Countrywide Financial, a major player in the subprime frenzy, put it, "If you had a pulse, we gave you a loan. If you fog the mirror, we give you a loan."[26] Soon, increasingly exotic and untenable loan products were floating around, from loans with initially low "teaser" rates with payments that increased spectacularly after two or three years, and what were called "NINJA" loans ("no income, no job, no assets—no problem").

What does this have to do with race? Everything. With a commission system that rewarded salespeople for making the most outrageous possible loans, real estate brokers and subprime mortgage lenders saw black—as well as Latino—communities, with their historically low homeownership rates, as a huge profit opportunity. As Emily Badger writes, "Banks that once ignored minority communities were targeting them now to make money, a practice that's been bitterly referred to as 'reverse-redlining.'"[27] As a one-time Wells Fargo loan officer testified, they "had an emerging-markets unit that specifically targeted black churches, because it figured church leaders had a lot of influence and could convince congregants to take out subprime loans."[28] Black churches and other community groups were offered and readily accepted payment to host "mortgage fairs" and "real estate seminars" organized by lenders.

Detroit shared in the frenzy. Mortgages flowed like water, home prices rose slowly but steadily from 2000 to 2006, and the number of home sales rose dramatically, going from 5,000 in 2000 to nearly 30,000 in 2006. But the underlying reality was still that Detroit was hemorrhaging jobs and people, and for all the glitter spread by young "hip-hop mayor" Kwame Kilpatrick, whom the Democratic Party named one of the nation's "10 young Democrats to watch" in 2000,[29] the city was rapidly losing ground fiscally and economically. When the mortgage bubble burst, followed by the Great Recession, the city's house of cards abruptly collapsed, as figure 4-6 shows vividly.

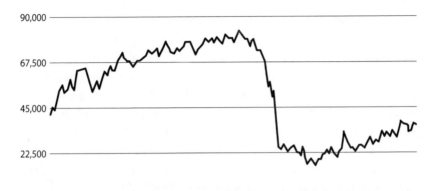

Figure 4-6 Detroit's boom and bust: median sales prices for homes in Detroit, 1998–2016. (Source: Zillow.com)

House prices plummeted and foreclosures skyrocketed. Meanwhile, since the local tax assessor refused to reduce people's property-tax assessments to reflect the reality that their houses had lost 80–90 percent of their value, homeowners were finding themselves with annual property tax bills of $3,000 or $4,000 on houses they'd be lucky to get $15,000 for if they put them on the market. By 2011, even as mortgage foreclosures were starting to slow down, tax foreclosures were taking off.

With thousands of homeowners losing their homes at foreclosure sales and tax auctions, a new breed of predatory investor began to show up. These investors did their arithmetic. They knew that it took at least three years of not paying taxes before the county took your property away. They realized that if you bought a house for $15,000 and rented it out, no questions asked, for $750 a month or $9,000 per year, and you didn't pay your taxes or do any repairs that took more than duct tape, then at the end of three years you had gotten close to $27,000 back from rental of the house. That works out to a profit of $12,000 over three years, a nice return of better than 25 percent a year. At that point, you wouldn't hesitate to walk away from the house, which by now was probably a near-total wreck, because you'd made your money. The people who were now buying houses in Crary-St. Mary's were the people who'd done that arithmetic.

Detroit was now caught up in a vicious cycle of its own. As property values plummeted, and as the Great Recession took hold, municipal revenues fell. As revenues fell and employees were laid off, services declined. In 2001, Detroit had over 1,500 public-works employees, 665 workers in the recreation department, and 244 people running programs for children and youth. By 2012, the city had barely 500 people in public works, with 200 left in recreation, which now included what few youth programs the city still offered.[30] Parks and playgrounds were abandoned, streetlights went out, and potholes never got filled. Even worse, the number of uniformed police officers went from 4,330 in 2001 to barely 2,700 by 2012; that year, Emergency Manager Kevin Orr cited FBI data that the Detroit police had solved only 11.3 percent of the murders, 8.1 percent of the robberies, and 12.8 percent of the rapes that took place in the city the year before.[31]

Like their white counterparts, some black middle-class families had been moving from cities to suburbs for years. Many others, though, held on, driven by pride in their neighborhoods and loyalty to their city. Nowhere was that loyalty stronger than in Detroit. As things got worse, though, those ties frayed and broke. Detroit activist Lauren Hood, whose parents moved out of the city in 2013 after being held up at gunpoint in the home they'd owned for forty-five years on the city's northwest side, wrote that "the city is now losing those that stood by its side for the longest, those that toughed it out in the neighborhoods until the last possible second, the second a gun was pointed at their heads! I become enraged when I hear people say the way to improve the city is to increase the tax base. . . . Detroit is hemorrhaging tax base every time a family like mine, and that of [my] dad's new friend, flees, traumatized, to a 'safer' suburb."[32]

In 2005, Detroit had more than 68,000 middle-class black households, families making $50,000 or more. By 2015, the number (with the floor adjusted to $60,680 to account for inflation) had dropped to 35,500—barely half as many. While it would be an oversimplification to say that fully half of the city's middle-class black families had moved out of the city in ten years—some may have lost income, and others passed away—it is safe to say that a very large number did leave, mostly for affordable suburbs like Southfield or Farmington Hills.

Detroit is an extreme case, but the same pattern can be found in city after city; as the *Economist* put it in 2011, "from Oakland to Chicago to Washington, DC, blacks are surging from the central cities to the suburbs."[33] Speculating on the reasons for the exodus, Akiim deShay of BlackDemographics.com, says, "Crime is one of them, a big one. Schools are a big one, as well. . . . You have a whole upwardly mobile group who can afford a better life, and they are pursuing it." DeShay adds that he moved his family from Rochester to the suburbs more than fifteen years ago. "When we left, I felt guilty, because I felt like I was contributing to the problem," he said. "And in a sense, I was."[34]

The upshot is that the black population of America's older cities is shrinking, and it is growing poorer. From 2000 to 2015, the African American population fell in almost every city, in some cases by a small number, but in others by hundreds of thousands, as in Detroit and Chicago.

The juxtaposition of black middle-class flight with the in-migration of the largely white Young Grads has created a situation in which the black-white income gap in the cities, wide to begin with, has grown steadily wider since 2000. Of twelve large cities shown in figure 4-7, white income gains outstripped those of black families in all twelve;

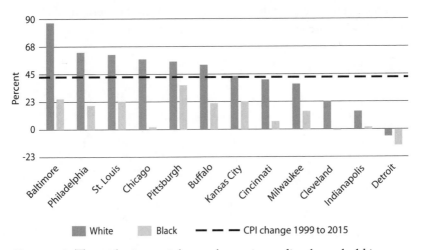

Figure 4-7 The widening racial gap: change in median household income by race, 1999–2015. (Source: US Census)

moreover, when measured in real dollars adjusted for inflation (the horizontal dotted line), black families *lost* income in every city, coming close to breaking even only in Pittsburgh. White families, on the other hand, held their own against inflation in eight of the twelve cities shown.

The widening racial income gap has fueled the economic and racial polarization of these cities. In 2000, the median black family in Baltimore earned 61 percent of the income of the median white family. By 2015, this figure had dropped to 48 percent. The typical white family, not only in Baltimore, but in Chicago, St. Louis, Pittsburgh, and Kansas City, earns more than twice as much—in Chicago and Cincinnati, nearly three times as much—as their African American counterpart. And, as the remaining black populations in the cities became poorer, they became increasingly stuck in place, in Patrick Sharkey's phrase, in ghetto areas of concentrated poverty, increasing racial polarization in space along with income. Baltimore is no longer legally segregated as in George McMechen's day—at least a handful of African American families live in every part of the city—but the reality is not that different.

The flight of the black middle class, and the increased concentration of the remaining African American population into concentrated poverty ghettos, is significant not only in terms of the demographics and economic makeup of the reviving legacy city, but is likely to have equally significant effects on the distribution of power, influence, and identity in these cities. Those effects are just beginning to emerge.

Chapter 5

Gentrification and Its Discontents[1]

Pittsburgh's Lawrenceville neighborhood is definitely where it's at. "Gus's Café gives you a chance to show your DJ prowess at Open Turntables every Monday," writes Chloe Detrick in *NEXTpittsburgh*, a publication that bills itself as the source of information about cool stuff in Pittsburgh. "On Wednesday, head over to Brillobox to test your knowledge at Pub Quiz night. If you like improv, keep an eye on Unplanned Comedy's calendar."[2] Lawrenceville has a dog park and a place where you can launch your kayak into the Allegheny River, right under the 40th Street Bridge. On Butler Street, the neighborhood's main drag, hip new stores and restaurants are supplanting the delis and hardware stores.

On one block, channeling two of the principal passions of the Young Grads we met in chapter 2, a yoga studio and a bike store sit side by side. Across the street in the next block are Café Gepetto, Gerbe Glass (a glass artists' studio), and Bierport, which bills itself as "Pittsburgh's great beer destination," with nineteen beers on tap and over 800 more bottled and canned beers to choose from. In addition to drinking beer, patrons of Bierport can participate in educational classes, brewmaster visits, and food pairings. Eight years earlier, Bierport was Starr Discount,

"Lawrenceville's largest convenience store," Gerbe Glass a hair salon, and Café Gepetto a shot-and-beer joint.

In 2000, despite a few urban pioneers here and there, Lawrenceville was an aging white working-class neighborhood, where 36 percent of the residents were over sixty-five. The numbers tell the story. Looking at the heart of what is known as Lower Lawrenceville,[3] from 2000 to 2014 median household incomes more than doubled, going from $19K to $49K—while citywide, they went from $29K to $40K. The share of college graduates in the area's population went from 14 percent to 36 percent, and the millennial share from 11 percent to 23 percent. In other words, over little more than a decade Lawrenceville flipped. It became a neighborhood of younger and increasingly affluent people. In other words, one might say it was gentrified.

If there is one word that has come to stand for all of the conflicts, controversies, and the sheer existential angst associated with the twenty-first-century urban revival, it is *gentrification*. While its roots may be economic, gentrification is far more than an economic phenomenon. It raises sensitive social, political, and cultural issues, prompting complex questions about the power relationships that underlie urban change, and about to whom a city or neighborhood belongs—or whether that question should even be asked. To understand gentrification, and the role it plays in the changes currently going on in America's industrial cities, we need to parse these different meanings and subtexts.

The word *gentrification* itself was coined in 1964 by British sociologist Ruth Glass, looking to put a name to her observation that "one by one, many of the working-class quarters of London have been invaded by the middle classes. . . ."[4] From the beginning, as Glass's choice of words suggests, it was never meant to be an objective description of a neutral phenomenon, but a politically charged and indeed pejorative term. Georgetown law professor J. Peter Byrne writes that "the very word 'gentrification' implies distaste,"[5] while journalist Justin Davidson put it even more strongly: "It's an ugly word, a term of outrage."[6] For that reason, many people, myself included, have tried to avoid the term when talking about what may be going on in a given city or neighborhood. By now, though, it is too firmly grounded in how people talk about cities to be easily sidestepped.

At the same time, it is dangerously misleading when it is seen, as is often the case, as a phenomenon outside the context of the larger ebb and flow of neighborhood change, or as a frame for venting outrage over any of the many ways in which social injustice and inequity are perpetuated in American cities. *There is nothing inevitable about gentrification.* As long as there have been cities and those cities have had neighborhoods, they have been changing, some moving upward and some downward. In most of America's legacy cities, though, more hard-working families are seeing their quality of life erode and their home equity disappear as their neighborhoods decline than there are people living in places where affluent people are moving in and where house prices are going up. Still other neighborhoods are hollowing out as all but the poorest residents flee, and whole blocks of homes and storefronts are abandoned. To understand what's going on in our cities, we need to see gentrification as part of this larger picture.

At its core, gentrification is economic. In its most widely recognized form, it is the process by which a formerly lower-income neighborhood like Lawrenceville draws a growing number of more affluent residents, at some point reaching a critical mass that changes the character of the neighborhood in fundamental ways. Businessdictionary.com defines *gentrification* in a way that goes to the heart of the issue: "the process of wealthier residents moving to an area, and the changes that occur due to the influx of wealth."[7] While the term is sometimes used in other contexts, gentrification is most fundamentally about what happens in urban neighborhoods when they experience an influx of wealth in the form of higher-income households.

When it comes to growth in the number of wealthier households, American cities are a mixed bag. A handful of cities I like to call "magnet" cities, cities like Seattle and Washington, DC, are seeing an extraordinary influx of mostly young higher-income residents, profoundly changing those cities' social and economic profile. Figure 5-1 compares those two cities with four legacy cities. It shows how the number of people in upper-income households, earning 25 percent more than the national median income, or roughly $70,000 per year or more in 2015, and the rest, the middle- and lower-income households, have changed between 2000 and 2015.

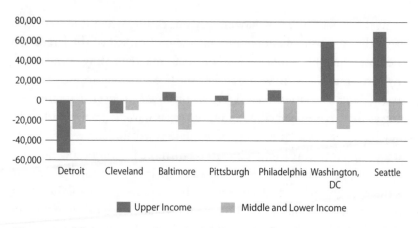

Figure 5-1 The uneven influx of wealth: change in number of households by income, 2000–2015. (Source: US Census Bureau)

Wealth is reshaping Seattle and Washington. Since 2000, upper-income households have been growing by 4,000 a year in Washington, DC, and almost 5,000 a year in Seattle. By comparison, while the fact that there is *any* net influx of even moderately wealthy people into Baltimore and Pittsburgh after decades of decline represents a dramatic shift from the past, the fact remains that this influx is still small, and far less than the continuing outflow of less affluent families. Finally, Detroit and Cleveland are seeing a net outflow of all family types, affluent and otherwise.

The graph is a quick and dirty way of getting a handle on the extent to which gentrification, in the sense described above, is likely to be taking place. Neighborhoods in Washington, DC, and Seattle are changing virtually overnight. Large parts of those cities have already been or are being gentrified, and thousands of new homes and apartments are being constructed. Even in areas like Anacostia, Washington's poorest neighborhood, where little demographic change has taken place to date and where the residents are still largely poor and near-poor, the sheer pressure of growth has pushed house prices upward. As I write this in December 2016, a developer is offering a new house for $600,000 on a block of modest frame houses in a section of Anacostia where the average family earns barely $20,000 a year:

Existing structure will be razed and a FABULOUS NEW 4-SIDED BROWNSTONE HOME will be built. Delivery in February 2017. This home will boast AMAZING VIEWS of DC. It will feature 4 large bedrooms, 4.5 luxurious bathrooms, a chef's kitchen, and fine finishes. 2,700 SF above grade. With an "optional elevator," this home will be a dream come true.[8]

Washington, DC, and Seattle are outliers among American cities. The picture is very different in Baltimore and Pittsburgh. Both cities are seeing gentrification, but it is confined to small parts of both cities—mainly areas near downtown, major universities, and medical institutions—and is not spilling over much to other neighborhoods, the way one sees in Anacostia. In Baltimore, it's only a short walk from thriving Bolton Hill to Sandtown-Winchester or Mondawmin. While a row house will sell for $500,000 or more in Bolton Hill, a seller in Mondawmin, where boarded-up, abandoned houses can be seen on almost every block, might be lucky to get $20,000 for what is basically the same house.

Will Sandtown-Winchester or Mondawmin ever gentrify? It is impossible to tell for sure, and ever is a long time, but despite the rhetoric of those who see every empty house as a stalking horse for gentrification, the likelihood is vanishingly small, at least in the foreseeable future. Wealth in Baltimore is growing, but it's growing slowly, and there are lots of places available to even moderately affluent young people which don't nearly require such a leap of faith. Elsewhere, the threat or the promise of gentrification, depending on one's perspective, remains remote.

The same is true in Pittsburgh. To measure gentrification in Pittsburgh, I looked at change in two features for each census tract: an increase in median household income at least 25 percent greater than the citywide average increase, and an increase in median house value at least 25 percent greater than the citywide average increase, between 2000 and 2015. Then I included only those tracts that were low- or moderate-income areas in 2000. Only eight out of more than one hundred census tracts in Pittsburgh met all the criteria, shown in figure 5-2. They may not be the only areas in Pittsburgh where prices and incomes are rising, but they're the only areas where it's happening that were not already fairly well-to-do in 2000.

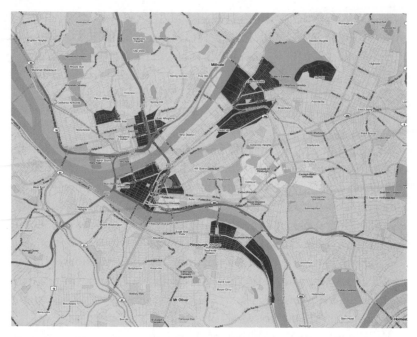

Figure 5-2 Gentrification in Pittsburgh, 2000–2015. (Source: PolicyMap)

If gentrification is a remote prospect for distressed areas in Baltimore or Pittsburgh, it is even more so in Cleveland or Detroit, where more wealth is still flowing out of those cities than is flowing in. While small pockets of revival exist in both cities, like Tremont in Cleveland or Corktown in Detroit, they are small and few in number. Decline is a far more pervasive reality, not only in areas that have long been distressed and disinvested, but even in areas that were healthy neighborhoods until recently, as I'll describe in the next chapter. To the extent that wealth is flowing in, little of it is going into residential neighborhoods. Instead, almost all is going into areas like downtown Detroit or University Circle where few people lived before. In city after city, downtowns are becoming the new upscale neighborhoods.

What has been going on in downtowns like Detroit's may actually be the biggest transformation story in America's once-industrial cities. To understand why, we need to step back briefly into the history of American downtowns. The early-twentieth-century American downtown was a bustling, crowded, dynamic place, which downtown historian Robert Fogelson has described as "an extremely compact, highly centralized, *largely depopulated* business district to which nearly all the residents, even those who lived far away, would come every day to work, to shop, to do business, and to amuse themselves" (emphasis added).[9]

While in the small cities of the early years of the American republic downtowns and residential areas were not clearly distinguished, that changed dramatically during the late nineteenth century, as the growth of cities, and the business activity that came with that growth, gradually pushed residential uses out of downtowns. Most urban thinkers of the time saw this as a good thing; in 1871, Frederick Law Olmsted, the designer of Central Park, saw the "strong and steadily increasing tendency" toward the separation of businesses and residences as part of the "law of progress," and "a fixed tendency among civilized men."[10] The early-twentieth-century downtown was crowded during the day but largely abandoned at night. Except for a handful of janitors and the denizens of the skid rows that popped up on the edges of some downtowns, people lived elsewhere. They lived in the residential areas that were being built all around downtown and used the burgeoning networks of subways, streetcars, and street and elevated railways to get conveniently in and out of downtown.

The 1920s may have been the high point of the traditional American big-city downtown. Highly ornamented skyscrapers with spires, turrets, and exuberantly decorated lobbies went up by the hundreds. Downtown department stores were at their grandest. John Wanamaker's downtown Philadelphia store, which he had opened in 1874, was completely rebuilt in 1911, and reopened with 2 million square feet of space covering an entire city block, featuring a 150-foot-high Grand Court with the world's second largest organ and a great eagle recovered from the 1903 St. Louis World's Fair. With the Great Depression, though, downtowns, most heavily overbuilt from the 1920s' building boom, collapsed. Construction ground to a halt, values plummeted, and vacancies skyrocketed. In most cities, the tallest building in 1929 was still the tallest three decades later.[11]

Although downtowns were struggling, they were still the centers of urban life into the 1960s. When I moved to the Trenton area in 1967, downtown Trenton was not what it was, by all accounts, but it was still the place to be. It had three movie theaters, five department stores—although one closed just about the same time I arrived—and the local custom of driving into downtown and driving around and around on Saturday nights, in a sort of wacky motorized parody of the Spanish *paseo*, was still alive. Within ten years, though, it was all gone. The bustling city seen in figure 5-3 was gone. The movie theaters were closed, the department stores had closed or moved to the new suburban malls, and no one drove downtown on Saturday night anymore.

Figure 5-3 Downtown Trenton in the 1940s. (Source: Alan Mallach collection)

The solution, if that's the right word, that politicians, planners, developers, and downtown business people came up with was urban renewal. Large tracts of downtown business districts and nearby residential areas, usually low-income and often black, were cleared for new office towers, shopping malls, and highways. Expectations were high; as urban renewal chronicler Jon Teaford writes, "At the beginning of each project, planners presented drawings of a jet-age rebuilt city, with glistening high-rise towers in fountain-adorned plazas. Metropolitan newspapers faithfully reprinted these images, rallying support for proposals that seemed to promise a transformation from grit to glitter."[12] From one city to the next, large parts of the prewar fabric of downtown was obliterated in the name of progress, yet the results rarely lived up to expectations. Many projects never got built, while many of those that did turned out to be failures, either economically or aesthetically, or both. The highways seemed to do little or nothing to reverse downtown decline, as the remaining businesses continued to flee for the suburbs.

Luring upscale households to live in downtown was often part of the plan. Downtown housing, though, generally took the form of sterile, boxlike high-rise towers in a sea of parking, with few amenities beyond, perhaps, a deli and a dry cleaners establishment. A few, like Lafayette Park in Detroit, were big enough to create their own self-contained world, but most failed. As Teaford sums it up, "In one city after another, middle- and upper-income Americans shunned areas whose reputations had been so odious that they required renewal. With millions of new homes on the market during the 1950s and 1960s, there was no compelling reason to opt for life amid the bulldozed wastelands of once-blighted areas."[13]

That remained the picture over the next few decades. More office buildings were built during the eighties and nineties, and here and there an imaginative project like James Rouse's Inner Harbor project in Baltimore caught fire, but downtowns continued to be shunned by most people except as a place to work, while, even as new office buildings were constructed, the once-shining skyscrapers of the 1910s and 1920s increasingly stood empty, millions of square feet abandoned by tenants and, increasingly, by their owners. "By the early 1980s," architectural historian Michael Schwarzer writes, "downtown appeared a lost cause. It was burdened by aging, emptying office buildings, struggling discount retailers, and vanishing entertainment complexes."[14]

Exactly when and how things started to change is hard to tell, and a lot of it has to do with the Young Grads we met in chapter 2 moving to the cities first in the 1990s, and then in even larger numbers after the turn of the millennium. The story of St. Louis's Washington Avenue illustrates their role, but also highlights the importance of many other players. I mentioned Washington Avenue briefly in chapter 2, the one-time garment and shoemaking district shown in its heyday in figure 5-4.

Figure 5-4 St. Louis's Washington Avenue in the early 1900s. (Source: Missouri History Museum, St. Louis)

By the early 1980s, all the factories had moved out, leaving block after block of magnificent early-twentieth-century five- and six-story factory buildings behind.

Washington Avenue never emptied out completely. Even as the last factories were still winding down, one or two property owners had started to make just enough improvements to a couple of the buildings to make it legal for them to rent out cheap live/work space to artists. By the early 1990s, the avenue was mostly empty, but with just enough artists, galleries, and funky shops scattered here and there to make it a hub of St. Louis's small counterculture scene. By that point, a few people were starting to pick up buildings on the avenue for pennies. One of them was a sculptor named Bob Cassilly, who bought a 250,000-square-foot building for sixty-nine cents per square foot and opened it in 1997 as the City Museum, an eclectic hodgepodge of everything and anything, which *Mental Floss* blogger Erin McCarthy calls the "coolest—and most entertaining—place on earth."[15] Meanwhile, in 1996, using federal housing subsidies, another developer had converted the Frances Building at the corner of 16th Street to Arts Lofts, live/work spaces for sixty low-income artists.

Developers started to realize that there were quite a few people interested in moving into old loft buildings along Washington Avenue. Their problem was that the rents they could charge weren't high enough to cover the cost of restoring these magnificent old buildings—perhaps cheap to buy but expensive to restore. In 1997, though, the state of Missouri enacted what is called a Historic Tax Credit, a program that gave developers a major tax break for restoring and renting out historic buildings. Combined with the existing federal historic-preservation tax credit, the program meant that, with any luck, a developer could recover one-third or more of her cost from these tax breaks, meaning in turn, that she could charge the lower rents that the market demanded, and still make a decent profit.

That opened the floodgates. Before the end of 1999, eight separate redevelopment projects had been announced along Washington Avenue. By the end of 2000, nearly 500 apartments were under construction, and another 800 planned. By the end of 2004, 1,400 apartments had been completed since 1999, and another 1,000 were on the way.[16] As buildings were restored, stores and restaurants opened their doors, with eighteen bars and restaurants along the avenue between 10th and 14th Streets alone. By 2007, although a building here or there still awaited renovation, the transformation of Washington Avenue was effectively complete. It took only twelve years, almost overnight in the real estate world.

What happened along Washington Avenue has its counterparts in the downtowns of every major older industrial city, and a fair number of small ones as well. In struggling Youngstown, Ohio, local developer Dominic Marchionda has turned five downtown office buildings into apartments, renting to a mix of Youngstown State University students, Young Grads, and a few retirees. What is behind this is that the physical shape and layout of traditional American big-city downtowns turns out to be the Young Grads' dream environment. The density, the activity level, the combination of stores and restaurants on the ground floors and apartments or lofts overhead, the ability to get around on foot or by public transportation, all make it easier to create the "scene" I described in chapter 3, ultimately becoming a self-sustaining chain reaction.

The areas, though, which are drawing people back are not the areas that were "improved" through urban renewal in the fifties and sixties. In fact, the opposite. Washington Avenue was one of the few parts of down-town St. Louis to escape the urban renewal wrecking ball, something that is equally true of reviving downtown areas in Cleveland, Philadel-phia, and elsewhere. The theory behind urban renewal, that cities had to rebuild themselves around the automobile in order to thrive, turned out to be no more sound than the medieval idea that the sun revolved around the earth. It was actually the opposite. Cities needed to maintain their *urban* character—their density, their diversity of buildings and people, and their mixture of uses and activities—to thrive. It was an expensive, painful lesson to learn.

Washington Avenue is not the only reason that the number of Young Grads in the city of St. Louis has been going up by 1,500–2,000 each year since 2010—up from 500 each year between 2000 and 2005—but it's an important part of the picture. Since 2000, the population of the three census tracts that make up downtown St. Louis has more than tripled, going from 3,400 to 12,600. During the same period, the downtown population of Cleveland more than doubled, from 5,000 to 11,300.[17]

Every city has its own story that parallels the Washington Avenue story. In Detroit, downtown revitalization has been given a jump-start by billionaire Quicken Loans founder Dan Gilbert, to the point where some critics are calling downtown Detroit "Gilbertville." A tally by the *Detroit News* in the spring of 2016 found that Gilbert-connected entities had spent $451 million to buy downtown properties, with at least eleven more deals still in the pipeline, and untold hundreds of millions more to restore the properties, converting them from office space to apart-ments—all in all probably over $2 billion.[18] Along with the apartments, Gilbert's buildings are drawing retailers popular with Young Grads, such as Nike, Under Armour, Moosejaw, and Warby Parker.

Whether Gilbert and his investors will get their money back, and if so, by when, are open questions. What is not in question is that his buildings are filling up, as Detroit has started to catch up with other cities like St. Louis and Pittsburgh in drawing Young Grads. On a balmy fall night in 2016, I found myself walking down Woodward Avenue, downtown Detroit's main street. It was nearly 10:30 on a weeknight, but restaurants were open, young people were sitting at outdoor tables, knots of young people were gathered talking on the wide, brand-new sidewalks, and from time to time a jogger would come running by. For those like me who remember the emptiness of downtown Detroit only five or six years earlier, this was a sea change.

Is this gentrification, or something else entirely? Clearly, downtowns are not the "working-class quarters" Ruth Glass was writing about, and if displacement, direct or indirect, is one's touchstone for gentrification, it is hard to make the case that that is going on to any extent in the course of what might be called the "residentialization" of downtown. At the same time, it is a form of transformation, not only physical but social and economic, as fundamental and as far-reaching as any neighborhood change characterized as "gentrification."

In fact, the implications of downtown revitalization may be even more profound. Downtowns, at least in part because they were *not* residential areas, were historically a common ground within the city, nobody's turf and open to all. In many cities, historically fragmented into a jigsaw puzzle of ethnic and racial enclaves, downtowns may well have been the *only* common ground those cities could offer. The significance of that common ground has frayed over decades of decline, but was never completely lost. As downtowns, though, become increasingly residential and redefine themselves as upscale neighborhoods, that could easily disappear, further cementing the spatial polarization that is increasingly the new reality of urban America. If only for that reason, the transformation of downtowns needs to be discussed in the same breath as gentrification, as another manifestation of how revival and inequality go hand in hand.

Another question has to do with spin-offs. While downtown residentialization may not displace anyone, the course of downtown revival can trigger powerful spin-offs, and a disproportionate number of gentrifying neighborhoods are in fact adjacent to reviving downtowns. This reflects what we know about which neighborhoods are more likely or less likely to gentrify.

Reviving neighborhoods tend to have a number of features that distinguish them from other areas, of which the first, and most important, is location. Revival does not jump around, leapfrogging from one area to another. It moves incrementally from areas that are already strong or from major nodes of activity, such as a downtown or a university campus. Exceptions to this rule are few and far between.

In Baltimore, gentrification has moved gradually east and south of the inner harbor from Fells Point to Canton and Patterson Park, and north of downtown toward the Johns Hopkins campus, as well as in a growing band of neighborhoods around the campus itself. Figure 5-5 shows what one might call Baltimore's gentrification vectors; thick arrows show established middle- and upper-income areas—some of which are the product of earlier waves of gentrification in the 1970s or 1980s—and narrow arrows show areas that appear to be experiencing revival today. All of the vectors flow from one or another of three nodes—Johns Hopkins, downtown, and the Inner Harbor.

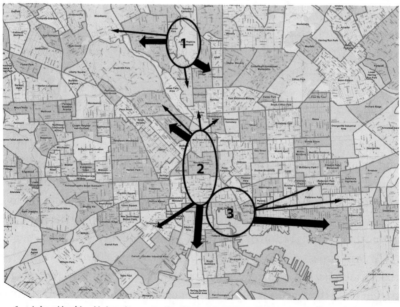

1   Johns Hopkins University   2   Downtown/Central Core   3   Inner Harbor

Figure 5-5 Baltimore's gentrification vectors. (Source: base map from City of Baltimore Department of Planning, overlay by author)

The second feature is what designers call the neighborhood's "fabric"—the weave of houses, small apartment buildings, and storefronts that collectively create the built landscape of the traditional urban neighborhood. In areas that gentrify, that fabric is still largely intact. Vacant lots, where houses have been demolished, are few in number. The houses themselves may not be architectural gems, but are generally attractive, if perhaps run-down, and reasonably close together. Such areas often have a shopping street running through them, built for walking rather than driving, as most places had before the automobile era. They almost always predate World War II, having been laid out before we started to design neighborhoods for cars rather than people.

Gentrifying areas are rarely the most distressed areas of a city, particularly those where the cumulative effect of demolishing vacant buildings has undone the neighborhood's fabric, as can be seen in the street scene from North City St. Louis in the last chapter. Indeed, the idea one hears that urban demolition is a stalking horse for future gentrification is yet another urban myth; in reality, it more often creates a moonscape of vacant land that all but guarantees gentrification will *not* take place.

The third feature may come as a surprise to people who learn about gentrification from blogs and social media, but predominantly African American neighborhoods are *less*, not more, likely to experience gentrification than largely white, working-class neighborhoods. In a 2014 study of Chicago, sociologists Jackelyn Hwang and Robert Sampson found that "upward neighborhood trajectories tend to follow a pattern of Black and Hispanic neighborhood avoidance."[19] They found that neighborhoods that were more than 40 percent black or Hispanic were significantly less likely to gentrify than other similarly situated areas.

This pattern is not unique to Chicago; Todd Swanstrom and his colleagues in St. Louis found that only five out of thirty-five of what they called rebounding neighborhoods had more than 40 percent black population in 1970.[20] In Baltimore, a city that is nearly two-thirds African American, hardly any of the gentrification vectors point to majority African American areas; in fact, they are largely concentrated in what Baltimore scholar-activist Lawrence Brown has called the city's "White L," the L-shaped area clearly visible in figure 5-5 that tends to be predominately white, in contrast to the "Black butterfly" that makes up most of the rest of the city.[21] The same is largely true in Pittsburgh. Only two of the eight gentrifying census tracts shown earlier had 30 percent or more black population in 2000. One of those two is at most a borderline case of gentrification; although rising economically, it was still a poor area, and well below city averages in both income and house value in 2015.

Racial considerations are never far away in America's urban centers, many of which became majority-black communities during the second half of the twentieth century. Since gentrification by its nature starts out as an uncertain proposition—the first urban pioneers have no idea who, if anyone, will follow them—race can be seen to add another layer of uncertainty, particularly for the mostly white families and individuals likely to be putting their resources on the line.

What happens when a neighborhood starts to change is a function of how the market works, which is based on the all but inexorable laws of supply and demand. If more people want to live in a particular area, demand for the homes in that area goes up. If the supply of housing does not go up at the same time, more people are now competing for the same pool of homes and apartments. If the people who now want to live there have more money to spend on housing than those who have previously done so, they will bid up the prices—whether sales or rental—of the housing. As prices rise, some people who already live in the neighborhood may be unable to stay, and more often, people like them will be less able to move in.

That is a very bloodless, abstract description. It depicts the underlying economic reality behind gentrification, but does not reflect the messiness on the ground. The process may be gradual and quiet, with a minimum of overt pressure or visible strain; or it may be faster and be accompanied by overt or covert conflict, ranging from the tensions of contrasting life-styles and values to speculation, flipping, and intimidation. In cities like Pittsburgh or St. Louis, it is likely to be slower, in Washington or San Francisco, faster and with more visible conflict.

The initial stages of gentrification are usually fairly gradual, involving people making individual choices to buy or rent in a traditionally lower-income neighborhood; as Kalima Rose of PolicyLink writes, "At first, this causes little displacement or resentment. This process may occur over several years, and initially may cause little change in the appearance of long-disinvested communities."[22] While public investment in housing rehab, beautification, or transit may sometimes fuel gentrification, few if any cities have a grand design or plan for gentrification, even though it may sometimes seem otherwise to people living in gentrifying neighborhoods in hot markets like Brooklyn or Washington, DC. It is more likely to be informal and spontaneous, taking local planners and elected officials by surprise. More often, once a neighborhood begins to show significant signs of gentrification, the city may start to think after the fact about how it can move the process along, gracing the area with park improvements or new street lighting, or selling city-owned land to developers.

Whatever the intentions of the families wanting to move into a neighborhood, the low-key, informal quality of the first stages of gentrification eventually ends. Either the effort fizzles, the pioneers fade away, and the neighborhood reverts to its earlier state, or the potential profits to be made from the demand for the houses in the area bring out the members of what a 2014 public radio report called the "gentrification-industrial complex," the "web of real estate leasing agents, listing agents, landlords, and investors whose business models are built on stoking and profiting from neighborhood change."[23] Individual actors, though, tend to be small operators marketing or flipping houses, or developers and contractors buying and restoring individual properties.

Large-scale developers usually come last, after the small fish have created an environment where lenders are now willing to put up the millions that developers need to get a major project off the ground. This may not be true in some "hot" cities like New York or San Francisco, where no neighborhood is immune from the intense market pressures at work in those cities, but it is generally true elsewhere. The first large-scale development to go up in Pittsburgh's Lawrenceville neighborhood, a mixed-use project with 243 apartments, retail space, and a pedestrian walkway leading to a new one-acre park, was only announced in 2016, well after the newly upscale character of the area had already been firmly established.

Local developer Bart Blatstein's role in the transformation of Philadelphia's Northern Liberties area is a big, and unusual, exception.

Northern Liberties, just north of Center City along the Delaware River, had been the "next hot neighborhood" in Philadelphia for decades. In fact, when my wife and I were house-hunting in the late 1970s, some of our hipster friends told us to look in that area. One Saturday morning, we drove around what was a wasteland of scattered clumps of row houses, vacant lots, and derelict industrial buildings, and quickly decided that it wasn't for us, even if it was within walking distance (albeit a scary walk in those days) to the restaurants of Old City. Perhaps it was up and coming, but it had a long way to go. We weren't *that* hip.

By the 1990s little had changed, except for a few contrarian artists here and there and a brief flurry of activity that was snuffed out by the real estate recession of the late 1980s. Blatstein, who had made a fortune building conventional shopping centers, saw the area's potential, and started buying properties there in the 1990s, culminating in his acquiring the landmark Schmidt's Brewery complex in 2000. With enough capital of his own so that he didn't need to rely on bankers, he began developing properties in the area.

Originally, Blatstein had planned to build another shopping center on the site and get out, but "then," he said, "the midlife crisis hit, and I thought, What do I do? Do I get the bright red Ferrari? And then I decided, Let me do the creative thing here. I have the opportunity to do something really cool here."[24] What he created was the Piazza at Schmidt's, since renamed Schmidt's Common, which opened in 2009. Inspired, Blatstein said, by Rome's Piazza Navona, the complex contains office space, stores, and over 400 apartments surrounding a nearly two-acre plaza or piazza, which has since become a popular gathering place for Philadelphia's Young Grads.

It's impossible to tell how often pressure of one sort or another is part of the gentrification process, but there's no doubt that it happens. As New York legal aid lawyer Scott Stamper says, "We've seen a real rise in landlords stalking, threatening, and badgering tenants with unwanted buyout demands. This isn't negotiation, it's harassment."[25] Homeowners receive letters from realtors, describing how much a nearby house sold for, and get notes slipped under their front doors, such as the one that appeared in Brooklyn, as described by Jerome Krase and Judith DeSena: "I am interested in buying your building. I will pay Cash now or in the future. Please give me a call if you are ready to sell."[26] Homeowners may receive calls from people trying to buy them out, or find would-be buyers on their doorsteps making their pitch in person. Harassment may never be too far away, while low-income, elderly homeowners with few other assets and painful debt burdens may easily be convinced to sell for less than the true value of their homes. At the same time, gentrification offers a rare opportunity for struggling lower-income homeowners who see the value of their sole asset rising to the point that it really means something, if they can realize that value.

Gentrification of a neighborhood brings benefits, but uneven ones. Once a neighborhood begins to change, it is easy to look back with rose-colored glasses and recreate an idealized image of the past. The bodega down the street that has been replaced by a coffee place had over-priced milk, and tired, often rotten produce. The young people clustering on the street corner were not always engaged in harmless pursuits. People remember the cookouts, but not the fear. Moreover, as City Observatory's Joe Cortright aptly points out, the idea that "if a neighborhood doesn't gentrify, it somehow stays the same" is a fallacy.[27] The reality is that today most neighborhoods that don't revive, go downhill.

As neighborhoods revive, they become safer, cleaner places. Vacant houses, which undermine the health and safety of residents as well as the value of their property, are rehabilitated and reused. New stores and businesses open; some may replace existing ones, but many others fill long-vacant storefronts. The yoga studio may have little appeal to longtime residents, but they are more likely to appreciate the new grocery store with its fresh produce. Neighborhoods that have seen all the problems of blight and concentrated poverty, with all of the devastating effects those conditions have on both child and adult life outcomes, have become less blighted and more integrated.

Public services may improve, not just because the area is becoming more affluent but because the newcomers are often more effective advocates for their neighborhoods. In one changing neighborhood in St. Louis, newcomers took the lead in starting City Garden, a Montessori charter school committed to maintaining an economically and racially integrated student body, which has since been recognized as one of the outstanding schools in the region. Over and above the direct benefits to neighborhoods, financially and economically stressed cities benefit from a more economically diverse population and higher tax revenues, which in turn enhance their ability to maintain their physical environment and provide better public services. These are not insignificant benefits, and there is evidence that in legacy cities they are shared by many gentrifying neighborhoods' longtime residents.

The issue is not only whether those benefits are shared to any meaningful extent by lower-income families, but whether they outweigh other damage done in the process. The critique of gentrification typically identifies three distinct forms of harm: displacement, loss of housing affordability, and what might be called cultural displacement. All three demand attention, but to see all change as inherently harmful is to fail to recognize the complexity of what is actually going on and what might or should be done about it. This is particularly the case in cities like Philadelphia or St. Louis where, in contrast to Washington, DC, or San Francisco, neighborhood transitions tend to be more gradual, with less of the feeding frenzy that takes place in magnet cities, and where rents and house prices even in gentrifying neighborhoods are rarely stratospheric. Indeed, it is striking how much of what a national audience reads about the evils of gentrification emanates from New York and San Francisco among the handful of magnet cities, and how little from the far larger number of legacy cities.

At one level, common sense would suggest that displacement is an inevitable product of gentrification. If prices go up to the point that they are no longer affordable to many of the area's residents, they will be displaced. It's actually far from that simple. It's important to distinguish between displacement in the literal sense—when a tenant is forced to move by gentrification, either as a result of a rent increase that renders her unable to afford her apartment, or some other form of pressure from her landlord—and longer-term loss of affordability. Despite individual horror stories, most of which seem to come from New York City, the former is rarer and much harder to establish than one might think.

Turnover of urban renters, particularly low-income renters, for all kinds of reasons, is extremely high. The median stay of urban renters in the same house or apartment is barely two years. Much of this turnover is involuntary, but for reasons unrelated to gentrification. As Matthew

Desmond has powerfully shown in his book *Evicted*, poor tenants, particularly single mothers with small children, face a constant struggle to come up with the rent every month for even the most modest house or apartment. Their lives are a desperate battle to survive on the edge of eviction, doubling up, and potential homelessness, a battle they often lose. This reality has nothing to do with gentrification. It is about what it means to be poor in America, and about the disgraceful way in which we as a nation fail to recognize, let alone address, the housing needs of the poor.

The issues are different for homeowners. The conventional wisdom is that lower-income homeowners are forced out of gentrifying neighborhoods as a result of skyrocketing property taxes, themselves the result of the dramatic rise in property values. Again, I would not suggest that this never happens; what little research has been done on the question, however, suggests that it is not that widespread. Some cities have tried to prevent it, although at a cost. Through its Longtime Owner Occupant Program, or LOOP, Philadelphia has provided tax relief for homeowners who have lived in their homes for ten years or more and are facing rapidly rising property tax bills; 17,000 people qualified for the program in the first two years.[28] This looks like a pretty blunt instrument, though. Given the generous income ceilings for the program—from $83K for a single individual to nearly $119K for a family of four—many of these families are at little risk of losing their homes. Instead, the financially strapped city is going without property taxes from a large number of people in order to benefit a much smaller number.

The real issue is well summed up by journalist Jarrett Murphy, who writes, "The issue isn't *dis*placement of the poor, but *re*placement."[29] In a poor neighborhood, when a lower-income tenant leaves her current home—by choice, eviction, or otherwise—she is usually replaced by another low-income tenant, someone much like her. In a neighborhood that is seeing growing demand from higher-income people, she is more likely to be replaced by a higher-income tenant, or perhaps—if the home is a single-family house, rather than an apartment—by a home-buyer. Looking at a neighborhood as a whole, this process is likely to take place gradually, over the course of many moves by many tenants over many years. The question is, though, under what conditions should this be seen as a problem associated with gentrification?

While replacement may be all but total in a neighborhood in the path of gentrification in Brooklyn, the picture is quite different in a city like St. Louis. In the St. Louis neighborhoods that Swanstrom and his colleagues studied, they found that "the influx of higher-income white professionals has not caused rents to soar to the point that poor populations are displaced entirely. [...] Rebound neighborhoods remain the most economically diverse neighborhoods in the region." Consistent with those findings, I found that while house sales prices had risen faster in a cluster of gentrifying neighborhoods than they did citywide in St. Louis from 2000 to 2015, rents actually went *down*, although very slightly, relative to the city as a whole. Even then, house prices were still far from out of reach of most people, with houses selling in most of these neighborhoods for prices from around $150K to not much more than $200K. Swanstrom also points out that over the forty-year period he studied, from 1970 to 2010, "Only 5,816 people live in census tracts that transitioned . . . from high poverty to low poverty, whereas 98,953 live in neighborhoods that became newly poor during that period."[30]

Figuring how much harm replacement does hinges on two separate issues: first, whether nearby areas provide housing that is as affordable as where the tenant previously lived, and second, the way in which it changes the neighborhood and how those changes affect people. On the first issue, we must once again distinguish between magnet cities and legacy cities. In a city like Washington, DC, prices and rents are going up all over the city, and finding affordable housing anywhere in the city can be increasingly difficult. Families double up, put up with overcrowding, or move out of the city entirely to Prince Georges County or even farther afield. In Baltimore or St. Louis, they may have to do little more than move a few blocks to find housing no more expensive than their last home.

If the family involved is poor or near-poor, that does not mean that they will find high-quality housing at a truly affordable price, unless they are among the chosen few who win the affordable-housing lottery and get a housing voucher or an apartment in a high-quality affordable-housing project. But, again, that is *not* the result of gentrification; it is the result of poverty and systemic housing costs that all but guarantee that even crumbling, roach-infested housing is too expensive for a poor family to afford without hardship. It is also the result of our nation's failure to come up with a housing policy or provide the resources that might make the pledge Congress made back in 1949 of "a decent home in a suitable living environment for every American family" more than empty rhetoric.

The replacement triggered by gentrification does not only change people's lives, it also changes the neighborhood and creates a neighborhood populated by an increasingly heterogenous group of people, black and white, young and old, well-to-do and struggling, with different values, tastes, and norms. Even more, it means that a neighborhood that people thought of as their more or less clearly defined territory is no longer theirs. This can mean many things. It can be as fundamental as identity, as Michelle Lewis, a black former resident of one Portland neighborhood told a reporter: "It's a horrible feeling, to come to a neighborhood where you grow up in, and have the people there look at you as if you don't belong." The reporter added that Lewis "recalled . . . the funeral home where she buried her grandfather. Little Chapel of the Chimes is now a craft beer pub."[31]

In a 2014 gentrification rant that went viral, film director Spike Lee put it differently: "You just can't come in the neighborhood. I'm for democracy and letting everybody live but you gotta have some respect. You can't just come in when people have a culture that's been laid down for generations and you come in and now shit gotta change because you're here?"[32] Newcomers bring different norms and preferences with them. Conflicts can arise over almost anything—noise, trash, or as one longtime resident of a changing St. Louis plaintively said, "Why can't we do what we do? Why can't we put chairs outside of our houses?"[33] It can be about less tangible matters like attitudes, as in the words of Bill Francisco, a longtime resident of Philadelphia's gentrifying Fishtown neighborhood: "There are too many real problems in life in general to be weird about a bar or a restaurant. It's about respect, that's all."[34]

It is impossible not to sympathize with the sense of loss that's reflected in these comments. At the same time, change is a constant in American neighborhoods, and while respecting the passion and pain in Spike Lee's voice, the reality is that shit does change one way or another all the time, and that the pain and loss are just as real and maybe worse for people living through decline as a neighborhood they remember as warm and supportive deteriorates, houses are abandoned on once-stable blocks, crime increases, and families no longer allow their children to play outside. Decline gets far less ink than gentrification, for reasons which I will explore in the next chapter.

Why people react to gentrification the way they do, though, is driven by a separate but closely related issue that in turn is part and parcel of the racial dimension that plays such a large role in this conversation. My friend Paul Brophy, one of the wisest thinkers about these issues I know, taught a graduate seminar at Washington University in St. Louis a few years ago and told me a story that captures this better than anything else I can think of. A young African American student in the class was clearly unhappy with much of his presentation; finally, he made his point directly. "Listen, professor," he said. "When you talk about gentrification, you talk about numbers, about incomes and house prices and such. When *we* talk about gentrification, it's about powerlessness."

The question of power is never far from any discussion of urban change, whatever one's ideological stripes. If you are poor, it is hard not to believe that the system is rigged against you. If you are poor and black, infinitely more so. It is hardly surprising that perhaps the greatest disparity between the rhetoric of gentrification and the reality of it on the ground is in Detroit. Over 80 percent of the city's population is African American, and yet almost every decision that has any significant bearing on Detroit's future is made by a small group of white men. Detroit is also a place where the deeply offensive proposition that it is a blank slate waiting to be brought back to life by newcomers has become a recurrent media theme.

In that context, *gentrification* becomes a powerful code word, as reporter Jake Flanagin writes: "The most unsettling thing about gentrification, however, is how it reflects the utter and complete lack of control the poor and the nonwhite have in where they are permitted to live. And this potential Great Return to Detroit is a high-contrast, technicolor example."[35] In a similar vein, a woman protesting against the city's policy of shutting off water service for nonpayment asserted that "the Detroit water shut-offs are gentrification on steroids."[36] To that protestor, the meaning of gentrification has long since transcended any connection to neighborhood change; to her, it is any policy that further impoverishes and marginalizes the already poor and marginalized members of society. The reality that far more middle-class families and individuals are moving out of Detroit than are moving in is, from this perspective, irrelevant.

In the final analysis, gentrification is about neighborhoods, but it is also about much more than neighborhoods. At its most fundamental level, it is about the changes that take place in lower-income neighborhoods when more-affluent people begin to move in, house prices go up, and coffee places and craft beer pubs open up. That is a complicated enough matter, which can be both good and bad for people, but often not for the same people. At a second level, though, neighborhood change reflects a larger change in the cities themselves, part and parcel of the larger economic transformation that saw those cities go from an economy based on people's strength and willingness to do hard physical labor, to one based on specialized skills and higher education, a change that is increasingly sidelining thousands of these cities' residents and erstwhile workers. While the changing urban scene is indeed bringing gentrification to many neighborhoods, it is bringing accelerated decline to still more. Finally, though, it is about power, and how economic polarization breeds political polarization, and how both become increasingly racialized, shifting the ways in which the reins of power are distributed in the city. It is the *cri de coeur* of the thousands of people who rightfully feel marginalized by their city's transformation.

That said, it is still also about neighborhoods. And when we look at the neighborhoods in America's legacy cities, as I said at the beginning of this chapter, the story of neighborhood decline is a far bigger one, certainly in terms of the sheer number of people, homes, and city blocks affected, than gentrification. In the next chapter, I will first look at the numbers and show how decline and gentrification compare in a few cities, and then delve into why, even as one might say that many of these cities are prospering beyond even their boosters' wildest dreams, neighborhood decline is not only still present, but a growing crisis.

Chapter 6

Sliding Downhill: The Other Side of Neighborhood Change

In the summer of 2016, I spoke to some people engaged in community development work in Indianapolis. There was a lot of controversy in Indianapolis about gentrification, they said, and they were concerned that it wasn't the complete story about what was happening in the city's neighborhoods. They asked me to look at this question, and then come to Indianapolis to talk about what I found. I agreed, and went to work with the data.

My measures were household income and house values. There are about 200 census tracts in Indianapolis, and I looked at each to see how those two factors had changed from 2000 to 2014. I looked at census tracts that were low-income (where the median income was 80 percent or less of the regional median income) in 2000, looking for the ones where both measures had gone up significantly faster than citywide, to get a sense of whether gentrification was taking place. I found a total of five census tracts that appeared to be gentrifying. Four out of the five were immediately adjacent to downtown, while the fifth was an area known as Fall Creek Place, a short distance to the north, where the city had led a major transformation of the area starting in the late 1990s (fig. 6-1).

Figure 6-1 Census tracts that gentrified in Indianapolis from 2000 to 2015. (Source: base map by PolicyMap, analysis by author)

Then, I flipped the measures. Instead of looking at areas that had seen significant *improvement* in incomes and house values, I looked at areas that showed comparable *decline* in incomes and house values over the same period, and were either low- or middle-income today (up to 120 percent of the regional median income). While five census tracts showed signs of gentrification, *over sixty* declined between 2000 and 2014. As the map shows, they were spread across much of the city, with large clusters of decline in the eastern and western parts of the city (fig. 6-2).

Indianapolis is widely considered one of the more thriving cities in America's Rust Belt. Over the past fifteen years, it has been adding people and jobs at a decent rate. If you compare it to most other big Midwestern industrial cities on just about any index—poverty, house prices, share of college graduates—it does fairly well. And yet, while only a small pocket of the city close to downtown is gentrifying, nearly a third of the city's neighborhoods are trending downward, with families becoming poorer and houses losing value.

Indianapolis is not an outlier. In Baltimore, a widely heralded urban-revival success story, four people live in a declining neighborhood for every one who lives in a reviving or gentrifying area. As we mentioned in the last chapter, researchers found that in St. Louis, the ratio

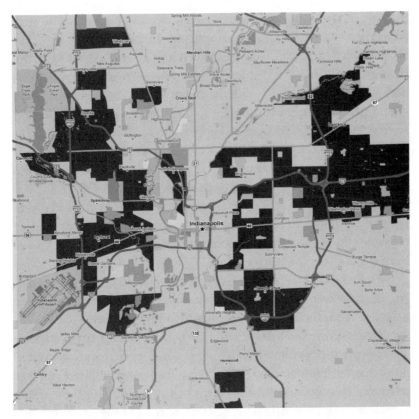

Figure 6-2 Census tracts that declined in Indianapolis from 2000 to 2015. (Source: base map by PolicyMap, analysis by author)

was more like seventeen to one. A lot of these declining neighborhoods were still reasonably healthy places not that long ago.

Two side-by-side neighborhoods in North Central Baltimore, Pen Lucy and Wilson Park, are fairly typical. In 2000, with their well-maintained brick twins and row houses, and small but well-kept front yards, they were both healthy neighborhoods, with incomes and home prices above the citywide average. Since then, both incomes and prices have dropped relative to the rest of the city. In parts of these neighborhoods, you can buy a house for as little as $30,000.

Pen Lucy and Wilson Park are still neighborhoods, not the devastated areas rife with boarded-up houses, vacant lots, and concentrated poverty that one can see in many parts of East and West Baltimore. Those areas are a different story, as I discussed in chapter 4. Most houses in Pen Lucy and Wilson Park are still well maintained, and most yards well kept. But the signs of decline are visible. An overgrown yard and a house that's been sitting empty for a few months or over a year. Another house with a grubby packed-dirt front yard where neither the landlord nor the tenants seem to care about either grass or appearances. More and more chain-link fences marking off families' front yards to keep people off their property. Here and there, a vacant lot, where a derelict house has been torn down. Homeownership has gone down, and poverty up. From 2000 to 2014, the share of families below the poverty level in Pen Lucy went from 19 percent to 29 percent, a jump of more than 50 percent. During the same period, the number of homeowners in Wilson Park went down by nearly 200, or more than a third.[1]

No one should write these two neighborhoods off. Both contain many families who keep up their properties and care about the welfare of their neighborhood. The Pen Lucy Neighborhood Association and the Wilson Park Improvement Association are both working hard to stabilize and improve their communities. An aggressive city strategy to get vacant properties back into use has gotten property owners and developers to rehab and reoccupy nearly sixty vacant houses since 2010. These efforts may slow down these neighborhoods' trajectory, but the trajectory itself is clearly downward. People keep walking away from houses. Despite the city's success getting vacant houses reused, both neighborhoods have more vacant, abandoned houses today than they did in 2010.

Baltimore has more neighborhoods like Pen Lucy and Wilson Park than it has areas like Fells Point or Hampden. This is not true in Washington, DC, or Seattle, but it is true pretty much across the board in the legacy cities of the Midwest and Northeast. For these cities, as a Detroit activist friend told me, this may be "the biggest issue that nobody's talking about." Why is this happening?

As I've discussed earlier, a lot of what is going on has to do with larger forces in American society that affect everyone, but affect the cities even more strongly. Both the hollowing of the middle class and the sorting of people by economic status, which are going on across the country, are important parts of the picture. The American industrial city of the 1950s was far from an egalitarian commonwealth, but it was far closer to one than the same city today.

Pittsburgh is a good example. In 1960, at the height of its manufacturing prowess, nearly half of all the families in Pittsburgh were middle-income families, meaning that their income was between 80 percent and 120 percent of the citywide median income, with the rest divided between lower- and upper-income families. By 2015, the share of middle-income families had dropped to a quarter, and the number of low- and upper-income families had grown in proportion. During those years, Pittsburgh lost over 37,000 middle-income families (fig. 6-3).

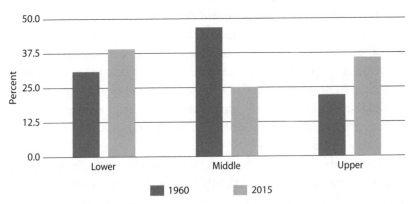

Figure 6-3 Change in income distribution in Pittsburgh, 1960–2015. (Source: US Census Bureau)

Fifty years ago, most people, not just middle-income families, tended to live in middle-income neighborhoods, many of them ethnic neighborhoods where people of all economic levels and social classes lived cheek by jowl, linked by their shared ethnic identity. Daniel Kay Hertz, a brilliant young Chicago-based researcher, has tracked how that city's neighborhoods have changed over the years. In 1970, most of Chicago was made up of middle-income areas. There were a handful of wealthy areas, mostly just north of the Loop along the lakefront and along Chicago's northern border, and a few more poor areas on the south and west sides. But middle-income areas predominated.

By 2012, the picture had utterly changed. There were few large middle-income areas left, except in Chicago's far North Side and pockets in the city's southwest. Wealth had spread strikingly to the north and west, taking in large parts of the Near North Side and moving inland. That growth paled, though, compared to the spread of poor neighborhoods, which now filled much of the rest of the city. Aptly, when Dan published his maps in 2014, he gave his piece the title "Watch Chicago's Middle Class Disappear before Your Very Eyes."[2]

The waning of the middle class, and the decline in the number of childrearing married couples that represents one of the most powerful demographic shifts of the past fifty years, are closely tied to one another. In order to understand the role that the decline of those families has played in the collapse of the urban neighborhood, though, we need to take a step back and look at how these neighborhoods came about, and the kinds of places they actually are, something I touched on briefly in chapter 2. To begin, the popular image of the traditional early-twentieth-century urban neighborhood as blocks of tenements is wildly misleading. Rather than reflecting reality, it reflects the extent to which images of New York City—or rather, Manhattan—dominate how we think about American cities.

The archetypal urban neighborhood, outside parts of the Northeast, is a neighborhood of single-family homes. Neighborhoods in many Northeastern cities like Newark, New Haven, or Boston are made up instead of two- and three-family homes, sometimes known as double-deckers or triple-deckers, in Newark sometimes derisively called "Bayonne Boxes." The owner usually lived in one of the apartments, and rented out the others, often to members of her extended family or to fellow immigrants from the old country. For various reasons, that model never caught on in the cities to the south like Philadelphia and Baltimore, or in the Midwestern cities like Detroit or Pittsburgh that didn't start to grow until the nineteenth century. They all became single-family cities.

All of these cities have a central downtown core, and some have a second core area where the major universities or medical centers are situated, like University Circle in Cleveland or Oakland in Pittsburgh. When you add up those areas, though, they rarely make up more than five percent of the city's land area. The rest is all single-family residential neighborhoods, along with what's left of the factories, railyards, and gasworks that once sustained the city's industrial economy. Even after decades of attrition, nine out of ten residential structures in Baltimore and Philadelphia today are single-family homes, and eight out of ten in Cleveland.

The first settlers of Philadelphia and Baltimore built brick row houses modeled after the houses in the English cities these people came from. As their cities grew, they continued to follow that model. As western cities were settled in the nineteenth century, though, their builders tended to build separate or detached houses. At first, they often used brick, but as time went on they shifted to building wood-frame houses that were easier and often less expensive to build, yet remarkably durable and comfortable when properly maintained.

Either way, America's urban neighborhoods, as they were built over the century following the end of the Civil War, in ecological terms could be called "monocultures" of single-family houses, like a field where only one crop is planted. That can be vividly seen in figure 6-4, an aerial view of a piece of Cleveland's West Side. They were and still are vast expanses of single-family homes, interspersed with convenience stores

Figure 6-4 The single-family monoculture: Cleveland's West Side. (Source: Google Earth)

and crossed at intervals by wider streets or avenues. Some of these avenues were lined with grander houses, but more often with the host of small stores, taverns, and businesses that served the people who lived in the single-family houses on either side.

Who lived in these houses? People of all social levels. From large, elaborately decorated homes for prosperous managers and merchants to small, plain dwellings for factory workers, whatever their residents' status, the people who lived in them were almost always married couples who would spend much if not most of their life together rearing children. The neighborhoods were well designed to provide a supportive environment for those families. Each family had the privacy of a separate house and small backyard, but at the same time, the homes were close enough to one another to encourage walkability and neighborliness. Except in the toniest areas, the commercial strips where people could find their grocer, butcher, baker, and tavern were rarely more than a short walk from most people's homes, a necessity in an era before car ownership became widespread. Children walked to the neighborhood public school or to the parochial school attached to the neighborhood parish church. Some neighborhoods clustered around factories, where most of the neighborhood's men worked. For others, their jobs were only a streetcar ride away. Urban neighborhoods were far from idyllic places, but on the whole they performed pretty well the function for which they were designed.

The big change began in the 1960s. The demographic and cultural changes in American society that I described in chapter 2 were beginning to undermine traditional family patterns at the same time that hundreds of thousands of white urban families were abandoning the cities for the lure of the suburbs. Between 1960 and 1980, the number of childrearing married couples in Cleveland went from 102,000 to 45,000 and in St. Louis from 76,000 to under 29,000. Those were the years when these cities first saw houses being abandoned *en masse*, and whole neighborhoods in North City St. Louis or Detroit's East Side begin to turn into the derelict near-prairies that haunt these cities today.

That was not the whole story, though. At the same time that some neighborhoods were devastated by suburbanization and white flight, or torn apart by urban renewal or freeway construction, many others survived, and some even thrived. In Detroit, middle-class African American families moved into and stabilized many of the neighborhoods their former white neighbors had left behind. Many white South City St. Louis neighborhoods stayed intact and slowly became more racially integrated over the coming decades. Although most ethnic communities dispersed, others resisted white flight. Here and there, through governmental or nonprofit initiatives or through the determined efforts of home-buyers and residents, a neighborhood would rebound and regain its vitality. Even as the cities' future looked bleakest, large parts of the cities remained intact, vital neighborhoods.

But the erosion continued. More and more of the jobs that traditionally sustained neighborhood breadwinners disappeared, while the new jobs that emerged demanded skills and education beyond what they could offer. Cleveland lost over half of its married couples with children between 1960 and 1980 and almost half of the rest between 1980 and 2000. Over half of those families left in 2000 were gone by 2015. By that point, of the 102,000 childrearing married couples in the city in 1960, only 12,000 were left. The picture was similar elsewhere. Neighborhoods like Pen Lucy in Baltimore, Dutchtown in St. Louis, or Price Hill in Cincinnati, which had survived the worst years of urban decline seemingly in good shape, were now visibly in decline.

The heart of the problem for these neighborhoods is that, as the demographic for which they were designed has shrunk, there are few people waiting in the wings to take their place. Most Young Grads or affluent empty-nesters are looking for very different types of places— the high-density, mixed-use areas close to downtowns, universities, and amenities like Baltimore's Inner Harbor waterfront. While a few of the denser neighborhoods close to the core, with distinctive older homes, like Shaw or Lafayette Square in St. Louis, may appeal to them, those are the exceptions. A few areas may be revived by immigrants like Detroit's Banglatown, but America's legacy cities are not seeing a large-enough immigrant influx to repopulate more than a handful of their struggling neighborhoods. Meanwhile, the young working-class couples that might have chosen to buy homes in these neighborhoods find it all but impossible to get a mortgage, and if they can, they are more likely to opt for one of the many price-competitive suburbs around cities like Detroit or Cleveland.

To the extent that these blocks and blocks of single-family homes depend heavily on childrearing families, the only significant alternative would appear to be female-headed families with children, whose numbers have grown since the 1960s. But their growth has been far less than the decline in childrearing married couples. Nationally, between 2000 and 2015, the number of female-headed families with children grew by one million, but the number of married couples with children dropped by *three* million.

But there's another reason that female-headed families don't offer much hope for these neighborhoods, which has nothing to do with numbers, and everything to do with economic inequality and the porous American social safety net. Single mothers are the poorest demographic group in America, and the single mothers who live in cities like Cleveland or Buffalo are the poorest members of that group. In most cities, single mothers earn only about a quarter of what married couples make. Since even two minimum-wage jobs are enough to lift a family out of poverty, few married couples with children live in poverty. Single women raising children are another story. Even though most of them work, they are typically trapped by low skills, limited education, and limited transportation options into poorly paying, low-level, often transitory employment. In 2015, 60 percent of all families headed by single mothers in Buffalo and 56 percent in Cleveland were below the poverty level.

To be poor in an American city is to live a life of almost constant instability and uncertainty. Job insecurity, unreliable transportation and child care, unpredictable health costs, and, as Matthew Desmond has brilliantly depicted in his book *Evicted*, rents that vastly exceed what they can afford even for poor-quality housing, all play their part. "The majority of poor families in America spend over half their income on housing," Desmond writes, "and at least one in four dedicates over 70 percent to paying the rent and keeping the lights on. Millions of Americans are evicted each year because they can't make rent. In Milwaukee, a city of fewer than 105,000 renter households, landlords evict roughly 16,000 adults and children each year."[3] Those numbers don't even take into account the thousands of "informal evictions," foreclosures, condemnations, as well as only nominally voluntary moves one step ahead of the landlord or the housing inspector. Not surprisingly, in these cities the average length a renter stays in the same place is barely two years.

Their intense poverty and the tragic instability and insecurity of their lives drastically curtail the role single mothers can play in sustaining the economic vitality or stability of their neighborhood. Their poverty means that most cannot realistically aspire to become homeowners, or if they are homeowners, to *stay* homeowners. If they are already home-owners, they often lack the money and skills to maintain aging houses that demand regular, expensive repairs and replacement. Their transitory existence, largely against their will, makes it difficult for them to sink roots into a single community, while their continual financial strug-gles sap their energy, leaving little for any involvement in the life of the neighborhood or their children's schools. There are exceptions, and they are real and important, but there are not enough of them to fundamen-tally alter this picture.

Homeownership is an important part of the glue that holds single-family neighborhoods together. Although in recent years there has been something of a tendency to suggest, as one colleague of mine put it, that we "get over homeownership," that would be a mistake. The evidence is compelling that homeownership matters. For decades, people have been studying the effects of homeownership on everything from home prices to juvenile delinquency. While no single study offers conclusive proof of the connection between homeownership and neighborhood vitality, the sheer accumulation of evidence all points strongly in the same direction.

Homeownership, even after controlling for social and economic dif-ferences like family type or household income, matters in many differ-ent ways that affect the health and vitality of neighborhoods. Higher levels of homeownership are strongly associated with higher property values, better maintenance and greater investment in properties, greater residential stability, more-positive child outcomes, and greater social capital, including greater involvement in neighborhood activities and greater readiness to become involved in tackling neighborhood prob-lems like crime or disorder. Vital urban neighborhoods typically have high homeownership rates, with well over half of the single-family houses in the neighborhood occupied by their owners. There are excep-tions, but not many.

In the past decade, though, traditional homeownership patterns have come undone, profoundly destabilizing many still-intact neighborhoods. The biggest factor in undoing urban homeownership was the insanity that possessed mortgage lending, beginning near the end of the last century, and its aftermath.

As I discussed in chapter 4, starting in the 1990s, a dramatic change came over the world of mortgage lending. People were enticed into becoming home buyers by low teaser rates and promises of future refinancing, while older home owners were urged to cash in by refinancing their existing mortgages. Shady products were aggressively marketed to unsophisticated lower-income and minority borrowers, who leapt at the chance to become homeowners or to get money out of their homes to use for their retirement or their dream vacation. With capital available to anyone on any terms, speculators had a field day.

Newark, New Jersey, was one epicenter of the subprime mortgage bubble. From 2000 to 2006, the number of mortgages made in Newark nearly tripled, while the median house price soared from $118,000 in 2000 to $307,000 in 2006. With hundreds of acres of vacant land still available in parcels where houses had been demolished in the 1970s and 1980s, the number of building permits for new homes also tripled. None of it made any sense. People weren't earning any more than before, new jobs weren't being created, crime was still rampant and the city's quality of life wasn't getting any better. The only thing that had changed was that lenders were handing out money for the asking. Of course, it was being handed out on terms that meant that most borrowers would never be able to repay the loans. When the music stopped, the bubble burst. People stopped making mortgages, house prices collapsed, and building projects were canceled. Nearly a decade later, Newark's real estate market, outside of a few pockets, is not even close to recovery. In 2014, building permits were half of what they were in 2000, mortgages barely one-third, and sales prices back to the 2000 level—but almost 40 percent below 2000 when adjusted for inflation (fig. 6-5).

The bursting of the subprime bubble devastated neighborhoods that may have been struggling, but still had their heads above water. Foreclosures skyrocketed. Newark has about 50,000 separate parcels of property. The number of foreclosure filings went over 2,000 in 2007, and stayed

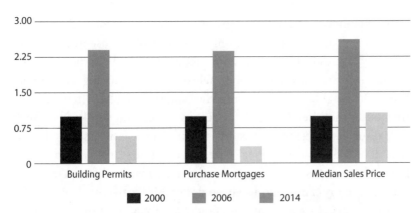

Figure 6-5 Newark's real estate boom and bust. Data shown relative to 2000, not in absolute numbers. (Source: house price data for Newark from Boxwood Means on PolicyMap, mortgage data from Home Mortgage Disclosure Act, building permit data from US Census Bureau)

above 2,000 per year for four years.[4] By 2014, one out of every three homes in the city had received a foreclosure notice. Newark, which has never had a high homeownership rate, has 20 percent fewer homeowners today than ten years ago. Homeowners who managed to save their homes were only slightly better off. Their equity was wiped out and they were now underwater, meaning that their house was worth less than the amount they owed on their mortgage. For the working-class families whose only possession of real value was their home, their entire wealth, modest as it was, had disappeared. In Newark, as elsewhere, the hardest-hit neighborhoods were not the worst areas, but the places people from those areas had moved into, the struggling but still vital middle neighborhoods in the city and its nearby affordable suburbs.

After the collapse, lenders tightened their standards, making it harder than ever before for an average working-class family to get a mortgage. This is particularly true in these middle neighborhoods, where house prices are low compared to reviving neighborhoods, and even more so compared to growing coastal areas; as housing finance expert Ellen Seidman says, "Getting a mortgage loan for less than $50,000 has never been easy, but it's becoming next to impossible."[5] This makes it even harder for these areas to recover. Young families who might want to buy a home in the neighborhood end up renting, or going elsewhere. And when houses come on the market, the only buyers are often absentee investors who buy houses to rent out as an investment, and who either pay cash or have informal or nonconventional sources of financing. A few may live in the neighborhood, but most live somewhere else, often far from the houses they are buying. As prices skyrocket in areas like New York or California, investors have started to see legacy cities as bargains; in the fall of 2016, Cleveland real estate agent Anne Callahan said "in the last twelve months, I've seen more cash buyers from California than I've ever seen in my career, and I've been doing this for twenty-five years."[6]

Since 2011, three out of four single-family house buyers in Trenton, New Jersey, another city hit hard by foreclosures and collapsing house prices, have been investors, including rings of small investors organized by brokers and investment advisors like New Jersey's Avi Cohen, who calls his business "Outside In." Asked why in a 2015 radio interview, he responded: "I take people that were either not investors yet, or not in the Trenton market, and I . . . get them in—to become a Trenton investor. For as little as $15K, somebody can be a real estate investor in Trenton."[7] His deals offer investors annual returns of 12 to 14 percent, sometimes as high as 20 percent. Meanwhile, between 2007 and 2015, Trenton's homeownership rate dropped from 48 percent to 38 percent. Trenton, a city of fewer than 90,000 people, lost over 2,200 homeowners.

These sudden shifts in a neighborhood, as neighbors see house after house flip to absentee owners, are destabilizing in themselves, even when the buyers are responsible long-term investors. Many, though, are not. Urban neighborhoods, like some parts of Trenton, where one can buy a house for as little as $20,000 draw a different type of investor, who are better called speculators or what I call "milkers." Milkers aim to get as much money out of the property as they can for a few years while putting virtually nothing into it, and then walk away. Milkers are a disaster for a neighborhood, and in many cases they are aided and abetted by sloppy or nonexistent code enforcement. As graduate student and investor Darin McLeskey puts it about Detroit, a popular target of speculators, "with no code enforcement, it's the Wild West."[8] Detroit is now trying to remedy its code enforcement, but progress is slow. Their properties are dying a slow death in front of their neighbors' eyes, doing more damage in the process than if they were abandoned and left to the elements. And that, of course, is what usually happens in the end anyway.

All of this just adds to the underlying weakness of urban neighborhoods; namely, that for a family with children, whatever their income and educational level, the downsides of living in an older central city are many. Enabling their children to get a good education, in cities where the public schools seem to be failing more often than not, is a constant challenge. In some cases, that can be solved by finding a good charter school, or even sending one's children to a nearby suburban school district, as one can do in Michigan. The pervasive presence of crime is harder to work around. In some neighborhoods, it is the onset of gun violence and gang activity. In others, it may not be murders or gunshots, but what one might call the constant incivilities of city life—the break-ins, the car thefts, the petty vandalism, and the graffiti on the walls.

What makes it even harder is the widespread feeling of being abandoned by a big, indifferent city that doesn't even seem to be able to provide the services that one could once all but take for granted. Property taxes are high, yet every year there seem to be more potholes in the streets and more broken streetlights, and it seems to take longer for the police to show up after you call 911. If you live in a neighborhood like Pen Lucy, far from the high-profile developments in downtown Baltimore or Harbor East, and you see your neighborhood gradually slipping away, it's easy to get a sense that nobody really cares about either you or the fate of your neighborhood.

Once the downsides outweigh the factors that connect you to your home, your neighbors, and the desire to stay in the same place where you've lived for years, you are ready to leave. What is different about that, though, from what has driven families to move to the suburbs at any time over the past fifty years? In many respects, the factors involved are much the same, but there are some important differences. First, it is happening not as part of a larger trend of urban decline and disinvestment, but *despite* today's trends of urban revival and reinvestment. Second, it is more of an equal opportunity migration.

In contrast to the largely white flight that characterized the 1960s and 1970s, today's migration is as much about black flight, the accelerated departure of the black middle class from the nation's older industrial cities. Between 2000 and 2015, the number of African American married couples with children in Detroit dropped by 60 percent, and in Cleveland by 50 percent. While some of this decline reflects the passage of time, with children growing up and leaving the home, and the effects of divorce and separation, a very large part of it has to do with thousands of those families voting with their feet to leave the city that they, more than any other group, had helped to keep afloat over the hard decades preceding the end of the millennium. I touched on black migration in chapter 4, but will dig into it a bit more deeply here.

It is easy to leave a legacy city for its suburbs. In contrast to the Seattle area, where even a modest 1950s ranch house in a close-in suburb like Shoreline can set one back $500,000 or more, attractive houses in close-in suburbs of Detroit, St. Louis, or Philadelphia are widely available for under $100,000. One house I found on Zillow was a four-bedroom, 1,600-square-foot house in a leafy subdivision in Trotwood, a suburb of Dayton, Ohio, that was listed for $70,900. A buyer getting an FHA mortgage at the going rate at the end of 2016, with the minimum 3.5 percent down payment, can cover interest and principal, property taxes, and insurance for only $550 per month. Trotwood is not an upscale community, but both by reputation and by such data as is available it is a much safer place than Dayton, with public schools that are at least marginally better. Trotwood is one of dozens, if not hundreds, of majority–African American suburbs around cities like Dayton, Cleveland, or St. Louis that have emerged over the past few decades.

The bottom line is that as people leave, whether they pass away or move to the suburbs, their places are more likely to be taken by people poorer than they are, living in houses that are now owned by often faraway absentee investors. Often, though, the house they vacate may just stay vacant. To look at the effects of this migration, we can turn to another Baltimore neighborhood, zooming in on one census tract in Baltimore along Garrison Boulevard, mostly in the Dorchester neighborhood in the northwest part of the city. In 2000, this area was a stable African American middle-class area, with big old frame-built single-family houses and yards more typical of a Midwestern town than a row house city (fig. 6-6).

Figure 6-6 Houses near Garrison Boulevard in Baltimore. (Source: Google Earth)

No longer. As houses have been abandoned, or flipped to investors, the number of homeowners in the area has dropped by almost 400. There are few new home buyers. By 2015, the number of vacant dwelling units had gone from 378 to 647, an increase of over 70 percent. By 2015, over half of the area's homeowners were over sixty-five, and less than 1 percent under thirty-five. In a strange reversal of the normal way incomes are distributed, the incomes of the elderly residents of the neighborhood were almost twice as high as those of the younger newcomers, largely poor single mothers living in rental houses and apartments, often created by landlords carving up the big old houses. The median single mother in this neighborhood earned less than $15,000 per year.[9]

The neighborhood's decline has had serious consequences. Since 2006, as house prices have dropped by more than 30 percent, the 350 or so elderly, almost all African American homeowners in the neighborhood who own their homes free and clear have lost $11 million in their collective net worth, or over $30,000 each. One can only speculate on how much equity the other 350 owners, or the former owners who sold their houses for less than they may have paid for them, have also lost. Multiply this by the hundreds of other legacy city neighborhoods that have lost that much or more of their property values, and the losses mount into the billions. Neighborhood decline is not the only thing going on that is draining the wealth of millions of African American homeowners. It is inextricably interwoven with the effects of subprime lending and mortgage foreclosure.

The massive erosion of wealth disproportionately affecting African American homeowners is only part of the cascading series of problems triggered as neighborhoods find themselves in a downward spiral. As the number of vacant properties increases, the value of the remaining properties declines further, and the confidence of the remaining homeowners begins to disappear. Signs of disorder begin to appear, from litter in the gutters to graffiti on the walls of vacant houses or storefronts. Decline gradually undermines a neighborhood's ability to maintain its stability in the face of problems.

Strictly speaking, there's no such thing as a "stable" neighborhood. No neighborhood literally stays the same for long; people move in and move out, shops and restaurants open and close, houses come down and new ones are built, problems emerge and are—or are not—resolved. When people refer to a stable neighborhood, they are describing the effect of a form of homeostasis, in the ability of the neighborhood, like the human body, to maintain a level of social stability amidst change. As Jane Jacobs put it, in her seminal book *The Death and Life of Great American Cities*, "a successful city neighborhood is a place that keeps sufficiently abreast of its problems so that it is not destroyed by them."[10]

As people lose confidence in their neighborhood, the homeostasis breaks down. Jacobs continues, "An unsuccessful neighborhood is a place that is overwhelmed by its defects and problems and is progressively more helpless before them." Criminologist Wesley Skogan describes how neighborhood decline and disorder create a feedback system:

> For residents, disorder and crime lead first of all to withdrawal from the community. Daily experience with disorderly conditions creates anxiety; the prospect heightens fear. When communities finally become unpleasant to live in, and encounters leave people feeling uneasy and unsafe, many residents will try to leave. Those who cannot leave physically, withdraw

psychologically. [...] Such withdrawal tends to reduce the supervision of youths, undermines any general sense of mutual responsibility among area residents, and weakens informal social control. [It] also undermines participation in neighborhood affairs. [...] More, it contributes to the decline of local housing and business conditions. [...] Fewer people will want to shop or live in areas stigmatized by visible signs of disorder. ...[11]

For many of the families living in such a neighborhood, the decline goes far beyond the loss in their home's value and the disappearance of their modest wealth. It goes to their quality of life and their ability to live and raise children without fear, things that affluent suburbanites take for granted.

Decline is not irreversible. Some of the areas in Indianapolis that appear on the map at the beginning of this chapter may be beginning to stabilize and regain their vitality. Some may stabilize through the determined efforts of dedicated residents and civic organizations, while others may revive by attracting energetic, committed young people, or by becoming immigrant destinations like Detroit's Banglatown. Thoughtfully designed, well-executed public investment, as happened in Indianapolis's Fall Creek Place, may turn around a few more areas. At the same time, the sheer impact of all of the many factors working against the stability of legacy city neighborhoods means that, barring some new and unforeseen development, many will continue to decline over the coming decades. That will mean not only the loss of wealth and quality of life for thousands of struggling working- and middle-class families, but also the loss of thousands of salvageable homes, apartments, and commercial buildings, and the further decline of the cities' already inadequate tax base. That, then, raises another question: if the middle disappears, can a city with poor and rich people and fewer and fewer people in between remain a viable city? That is not a simple question, but I suspect that the answer is no.

While some scholars have looked at neighborhood decline—*Urban Geography* devoted a 2016 special issue to the subject—as have some planners and other professionals, this problem, for all its massive effect on tens of thousands of working and elderly families, seems to be prompting little sense of outrage or urgency on the part of most people in the cities where it is taking place, especially when compared to the gallons of real and virtual ink spilled on the subject of gentrification.

I'm not sure why this is so, but it reflects a worrisome disconnect between the reality of our cities and the rhetoric flowing from them. Some of this disconnect may come from the fact that there are fundamental differences in the nature of the forces behind gentrification and those driving neighborhood decline. Gentrification is widely seen as something that's being done by *someone* to *someplace* or *somebody*. In an increasingly tribal world, young white people with money, and the members of the gentrification-industrial complex working behind the scenes, are Them—a visible enemy on which to unload one's frustration and anger. Moreover, if one has a visible Them to aim at, there's always the possibility that one might actually be able to find a lever that will allow one to affect their behavior and thus deal with the problem in some fashion.

By contrast, neighborhood decline is painfully diffuse and impersonal. It is the product of a complex interplay of factors, many of which are difficult to tackle or even in some cases to define. Those include global and national increases in economic inequality, demographic shifts, changes in employment, aging of the urban housing stock, suburban out-migration of middle-class black families, and the continuing fallout from the foreclosure crisis and housing-market collapse of the mid-2000s. Some people get it, like Detroit activist Lauren Hood. She writes that she has "come to believe the 'G' word is kind of a distraction." "We've got our best minds thinking, writing, examining, dissecting, researching, and fighting against gentrification," she adds, "when those same thought leaders could be applying their intellectual prowess to some of the less sexy but more complex and widespread issues that are negatively affecting us/our neighbors."[12]

At the same time, it would be far too literal-minded not to recognize the complex relationship between gentrification and decline, and the fact that the overarching question of power transcends and subsumes both. It's not just about buildings and neighborhoods; as Detroiter Jerry Mangona says about his city, "Detroit is 140-plus square miles. Ninety percent of it will not be affected by gentrification for ten to twenty years, even if we're being optimistic. But what's important here is not the 'spoken' concern of gentrification. It's the 'unspoken' concern of how a community will cope, react, and adapt to a loss of power."[13] In that context, the continued decline of so many neighborhoods is simply the other side of the gentrification coin. The impersonality of the forces behind decline makes it that much more galling for those who lack the power to exercise any control over either one or the other.

Chapter 7

The Other Postindustrial America: Small Cities, Mill Towns, and Struggling Suburbs

The Monongahela River rises in the hills of West Virginia and flows north into Pennsylvania just south of Point Marion, where it is joined by the Cheat River and continues to flow north to Pittsburgh, tracing wide curves in the steep, verdant hills on either bank. At Pittsburgh, it meets the Allegheny, and the two become the Ohio River, continuing north for a while, and then making a sharp left turn to head west into Ohio, wandering westward for hundreds of miles to meet the Mississippi at Cairo, Illinois. To people unfamiliar with the area, few of the names of the towns that line the banks of the Monongahela or the upper reaches of the Ohio will strike even a faint chord: Donora, Clairton, McKeesport, Homestead, Braddock, Ambridge, Aliquippa, and Midland, to name just a few before the Ohio River even leaves Pennsylvania.

The valley that the Monongahela and the Ohio carved through southwestern Pennsylvania has been compared to Germany's Ruhr Valley, and dubbed "Steel Valley." All of these towns, nestled in narrow strips of flat land between the hills and the river, were factory towns, each one built around the mill that dominated the landscape. Of these towns, Braddock has received the most publicity in recent years, thanks to the larger-than-life personality of its six-foot-eight mayor, John Futterman, who, since taking office in 2008, has appeared on CNN, Fox News, CNBC, and the Colbert Report, and has been written up in the *New York Times*. Although the blast furnaces at US Steel's Edgar Thompson Works at the edge of town are still firing, the town itself hardly exists anymore. With a population of barely 2,000, only 10 percent of its 1920 peak of 21,000, it is a desolate place of empty buildings and vacant lots. Only fourteen houses sold in Braddock in all of 2015, for an average price of about $17,000.

Each one of these places has its own story, about coal, steel, and the river. Aliquippa was virtually a company town, created in 1909 after Jones & Laughlin built what would become the largest integrated steel mill in the world, which stretched seven miles along the river. To house the immigrants coming to work in the plant, J&L laid out a model community on the hills rising above the plant, designating each neighborhood as Plan 1, Plan 2, and so on up to Plan 12. Whether J&L officially steered people of different origins to the different "Plans" is unclear, but it worked out that way. Serbs and Croats lived in Plans 1, 4, and 9; Germans and Irish in 3 and 12; and Italians, Poles, and African Americans in Plan 11. Even today, when you ask someone from Aliquippa where they live, they'll tell you, "Plan 4" or "Plan 12."[1]

The plant closed in 1984, throwing 8,000 people out of work. Aliquippa today has only one-third of the 27,000 people it had in 1930. Once-bustling Franklin Avenue, the main street that led down the hill from the homes to the plant, is a shadow of its former self, with far more vacant lots, empty storefronts, day-care centers, and social service agencies than functioning stores and businesses. Aliquippa will survive in some fashion, though, because it is only twenty minutes from Pittsburgh International Airport to the south, and half an hour from the shopping centers and business parks of bustling Cranberry Township to the east, where most of the city's residents work. Survival, though is a low bar; as Pitt economist Chris Briem says, "Aliquippa's in a weird place, it's not the center of the region, it's not the city, it's not quite rural. What is the competitiveness of towns that used to have a reason for being—and don't anymore?"[2] Over the past forty years, Aliquippa has been battered by crime, racial conflict, unemployment, and the crack epidemic. Were it not for people's attachment to their scrappy high school football team that keeps punching above its weight and which has produced such NFL superstars as Mike Ditka and Tony Dorsett, the city might be little more than a low-rent dormitory for the low-wage workers the surrounding townships need to fuel their economy.

The story of Braddock and Aliquippa, although perhaps more extreme than most, shows a different side of postindustrial America from the story of Pittsburgh, Baltimore, or Detroit. While the industrial boom that began in the second half of the nineteenth century led to the rise of a handful of great industrial cities, it spawned many more small cities like Trenton, New Jersey; Canton, Ohio; Gary, Indiana; and Battle Creek, Michigan; and an even greater number of even smaller industrial places, not just those in the Mon Valley, but in upstate New York, in Ohio, and across the nation's industrial heartland. These towns and cities, as well as the struggling suburbs of the larger cities, tend to be far off the national radar. They get far less attention than the more exciting, upbeat stories coming out of cities like Pittsburgh, Baltimore, or Detroit.

Where to draw the line between big and small cities is hard to pin down, but the experience of the past few decades suggests that it's probably somewhere between 100,000 and 200,000 people. Population matters in itself, but matters even more as a stand-in for other factors. Small cities like Erie, Pennsylvania, or Canton, Ohio, don't look that different from big cities of the same era. They have downtowns with tall buildings and parking garages, many of them products of the urban renewal of the fifties and sixties, charming Victorian neighborhoods, as well as struggling depressed neighborhoods with more than their share of vacant, abandoned houses. Canton's downtown, the historic hub of a city that never quite reached 120,000 at its peak, and has barely 70,000 people today, doesn't look that different from the downtowns of larger cities.

Canton has actually done better holding on to its manufacturing jobs than larger cities like Pittsburgh or Baltimore. It still has 9,000 factory jobs, more than Pittsburgh and not quite half of what it had in the 1960s. While it has taken some hits in recent years, its flagship employer, Timken Steel, remains a vital part of the city's economy. Like Pittsburgh and Baltimore, though, most of Canton's economy today is based on eds and meds—education and health care. That comparison, although factually true, is also misleading.

The eds and meds sector in a city like Pittsburgh is a global industry and a powerful economic engine for the city. Tens of thousands of students from all over the world come to study in its universities, while the University of Pittsburgh Medical Center generates billions in revenues for medical care and research. They are export industries in the truest sense, bringing in billions of dollars from the outside to fuel the local economy, spinning off cutting-edge biotech and IT businesses and drawing others from the outside, while their students and well-paid employees fuel robust commercial spending, entertainment, and residential revitalization.

Canton's eds and meds sector, in contrast, is local. The city has two community hospitals and Malone University, an admirable but modest Quaker-oriented institution with fewer than 2,000 students. The hospitals meet the health care needs of the city and nearby communities, while most of Malone University's students come from the surrounding region, and only half live on campus. These, and their counterparts in similar small cities, contribute value to the community and provide a modest number of jobs, but add little more to the city's economy. From an economic perspective, if Pitt is New York's Central Park, Malone is a community playground.

This point is worth elaborating. What is it about a university that makes it a major economic engine? The number of students is important, to be sure, but many other factors also play important roles. One of the most important is how far away the students come from, and the extent to which the students actually live independently on campus or in the community, putting outside money into the local economy. A college that draws all or most of its students from the immediate area, most of whom live at home as they study, generates little or no spillover from those students' modest disposable income beyond a few pizzas and beers. That is a major reason why community colleges, although valuable for the educational opportunities they offer, have little direct economic impact on their communities.[3]

Major research universities, on the other hand, are fiscal and economic powerhouses. The University of Pittsburgh has over 11,000 full-time employees compared to Malone's 250, and an annual operating budget of $2.1 billion. Not only do research universities have large student bodies, faculty, and administrative staff, but their faculty and staff make far more, and in all likelihood spend more. The average full professor at Yale makes nearly $200,000 for her nine months' work, compared to $65,000 for her counterpart at Canton's Malone University, which means that she is likely to spend far more in the community where she lives, even after vacations and online purchases.

The major universities spend far more on research and development. Johns Hopkins University spent $2.3 billion on R&D in 2015, while the Pittsburgh duo of Pitt and Carnegie Mellon spent $1.1 billion.[4] That spending not only goes to support more hiring and purchasing, but also leads to valuable spin-offs in the form of start-up businesses like Pittsburgh's Ottomatika. Even large lower-tier universities generate little research activity; Youngstown State University's student body is half the size of that of Johns Hopkins, but YSU spent only $3.3 million on R&D in 2015, or slightly more than *one-thousandth* as much. When one adds all of these up, it becomes clear how vast the differences are among the economic impacts that various institutions have on their home communities.

Another important difference between larger and smaller cities can be found in what happened to their business establishments as regional economies first became national, and then global. The civic capitalism of the early twentieth century, based on an interlocking system of locally owned factories, banks, and other institutions, is long gone. As companies became national and then global, size mattered. The larger the city, the more likely it was to see its corporations stay home and its banks gobble up other banks rather than be gobbled up by them. Cincinnati and St. Louis are each home to seven Fortune 500 corporations, and Pittsburgh to six.

By contrast, the end of civic capitalism stripped most small cities of whatever local economic institutions they once had. Although there are a few survivors here and there, like Timken Steel in Canton or Boscov's department store chain, still based in Reading, Pennsylvania, most banks, department stores, and manufacturers were absorbed by national or international firms. The story of how Trenton's three big local banks were acquired and merged first into regional, and then into global institutions, as laid out in figure 7-1, can stand in for the story in dozens of cities.

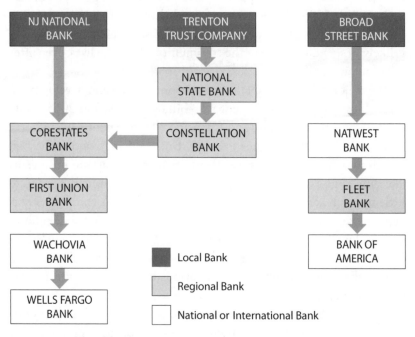

Figure 7-1 How Trenton lost its local banks.

Finally and most importantly, there is the matter, hard to pin down but inescapable, of critical mass, or what economists call agglomeration. As defined by Harvard economist Edward Glaeser, "agglomeration economies are the benefits that come when firms and people locate near one another together in cities and industrial clusters."[5] Again, size matters. Historically, economists first discussed the benefits of agglomeration as reducing the cost of transporting goods, but those costs matter less today. Thanks to shipping containers and other innovations, the cost of shipping manufactured goods from China to the United States has become little more than a rounding error in firms' balance sheets, but the value of agglomeration has become, if anything, even greater in the modern knowledge economy.

Firms benefit from clustering, both because more of the same type of firm in the same location multiplies each other's business activity, as in Manhattan's Diamond District or Philadelphia's Jeweler's Row, but also because the more similar firms in the same area, the stronger and more productive the infrastructure that grows up around those firms. Growth in small businesses in one place leads to more growth; as Stuart Rosenthal and William Strange write, "cities with vibrant small-business sectors will tend to continue to have vibrant small-business sectors. Those without much small business will have difficulty achieving takeoff."[6]

Clustering fosters knowledge spillovers, or the exchange of ideas among people in related fields, which in turn leads to increased productivity and activity among those sharing each other's ideas.[7] Those who expected the Internet and the tools it spawned to eliminate the benefit of face-to-face contact have found themselves rudely surprised; indeed, proximity has turned out to be more important than ever in the growth of the innovation economy. While *information* can be spread as easily at long distance, *knowledge* benefits greatly from proximity.

Berkeley economist Enrico Moretti tells the story of Danish entrepreneur Mikkel Svane, who cofounded the high-tech firm Zendesk in Copenhagen, "but soon realized that Copenhagen was too isolated. Two years later, he moved the company to the United States." First he tried Boston, but eventually he settled on San Francisco. "It is very exciting," Moretti quotes Svane. "Coming to San Francisco and working with the local people here and our advisors has made us think bigger and more aggressively and really pushed the envelope."[8] The serendipity between research universities and emerging technologies goes well beyond the spin-off companies that come directly out of those universities. Companies benefit from the talent the universities produce, hire their graduates, and thrive in the environment of creativity and innovation that surrounds them.

Clustering also helps workers, who benefit from what is known as labor-market pooling, or a "thick" labor market. "Thick markets," as Moretti puts it, "with many sellers and many buyers, are particularly attractive because they make it easier to match demand to supply."[9] If Sarah, for example, a new graduate with a specialized degree in bioinformatics, moves to a small city like Canton or Danville, Virginia, to work for the one firm in that city that has need of her specialty, only to discover to her dismay that the firm's culture is sexist and oppressive, she has little choice but to pull up roots and start all over again elsewhere. Sarah would have been far better off to have gone to San Diego, Austin, or Baltimore, where she would have found many different firms in need of her specialty. She will have more competition in San Diego, but if she is any good at all, she'll have many more options. Meanwhile, the biotech firms in San Diego and Baltimore can outcompete those in Canton and Danville because they have the luxury of choosing the best candidates, rather than having to settle for the few willing to move to the smaller city. Moretti sums it up: "a thick market is a win-win for workers and firms alike."[10] Sooner or later, the Danville firm, if it really wants to compete, will move.

In all likelihood, though, Sarah would never have seriously considered moving to Canton or Danville. As a member of Richard Florida's creative class, her choice would be dictated as much if not more by lifestyle than by employment. As Florida writes of his focus groups, "Many said they had turned down jobs, or decided not to look for them, in places that did not afford the variety of 'scenes' they desired."[11] Here, too, size matters. A scene needs a certain critical mass of supporters and participants to sustain itself, whether the scene takes the form of a major league hockey team, a symphony orchestra, or a cluster of Young Grad watering holes. Without that critical mass, efforts to build a scene wither and die.

That doesn't mean that people don't try. Small cities, particularly those with even modest universities, contain a cadre of people looking for the same amenities that are so readily available in Chicago or Philadelphia. A few years ago, I was in gritty little Youngstown, Ohio, spending a few days with the staff of the Youngstown Neighborhood Development Corporation, a remarkable organization which I'll talk about later. After a morning meeting at City Hall, I suggested to my host that it would be nice to get a cup of coffee before heading back to their office, fully expecting to end up in a coffee shop or diner, where I would get my coffee in the iconic blue take-out cup with Greek-style decorations running around the rim. Instead, we walked into a place that would have fit smoothly into Park Slope or Seattle, with its neo-industrial décor, jazz coming out of the speakers, tattooed barista, and a blackboard with tasting notes on the coffees they had roasted earlier that week. We got our (very good) lattes and left. When I looked for it a couple of years later, though, it was gone.

The point of this seemingly trivial story is twofold. First, even in small, struggling cities like Youngstown, there are people who will try to create a version of the hip urban scene of the larger cities; second, their efforts rarely add up to anything like a scene, and often fail—not for lack of will or ability, but for the absence of the critical mass needed to sustain them.

That doesn't mean that there's nothing happening in these small cities. Although one coffee shop may go out of business, others take their place. Youngstown has a new downtown coffee place, home base of an aspiring chain that has already opened outposts in Florida and Las Vegas, as well as another coffee place a few blocks to the north, next to the Youngstown State campus. The presence of Youngstown State, as well as a smattering of professionals and young entrepreneurs, is enough to enable Youngstown to support a couple of coffee places and an eclectic restaurant or two. Still, it is not enough to generate either the lifestyle attractions or the economic activity that is drawing thousands of Young Grads to Baltimore or Pittsburgh. And it does nothing for the one-time factory workers and their children, who see little hope for the future and whose lives continue to disintegrate.

In the small-city sweepstakes, Johnstown, Pennsylvania, has even less going for it. Site of the famous Johnstown flood, it sits on a tributary of the Allegheny River in the hills about sixty miles east of Pittsburgh. For over a century, it was a prosperous steelmaking city anchored by the vast Cambria Mill, reaching a peak population of nearly 70,000 in the 1920s. As was happening elsewhere, the mill gradually cut back during the 1970s and 1980s, and closed for good in 1992. But the hemorrhaging continued; between 2002 and 2012, Johnstown lost over one-third of its remaining jobs, and by 2014 two out of five of the jobs that were left were in health care or education. In 2015, the city's population dropped under 20,000 for the first time since the 1880s.

Over one-third of Johnstown's residents live in poverty, as do an astonishing 70 percent of the city's infants and toddlers under five. Over half of the city's residents 16 and over do not work at all, and one of every three dollars in income for Johnstown residents comes from Social Security, SSI, welfare, or pensions. Johnstown, indeed, is a poster child for what I call the urban transfer-payment economy, which I'll describe later in this chapter. It is hard to see a path to prosperity for Johnstown.

Not all small legacy cities are following the same trajectory. I've already described how New Haven has changed in recent years, thanks mainly to the overwhelming presence of Yale University. The same is true of at least a handful of small cities that, although they may not have a globally renowned university, have been able to take advantage of other assets to rebuild their economies. If we look at just one measure, change in the poverty rate from 2000 to 2015, we can see that a few cities, Bethlehem, Pennsylvania, and Lowell, Massachusetts, in particular, have done far better than the pack (figure 7-2).

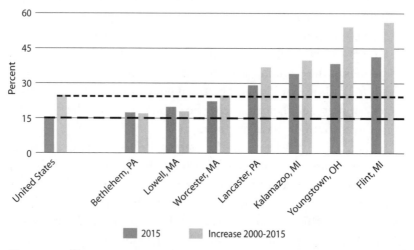

Figure 7-2 Poverty rate in 2015 and change in poverty rate since 2000: United States and selected small cities. (Source: US Census Bureau)

Much of this is likely to be what Michigan State researchers Laura Reese and Minting Ye call "place luck."[12] Lowell and Worcester are close to Boston, with good commuter rail service to that thriving metropolis. Both have solid if not globally acclaimed universities, as does Bethlehem, which is farther from New York City, but not so far that it doesn't benefit greatly from its proximity to that powerful economic center.

Flint is closer to Detroit than Bethlehem is to New York, but Detroit is not much of an economic engine, and it provides little or no economic lift to Flint. Even Philadelphia, with a local economy far stronger than Detroit's, still radiates little energy out to nearby cities like Camden, Chester, or Reading, all of which are in severe distress. Braddock is only twenty minutes from Pittsburgh, but the two places inhabit different worlds. On the whole, small cities in the Northeast are doing far better than those in the Midwest, largely because of the greater prosperity of the region as a whole, as well as their greater proximity to strong, grow- ing economic centers like New York or Boston.

Other small cities have held on to major manufacturing employ- ers like the Cummins Machine Company in Columbus, Indiana, or Timken Steel in Canton, Ohio. While some of these manufacturers are struggling, others are thriving. Hickory, North Carolina, a small city of 40,000 people in the Appalachian foothills north of Charlotte, has a booming furniture industry; Scott Millar, head of the county economic development agency, told me that their factories could hire 4,000 people tomorrow, if they could find them.

A strong mix of manufacturing, education, and the arts, along with a healthy infusion of Amway money, has propelled growth in Grand Rapids, Michigan. Lancaster, Pennsylvania, has rebuilt its economy around history, the arts, and its proximity to Amish country, a major tourist destination. Yet more cities, like Johnstown or Flint, seem to be falling behind, increasingly dependent on the urban transfer-payment economy. They won't disappear, yet the paths to revival that exist for a Pittsburgh or Baltimore, and potentially Detroit, seem remote for most of them.

Both Lowell and Bethlehem have taken advantage of other assets at their disposal. Bethlehem, whose economy and landscape was defined for over one hundred years by the Bethlehem Steel Works, which sprawled along the Lehigh River in the heart of the city, has made an impressive comeback since the mill closed. That comeback, fueled by a strong regional economy, heritage tourism, and, in the heart of the former steel mill, the Sands Casino—one of the few casinos that actu- ally seems to enhance the local economy rather than suck the life out of it—can be seen in the crowds on the streets, the bustling stores and restaurants; more concretely, in solid job growth numbers and a poverty rate barely above the national average.

Bethlehem also benefits from the presence of Lehigh University, which, although much smaller than Pitt or Johns Hopkins, is a substantial institution with a first-class engineering program. Lehigh, in turn, helps sustain a state-supported technology incubator called Benjamin Franklin TechVentures, based in a former Bethlehem Steel lab facility. Since its creation in 1983, the incubator has graduated sixty-four successful companies, creating over 6,400 jobs.

The prognosis is less promising for Midwestern cities like Flint, Youngstown, or the even more devastated city of Gary, Indiana. These cities have lost much more of their onetime population than most eastern cities, which have seen more immigration, particularly in recent years. Although Kalamazoo, Michigan, has a diversified economy, as well as two institutions of higher education—Kalamazoo College and Western Michigan University—that has not kept it from becoming a high-poverty city, with a citywide poverty rate more than double the national average.

Many of these cities, though, are working hard to tackle their problems and rebuild their economies and their physical fabric, with some amazing people and organizations on the job. The Youngstown Neighborhood Development Corporation (YNDC) is one of them. Its mission is "to transform neighborhoods into meaningful places where people invest time, money, and energy into their homes and neighborhoods; where neighbors have the capacity to manage day-to-day issues; and where neighbors feel confident about the future of their neighborhood."[13] Since its founding in 2009, YNDC has been unusually fortunate to have been headed by two visionary leaders, first Presley Gillespie and now Ian Beniston, the son of a Youngstown steelworker. YNDC puts most of its efforts, as Beniston puts it, into "those neighborhoods in the middle. Neighborhoods that have many signs of distress, but they're not to a point where we have 70 or 80 percent vacancy,"[14] while focusing on eliminating blight in the rest of the city by cutting grass and weeds, and boarding up and demolishing vacant houses.

On a budget of roughly $2.5 million per year raised through determined fundraising efforts, YNDC carries out a dizzying variety of activities to make Youngstown a better place, including mobilizing hundreds of residents and volunteers to clean and green vacant lots, securing and boarding up hundreds of vacant houses, rehabilitating other vacant houses and selling them to home-buyers, making microbusiness loans, making home repairs for low-income homeowners, fixing broken sidewalks, running a 1.7-acre urban farm, and far more. YNDC is determinedly entrepreneurial; when they realized a couple of years ago that too many of their prospective home-buyers weren't able to get mortgages, they raised the capital to make their own mortgages, and they convinced a local bank to service them at low cost. Above all, they engage the people who live in the neighborhoods where YNDC works, getting them involved in their blocks and thinking about their communities' future.

Danville, Virginia, a struggling former mill town far from the bustling Virginia suburbs of Washington, DC, is another place showing tenuous signs of revival. Thanks in large part to the effort and determination of the city's late visionary but pragmatic city manager Joe King, an unusual blend of drill sergeant and philosopher, its downtown is showing signs of life, while many of the old tobacco warehouses along the Dan River have been restored as apartments and the homes of start-up companies.

Beloit, a struggling small city in Wisconsin, has had its change fueled by the multimillion-dollar investments of Diane Hendricks, cofounder and owner of Beloit-based ABC Supply and, according to *Forbes* magazine, the second-richest self-made woman in the United States, with a fortune of nearly $5 billion. Between developing the Phoenix, a grandiosely named downtown mixed-use complex, and converting the old Beloit Corporation machine factory into the Ironworks complex, Hendricks has invested well over $50 million in the city.

Despite her efforts, as Alexandra Stephenson recently reported for the *New York Times*, "unemployment is still high, [and] a short drive south of the Phoenix and new buildings turn to boarded-up shops. Beloit remains deeply troubled."[15] The point is not that Diane Hendricks's investments have solved, or even seriously addressed, the problems of Beloit as a place and those of the people who live there, which they have not. But they may just possibly help create the environment in which the strategies that might address those problems could take root. Who knows whether with the right encouragement Hendricks could put some of her millions to work to help solve some of the underlying problems continuing to face Beloit's less-prosperous residents.

Not every small, struggling city has a billionaire willing to put up that kind of money toward its revival, but most have some capacity to foster change. Although some places may have few if any alternatives to continuing to survive on the urban transfer-payment economy, even within that economy's limited compass, in Youngstown, Danville, or Beloit the work of people like Ian Beniston, Joe King, and Diane Hendricks all show that there is room for change. At the same time, the limited scope of what the local economy offers imposes real limits on how far that change can go. Beniston is realistic. "It's the lack of resources," he points out. "One of the things we need more of here without a doubt is just jobs. That's the reality of it, that's why people leave. So until we can get to a point where we're attracting, developing, creating, even here locally, more jobs, we're going to be struggling to get to where we need to be."

If small industrial cities face a difficult challenge, the same is even more true of the mill towns that line the banks of the Monongahela and are scattered around the American heartland. If we drew the line between large and small cities between 100,000 and 200,000 inhabitants, the line between small cities and mill towns would probably fall somewhere between 20,000 and 40,000 people. Where the line is drawn, though, is not just about population but about the type of place it is. Cities, even small ones, typically have community colleges and community hospitals, some cultural life around an arts center, museum, or concert hall, and a downtown with the stores and businesses that historically—although perhaps no longer—served a hinterland beyond the city's boundaries. Mill towns have little if any of those features. They were there for the factory and the factory alone, and even in their heyday had little in the way of shops or civic spaces beyond what the factory and its workers needed.

Mill towns like Braddock, Pennsylvania, or Wellsville, Ohio, are in many respects the end of the line not just for an economy, but for a way of life. It is not just that the factories have closed, but that these communities, as described by commentator J. D. Vance, author of the memoir *Hillbilly Elegy*, are broken. Vance, who grew up in Middletown, Ohio, writes that "these are places where good jobs are impossible to come by. Where people have lost their faith and abandoned the churches of their parents and grandparents. Where the death rates of poor white people go up even as the death rates of all other groups go down. Where too many young people spend their days stoned instead of working and learning."[16]

As many have written since, these places were the bedrock of Trump's support in the 2016 election. Nowhere is this more true than along the Ohio River. A hundred years ago, East Liverpool, Ohio, was known as "Crockery City" and competed with Trenton for the title of pottery capital of the United States. The city's Museum of Ceramics keeps a roster with the names of hundreds of separate pottery firms that operated in the city at one time or another during its heyday. Today, East Liverpool, along with its smaller neighbor Wellsville, are struggling against the tide; all but a handful of the potteries are gone, and their collective population has dropped from 35,000 to 14,000. In 2016, East Liverpool gave Donald Trump 62 percent of its votes.

In ancient times, cities that lost their economic purpose as ports, trading centers, or mining towns simply disappeared. My favorite example is in central Italy, at the southern edge of the Po Delta, where a magnificent sixth-century Byzantine basilica stands in the middle of fields and pastures a few miles south of Ravenna. Generations of visitors have wondered why such a church, which clearly belongs in a major town, should sit in the middle of the countryside, as can be seen in figure 7-3.

The answer, of course, is simple. It was built in the heart of Classe, an important Roman port city on the Adriatic Sea. Although Classe suffered invasions and depredations over the years following the end of the Roman Empire, its deathblow came from Mother Nature. The Po River brought silt down from the mountains and the harbor gradually filled up, eventually beyond the point of no return. By the eighth century it was no longer usable, and the population drifted away. The city ultimately disappeared entirely, except for the church, which still stands, now four miles from the sea.

America's small industrial cities and villages will not disappear, though, even if they lose their last factory. Community hospitals and state universities will help sustain cities like Youngstown or Flint

Figure 7-3 The Basilica of Sant'Appolinare in the now-vanished Roman city of Classe. (Source: Google Earth)

through the money flowing into those facilities from the outside—Medicaid, Medicare, and Blue Cross payments to the hospital; state funds, Pell Grants, and federally guaranteed student loans to the university.

Even in a town like Aliquippa with no hospital or university, money still flows into the local economy. State, local, and county property taxes, sales taxes, and income taxes support schools and public services, although often poor or inadequate. Social Security, Supplemental Security Income (SSI), Section 8 Vouchers, and the Supplemental Nutrition Assistance Program (SNAP), formerly known as food stamps, inject additional resources into the local economy by putting at least a little money into the pockets of the area's low-income residents or the people who sell them food or rent them houses. Two out of every five households in Youngstown received food stamps in 2015, including more than two-thirds of the city's families with children.

Payments to hospitals, colleges, and local governments create jobs, which in turn generate consumer spending, while the money from SSI, Social Security, vouchers, and SNAP is spent in the community, in food stores or through rent payments. That spending, in turn, enables a few retail businesses and service providers to survive, and it generates some more jobs for bank tellers, grocery store clerks, and home health aides.

Not all this money stays in the community, of course, but much of it does. This is the urban transfer-payment economy, as I call it, and figure 7-4 shows how it works.

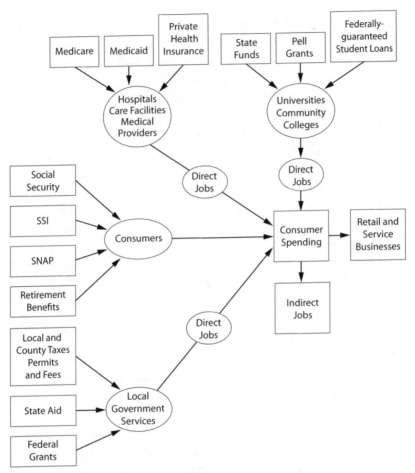

Figure 7-4 How the urban transfer-payment economy works.

Transfer payments create an economic floor for a community's survival, providing a regular and predictable flow of dollars. What they do *not* do is offer any shot at prosperity. They ensure a decent standard of living for the relatively small number of people with good jobs in city and county government, the hospital, and the colleges—most of whom live and do most of their shopping in the city's suburbs—and little more than subsistence for everyone else. Over 80 percent of the people who actually work in Youngstown—and nearly 90 percent of those making over $40,000 a year—live in the city's suburbs. The point, though, is that even in the most distressed community, there is *some* money coming in, and it's just enough to enable a core of people to continue to live there and for the community to survive, rather than vanish like Classe did over a thousand years ago.

Markham, Illinois, seems to have nothing in common with Youngstown, Braddock, or East Liverpool. A town of tree-lined streets, ranch houses, and split-levels, it looks like an *Ozzie and Harriet* suburb of the 1950s, where you'd expect to find Mom still standing in the kitchen ready to give the kids a glass of chocolate milk when they come home from school. Appearances are deceiving, though. Markham is one, although far from the most distressed, of dozens of suburban towns and villages in Illinois's Cook County, south of Chicago, that have seen their fortunes plummet in recent decades, and that have become centers of what the *Atlantic*'s Alana Semuels, borrowing a phrase from Michael Harrington, has called the "new American poverty."[17]

A few years ago, Elizabeth Kneebone and Alan Berube, two researchers at Washington's Brookings Institution, made an amazing discovery. During the 2000s, the number of poor people living in America's suburbs had come to outnumber those living in central cities.[18] While poverty rates are still far higher in the central cities, poverty is growing faster in the suburbs, and almost every older industrial city today has a cluster of high-poverty suburbs on its doorstep. In the Chicago area, that cluster is in South Cook County. The poverty rate in Markham is over 26 percent, higher than in Chicago itself. In Harvey, just east of Markham, it is 36 percent, higher than many inner-city ghetto areas.

Park Forest, a name familiar to generations of sociology students, lies a short distance south of Markham. In the late 1950s famed journalist and urbanist William H. Whyte wrote about Park Forest in his classic book *The Organization Man*. For Whyte, Park Forest was the natural habitat of the organization man, the class of college-educated, upwardly mobile white-collar workers that emerged after World War II. When its houses first came on the market, he wrote, "out came trainees for the big corporations, research chemists with the AEC, captains and majors with the Fifth Army, airline pilots, FBI men—in short, a cross section of almost every kind of organization man in America."[19]

"Chicagoland's COMPLETELY PLANNED suburb" as its developers dubbed it, became, in Whyte's words, a "hotbed of Participation," crammed with organizations, activities, and social gatherings of every stripe. With little sense of irony, the town's developers placed ads capitalizing on the town's growing reputation:

> A cup of coffee—symbol of
> PARK FOREST!
> Coffeepots bubble all day long
> in Park Forest. This sign of
> friendliness tells you how much
> neighbors enjoy one another's company—
> feel glad that they can share their daily
> joys—yes, and troubles too.
>
> Come out to Park Forest, where small-
> town friendships grow. . . .[20]

Another ad concluded, ". . . buying a home in Park Forest means buying *a better way of life.*"[21]

That was the fifties. Things have changed. Houses that sold in 1949 for $11,995, worth about $125,000 in today's dollars, are now selling for $30,000 or $40,000. As more and more of the houses are bought by investors and rented out, signs of disrepair have appeared on once-immaculately maintained blocks. Over a third of the Orchard Park Plaza shopping center is empty, and the rest includes a dollar store and a nail salon. As John Ostenburg, Park Forest's thoughtful mayor, observed recently:

> Few would have envisioned the day in Park Forest when one of its churches would operate a food pantry that feeds approximately 350 local families per week. [...] Few would have thought it necessary for two local churches to provide homeless

shelter twice a week from October through April, . . . and who
. . . would have believed that one day it would be necessary for
Habitat for Humanity to renovate Park Forest homes that had
gone into foreclosure . . . ?[22]

Park Forest and Markham are still hanging on. Some other towns in
South Cook County are in far more desperate shape, like Harvey, where
one out of four houses sits empty and which was described recently by
the *Chicago Tribune* as "arguably the area's most lawless community—
with high violent crime, subpar policing, and questionable cops."[23] Part
of the problem, indeed, is that there are too many cities, towns, and
villages in South Cook County. Illinois laws that make it easy for a
small but determined group of people to convince their neighbors that
they would be better off as an independent city rather than as part of
unincorporated Cook County have led to suburban Cook County being
carved up into 131 separate cities and villages demarcated by strange,
jagged borders, interspersed with pockets of unincorporated land where
the county is responsible for providing such few public services as
they receive.

The proliferation of tiny municipalities, many of which have little
more inside their border than low-priced houses and a handful of retail
stores, coupled with the fact that each one is expected to provide its residents with the full range of local government public services, has led to
South Cook County having some of the highest property tax burdens
in the United States. As financial maven Mark Glennon of *Wirepoints
Illinois Financial News* puts it, "Chicago's south suburbs are in a death
spiral and property taxes are central to the story."[24] What does he mean?

What a homeowner pays in property taxes relative to the value of
her house is known as the *effective* property tax rate. Nationally, average
effective tax rates range from a high of a little more than 2 percent in
New Jersey and Illinois, down to well below 1 percent in Alabama or
Delaware. On the average, the rate is around 1 percent. Thus, somebody
who owns a house worth $100,000 in the average town in the United
States will pay around $1,000 each year in property taxes.

In Park Forest, the effective tax rate—on paper, based on what
the Cook County Assessor has determined the value of the houses

to be—is 7.38 percent! That means that instead of paying $1,000 a year, a Park Forest homeowner with a house worth $100,000 would be paying $7,380 per year in taxes, more than seven times as much as the national average. But the situation is actually much worse. The fact is, property values—at least partly because of the high taxes—are steadily going down, and are much lower than what the Cook County Assessor claims. I went to Zillow, a wonderful source of real estate information, and pulled information for five recent house sales in Park Forest.[25] Instead of 7.38 percent, which would be bad enough, the *actual* effective tax rate for these buyers ran anywhere from 13 percent to 22 percent!

Crushing property tax burdens push property values down, because the cost of taxes gets factored into the value of the house. There was one house that sold for $40,000. The taxes last year were $5,917. Assume the buyer got a 4 percent mortgage with a 20 percent down payment. She'll be paying a total of $7,750 a year, or $646 a month, in taxes and mortgage payments. But, in a town where the property tax rate is 1 percent, she could spend $646 a month and buy a $138,000 house.

That triggers the death spiral. Astronomical property taxes depress market values, and as property values get lower and lower, the city has to keep raising the tax rate to cover its cost of services, so the taxes get higher and higher, or the services deteriorate—or more likely, some of both. Meanwhile, homeowners are reluctant to improve their properties because of how it would affect their tax bill. In the worst case, people simply stop paying taxes, walk away from their properties, and let them go into tax foreclosure.

At the height of the housing bubble in 2006, the median house in Park Forest sold for $118,000, or just about what it sold for as a brand-new house back in the 1950s after inflation. By 2010, after the bubble burst, the median price had fallen to $45,000. From that point, prices started gradually to pick up again in most parts of the United States, but not in Park Forest. By 2015, they had dropped even further, to a median price of $33,600. Meanwhile, from 2006 to 2015 the *number* of home sales dropped by nearly two-thirds, from 751 to 291. Park Forest is by no means the worst off; during the first quarter of 2017, the median sales price for houses in nearby Harvey was $14,500.[26]

Things are bad in South Cook County, but even nastier in that part of suburban St. Louis County known as North County, the suburban ring just west of St. Louis's North City neighborhoods. North County became briefly notorious nationally in 2014, after black teenager Michael Brown was shot by a police officer in Ferguson, one of the area's larger towns. One part of North County contains all or part of twenty-three separate incorporated cities and villages in just ten square miles. St. Louis County, which does not include the city of St. Louis, has a population one-fifth that of Illinois's Cook County, and ninety incorporated municipalities, twenty-one of them with populations under 1,000. While most of St. Louis County is white and affluent, North County is largely poor and black.

Missouri state laws cap local tax rates as well as most other ways small towns can raise money, so North County municipalities found a different way to balance their budgets, a way that is even more pernicious than South Cook County's outrageous property tax rates. Until the state legislature made some modest changes in 2016 in the wake of Michael Brown's killing, the one area where the state placed virtually no limits on a city's ability to make money was municipal fines and fees. As a result, struggling North County cities turned their police departments and traffic courts into money machines.

As *Slate* columnist Reihan Salam writes, "Towns too small or too starved of sales tax revenue to sustain their own local governments stay afloat by having local law enforcement go trawling for trumped-up traffic violations, the fines for which can be cripplingly expensive, and which only grow more onerous as low-income residents fail to pay them."[27] Until a 2016 state law capped the amount at 20 percent of total municipal revenues, some small cities were raising over one-third, and in Calverton Park two-thirds, of their municipal budget from fines and court fees. The city of Beverly Hills covers only sixty acres and has a population of fewer than 500 people living on thirteen city blocks. It has thirteen police officers, one for each block. Capitalizing on the fact that the city's northern boundary runs along Natural Bridge Road, a major east-west artery, the police issued over 3,000 tickets and the city's municipal court raised over $221,000 in revenues in 2013, or nearly $400 for every resident of the miniscule city.[28]

The city of Ferguson's practices received national attention after Michael Brown's killing. They were documented in careful language by a report by the US Justice Department. It's worth quoting at length:

> The City budgets for sizeable increases in municipal fines and fees each year, exhorts police and court staff to deliver those revenue increases, and closely monitors whether those increases are achieved. [...] The City's emphasis on revenue generation has a profound effect on FPD's approach to law enforcement. Patrol assignments and schedules are geared toward aggressive enforcement of Ferguson's municipal code, with insufficient thought given to whether enforcement strategies promote public safety or unnecessarily undermine community trust and cooperation. Officer evaluations and promotions depend to an inordinate degree on "productivity," meaning the number of citations issued. Partly as a consequence of City and FPD priorities, many officers appear to see some residents, especially those who live in Ferguson's predominantly African American neighborhoods, less as constituents to be protected than as potential offenders and sources of revenue. This culture within FPD influences officer activities in all areas of policing, beyond just ticketing. Officers expect and demand compliance even when they lack legal authority. [...]
>
> Ferguson has allowed its focus on revenue generation to fundamentally compromise the role of Ferguson's municipal court. The municipal court does not act as a neutral arbiter of the law or a check on unlawful police conduct. Instead, the court primarily uses its judicial authority as the means to compel the payment of fines and fees that advance the City's financial interests. [...] Most strikingly, the court issues municipal arrest warrants not on the basis of public safety needs, but rather as a routine response to missed court appearances and required fine payments.[29]

The Justice Department found what everyone in North County already knew, that if you are black, you are more likely to be targeted by the police, especially for minor, trivial offenses. If you are black and poor, and lack the money to hire a lawyer or to pay the fine immediately, it's much worse. North County pastor Timothy Woods laid it out to *FiveThirtyEight*'s Ben Casselman: "A low-income worker fails to pay personal property tax on a car. Aggressive policing makes him more likely to get pulled over and ticketed for that offense. Poverty makes him less likely to pay the fine. Pretty quickly, a minor offense turns into a warrant, then jail time. A criminal record makes it harder to find a decent job, which leads to continued poverty. You talk to half the people around here, they've got warrants."[30]

The real issues in North County, though, go deeper. As elsewhere, poverty and race are closely interwoven. While the area has some older, long-established small African American settlements, most of the increase in both African American and low-income populations in North County is the product of migration, as first the African American middle class, and on their heels, progressively lower-income families, fled North City St. Louis, looking for a place that would be at least slightly better than what they were leaving behind.

The postwar suburbs, not only in North County, were waiting for them. By the 1990s, the miles of modest single-family houses interspersed with inexpensive garden apartments built in the 1950s and 1960s that made up these places were going through a transition, as the people who'd first moved there when they were young were now aging, and the children they'd raised in those houses had grown and gone elsewhere. With affluent white families moving farther out into the western parts of St. Louis County and beyond, black families from North St. Louis became the default market for the homes and apartments in North County. As the St. Louis Fed's Michael Duncan writes, "A sweeping generational turnover took place, and a new class of moderate-income, black homeowners moved into these neighborhoods."[31]

Soon, North County became the epicenter for subprime lending in the St. Louis area. As in Detroit or Newark, when the housing bubble burst, things quickly fell apart. Looking at one small part of North County, Duncan found that "with only 6 percent of the housing units in the county, the area had 23 percent of the foreclosures." That added up to over 3,000 foreclosures, or one out of every seven homes in the area. As foreclosures mounted, investors bought up properties cheaply, renting them out to far-poorer families than had lived in them before. Home-ownership rates plummeted, and more and more poor black families moved out from North Side in hopes of improving their lives, or simply escaping the ghetto.

The move to the suburbs represented opportunity for some, but for many it was a move from one ghetto to another; as Casselman puts it, "being poor in the suburbs is in some ways more difficult than being poor in the city."[32] Transportation options are few and far between, and the public services, social support systems, and relationships that low-income families count on in the cities are far weaker in the suburbs. Other than their hypertrophied police departments, North County municipalities provide few services to their residents.

While some movers hoped that the move would at least help their children, they found that even that was doubtful. The Normandy School District, which serves much of North County and which was "98 per-cent African American, and 94.5 percent from impoverished families," according to then Superintendent Stanton Lawrence, lost its accredi-tation in 2013 after years of poor performance, low test scores, and low high school graduation rates.[33] Barely half of the district's high school students graduated in four years, and only one out of five of those grad-uates went on to any form of higher education. Although restructured under state control as the "Normandy School Collaborative" in 2014, it remained starved of resources and leadership; one year after the takeover, Mike Jones, vice-president of the state board of education, said that "these children and these families need to understand that they live in a state and a region that, despite some heroic individual efforts, collectively we have marginalized and dismissed them."[34]

North County St. Louis is deservedly notorious, a place where a toxic mix of economic hardship, social conflict, poverty, and destructive state and local laws, policies, and practices have come together to create an Gordian knot of entangled problems. The underlying problems that made North County what it is, though, of rising poverty and frag-mented, inadequate, and resource-starved governance are not unique to the St. Louis area but can be found in the suburbs of every older American city.

Not *every* suburb, to be sure. Although some urbanists have announced the end of the suburbs, the reports of their death, as Mark Twain once said, are greatly exaggerated. Some of the more apocalyptic predictions, such as those of urban cheerleader Christopher Leinberger, who wrote in 2008 that "the fate of many single-family homes on the metropolitan fringes will be resold, at rock-bottom prices, to lower-income families—and in all likelihood, eventual conversion to apartments,"[35] now look more like a knee-jerk reaction to the trauma of the real estate crash than anything else. Suburbs and single-family houses are still the lifestyle choice of most Americans, and while walkable suburbs with attractive downtowns and trains to nearby city centers like those of Philadelphia's Main Line or Montclair, New Jersey, draw the most well-to-do commuters, many other suburban areas are likely to hold their own for some time to come. That could always change, but it doesn't look likely for the near future.

But what's going on in the suburbs has uncanny parallels to what's happening inside the cities. The middle is disappearing. While some suburban towns and cities are becoming wealthier, their homes more expensive, and their downtowns full of expensive restaurants and boutiques, other suburbs are going in the opposite direction. They are becoming poorer as they become destinations for low-income people seeking a better life, but who, once there, find themselves adrift in a difficult and often hostile environment. Homes in these suburbs are selling for little more than in the most distressed urban ghetto neighborhoods; their shopping districts, often strip malls along nearby highways, are thinning out, with little but fast food outlets and dollar stores left, while their shrinking tax revenues are not enough even to support minimally adequate public services.

All three of these community types—small cities, mill towns, and struggling suburbs—face difficult challenges in the coming years. National trends, whether economic, demographic, or social, seem weighted, if not out-and-out rigged, against them. While a few, like Bethlehem, seem to have the special features that enable them to beat the odds, it would be easy to simply give up on many of the others. The fact is, though, that few of these places are giving up. Amazing people, like Presley Gillespie and Ian Beniston of the Youngstown NDC, which has given many of that city's neighborhoods new life; or Chris Krehmeyer of Beyond Housing, which is building hope amidst the most distressed pockets of North St. Louis County, are just a few of those who are fighting for these places and the people who live in them. The struggle is not over yet.

Chapter 8

Empty Houses and Distressed Neighborhoods: Confronting the Challenge of Place

I ndian Village is one of Detroit's few areas that can be considered an elite neighborhood. Magnificent 1920s mansions selling for $500K and upward flank tree-lined streets named, for some obscure reason, after Native American tribes. In 2014, the first house ever listed in Detroit for over $1 million—although it ended up selling for slightly less—was in Indian Village.[1] Yet if you walk two blocks east from Iroquois Street along St. Paul to Fischer Street, you find yourself in a very different world, one where vacant lots and vacant houses are the norm, and a habitable, let alone desirable, house is the exception.

The crumbling houses on Fischer Street are just a few of the 50,000 vacant, abandoned structures that surveyors armed with handheld computers found when they went out in 2013 to count vacant properties in the city. That number is on top of the 100,000 or more vacant lots in between and around them. It's not that Detroit isn't knocking down empty buildings as fast as they can. Of the 550,000 homes and apartments that existed in Detroit in 1960, over 250,000 are gone, in most cases replaced with the vacant lots that today dominate the landscape of most of Detroit's neighborhoods.

Unoccupied houses and vacant lots are the most powerful symbol and symptom of neighborhood distress. Not surprisingly, as they began to proliferate along the streets of the nation's legacy cities, people have tried to figure out how to deal with them, along with the underlying problems of the struggling neighborhoods where they proliferate.

The American industrial city of 1950 was a teeming, crowded place. With city populations at or near all-time highs, and with the home-building industry only beginning to recover from the war and the Great Depression, homes and apartments were at a premium. Cities had slums, but few vacant properties. That year, the Census found that in the city of Buffalo there were only 853 houses or apartments available to buy or rent in a city of nearly 600,000. Gradually, though, the cities began to empty out. Between 1950 and 1960, 93,000 new homes and apartments were built in the Buffalo metro area, 90 percent of them outside the city, and the number of empty homes and apartments available in the city had risen to over 5,000.

The fifties were the first decade in history in which Buffalo lost population. For many legacy cities, that was the beginning of a long decline that lasted for some of them until the end of the millennium, and that for others, including Buffalo, is still going on. Over the decades, cities steadily lost population and families as more people moved out and fewer and fewer moved in to take their place. As this went on, more and more of the houses and apartments they lived in, the stores they shopped in, and the factories and office buildings they worked in became empty.

The story of why neighborhoods declined so precipitously and houses, apartment buildings, and office buildings were abandoned is a long and complicated one, in which obscure laws and dysfunctional government programs, crime and vandalism, as well as predatory practices of all sorts, all played a part. In many cases, the driving force, though, was weak demand, driven in turn, as I've discussed earlier, by economic and social forces, but also by disinvestment and discrimination. For many different reasons, fewer people wanted to buy the homes vacated by people moving out or passing away, while landlords found it harder and harder to make money as their costs increased, and the pool of tenants became poorer and poorer. In other cases, though, neighborhoods that could probably have been saved were not.

By the 1970s, abandonment had become a flood and had gotten the attention of policy makers; as a 1974 law journal article put it, "During the past decade the phenomenon of abandoned residential property has surfaced as a menacing social problem."[2] The seventies were the years when hundreds of New York City apartment buildings were put to the torch and when then New York Housing Commissioner Roger Starr called for "planned shrinkage," arguing that the city no longer had the ability to deliver services to the areas that had become depopulated through abandonment.[3] Starr's proposal set off a firestorm that led to his being fired by New York Mayor Abraham Beame, but the issue did not go away.

The US Department of Housing and Urban Development commissioned a plethora of studies and reports on abandoned properties and neighborhood decline, including a 1978 survey of abandoned-property conditions in 150 cities that had lost population between 1960 and 1975. The largest numbers were in Philadelphia, which reported over 15,000 abandoned homes and 6,000 abandoned apartment buildings. Detroit reported that it now had 10,000 abandoned homes, 5,000 abandoned apartment buildings, and 1,600 acres of once-occupied vacant land. Buffalo, perhaps looking at itself through rose-colored glasses, reported only 650 abandoned houses, and 25 abandoned apartment buildings.[4]

HUD's 1978 vacant properties survey was published in 1981. By that point, the public's attention had already begun to drift away from the cities and their problems. It was now "morning in America." HUD programs were cut to the bone, and a new private-market-oriented ethos in local governments, filtering down from the Reagan Administration, was more interested in convention centers, arenas, and new downtown office buildings than neighborhoods and poor people. Meanwhile, homelessness had risen to the top of the urban agenda; the late 1970s and early 1980s were the years, as I wrote some years ago, when "the sight of homeless people sleeping on streets and park benches and in abandoned buildings triggered first outrage and then widespread action."[5] While activists' energy was redirected to the homeless, enough stadiums and office towers were being built in downtowns to give many Americans the mistaken impression that the cities were on the mend.

Around the end of the century, though, a new wave of city officials and others began to take notice of the fact that despite the nascent urban revival, vacant, abandoned properties seemed to have become a permanent fixture on the urban scene. A leading member of that new wave was Dan Kildee, a Flint, Michigan, politician who won his first election, to his city's school board, at the age of eighteen in 1977. As Genesee County treasurer, an office to which he was first elected in 1996, he spearheaded an effort to address vacant properties in Flint. Picking up on an idea that had first emerged in Cleveland, St. Louis, and a handful of other cities in the seventies, he convinced the state legislature to allow Genesee County to create a county "land bank," a quasi-governmental agency that would have the ability and the legal powers to get control of vacant properties, maintain them, and ideally, get them reused in the way that would most benefit the community.

The land bank idea, actively promoted by Kildee first as county treasurer and then as the founder of the Center for Community Progress, a national organization that works with towns and cities dealing with vacant and other problem properties, took off. Over the next decade, following Michigan's lead, state legislatures in Pennsylvania, New York, Ohio, Georgia, and half a dozen other states passed similar laws allowing cities and counties to create land banks to take on their communities' vacant-land challenges. By 2017, over 150 separate land banks were up and running in cities and counties around the country.

Detroit has the nation's most ambitious land bank. After being elected in 2013, Mayor Mike Duggan made the Detroit Land Bank Authority (DLBA) his go-to agency for anything having to do with vacant land and buildings in the city. With thousands of owners letting the county take their properties every year through tax foreclosure, within less than three years the DLBA had taken title to over 100,000 properties. As of the spring of 2017, it owned 98,302 properties, roughly one out of every four parcels in the city.

Mayor Duggan likes to see results, and the DLBA is his vehicle for getting them. The land bank has created a smorgasbord of programs aimed at eliminating blight and spinning off properties to private owners. In little more than three years, they have demolished 12,000 vacant houses and sold over 8,000 vacant lots for $100 each to the owners of the houses next door. Before Duggan, people who wanted to buy the vacant lot next door had to go through a process that required city council action and could take years. Now, all a would-be buyer has to do is fill out an online form or attend a side-lot fair held by the DLBA, and the property is hers a week later.

Realizing that would-be buyers in urban neighborhoods often have trouble finding older houses that don't need a lot of work, the DLBA came up with a program they call "Rehabbed and Ready." Under this program, they hire contractors to bring vacant homes they own to move-in condition, which the DLBA then sells to first-time home-buyers at prices that typically range from $60,000 to $100,000. Through an agreement with Quicken Loans, would-be buyers can get speedy mortgage pre-approvals. Meanwhile, other properties are sold as-is at nominal prices through an eBay-style, time-limited online auction. Finally, under their Community Partner program, the DLBA sells properties to nonprofit groups for uses that have included community gardens, artists' studio space, and a community center for the city's growing Yemeni population.[6]

The DLBA is trying hard to come up with uses for vacant properties that also help rebuild housing markets in the city's distressed neighborhoods. The reality, though, is that despite their efforts, the number of vacant properties in Detroit vastly exceeds the number that can be put back to use. Even after selling off 8,000 side lots, the DLBA still owns 64,000 vacant lots, with more coming on line daily as they continue to knock down vacant houses. Every legacy city has the same problem. Field surveys in 2015 counted 28,000 vacant lots in Cleveland and 25,000 vacant lots in Gary, Indiana, a much smaller city than Detroit.

Nobody's going to build a new house or anything else on all but a handful of these lots in the foreseeable future. There isn't a lot of demand for new houses in cities like Detroit or Cleveland outside a handful of neighborhoods near downtown or near major universities that have the old housing and the other amenities people are looking for. Meanwhile, the cost of building a new house on a vacant lot is likely to exceed $150,000, a near-absurdity in neighborhoods where existing houses are selling for as little as $20,000 or $30,000. At the same time, to simply leave a vacant lot to turn into a trash-strewn mixture of dirt, rocks, and unsightly scrub vegetation is little better than leaving a vacant, derelict house standing.

A body of ideas about vacant lots that started to percolate during the 1990s has come to be known as "greening." Instead of hoping in vain for developers to come and build on these lots, the core idea is to turn them into attractive and often usable green space. As with so many other ideas, there's nothing fundamentally new about it. Allotment gardens, where apartment dwellers could have small plots to cultivate, go back to nineteenth-century Europe, and they can be seen today in urban neighborhoods and on the outskirts of many European cities. Some older people may still remember the "Victory Gardens" of World War II. The difference is that now it's about figuring out how to use the vast surplus of vacant lots that have come into being over the past decades. Fresh food, though, is often a welcome by-product.

As vacant lots started to pop up in older American cities in the 1980s and 1990s, community gardens were actively promoted by community groups and horticultural associations. They were often encouraged by local officials, who generally saw them as a temporary use for properties that they hoped to redevelop sooner or later. Community gardens, however, depend on dedicated volunteers, who come and go over time. By the dawn of the millennium, with vacant lots continuing to proliferate, people were looking to other ways in which lots could be used.

Terry Schwarz, the wiry, intense director of Kent State University School of Architecture's Cleveland Design Collaborative, was one of the pioneers. In 2008, she laid out a vision in a pamphlet entitled *Re-Imagining a More Sustainable Cleveland* describing how the city's thousands of acres of vacant land could become a future asset for the city. Putting meat on the vision's bones, she and her team published the *Cleveland Vacant Land Reuse Pattern Book*, a catalogue of different green uses for vacant land, from rain gardens to geothermal wells, laying out what each would cost and what materials were needed.[7]

Using the *Pattern Book*, in 2009 a citywide nonprofit called Cleveland Neighborhood Progress and the city of Cleveland announced the "Re-Imagining Cleveland" competition, inviting people throughout the community to come up with ideas to turn vacant lots in their neighborhoods into attractive, productive green space. With $500,000 to work with, they awarded small grants to fifty-six different projects, including environmentally oriented projects such as pocket parks and rain gardens, as well as agricultural projects including gardens, orchards, and farms. One project was a vineyard in the heart of the Hough neighborhood, still scarred by the riots of the 1960s, created by a charismatic ex-con turned writer, activist, and incidental vintner named Mansfield Frazier.

Cleveland was not the only city thinking about the potential of vacant lots. A second city thinking along the same lines was Philadelphia, where the leading role was taken by the Pennsylvania Horticultural Society, an august organization founded in 1827 and best known for what is probably the nation's preeminent flower show, held every year since 1829. Although PHS was already supporting Philadelphia's community gardens, in the eighties and nineties they started thinking about how to play a larger role in greening the city's as many as 40,000 vacant lots. They began to work with nonprofit community development corporations like the Asociación de Puertorriqueños en Marcha (APM), which was building housing and a shopping center in eastern North Philadelphia. In 2001, PHS announced its Green City Strategy, an effort to "address all of the open spaces and vacant land in the city of Philadelphia."[8]

While PHS's strategy has many facets, one is particularly notable. For all the gardens, vineyards, mini-parks, or farms that people can get going, the reality is that the number of vacant lots vastly exceeds the number of dedicated organizations or volunteers ready to turn them into gardens, vineyards, or parks and maintain them for the long haul. At the same time, allowing vacant lots to remain derelict means that their neighbors suffer continued blight. To solve this problem, PHS came up with a simple and inexpensive low-maintenance approach to vacant lots, using no more than basic sodding, tree planting, and putting up a simple split-rail fence on the lot, as seen in figure 8-1. It's called the LandCare program.

With support from the city of Philadelphia, PHS maintains Land-Care treatments on over 7,000 vacant lots across the city, 285 of which are in the area where APM is building their new housing. "To build housing, a community development corporation or CDC has to attract residents into the area," said Bob Grossman, then director of PHS's Philadelphia Green program. "When we came in these lots were full

Figure 8-1 A LandCare lot in Philadelphia's Mantua neighborhood. (Source: Google Earth)

of trailers, toilets, cars. They were horrendous. Nobody is going to buy a new house across the street from an overgrown lot filled with rats."[9] A research team led by University of Pennsylvania public health professor Charlie Branas has found that cleaning and greening vacant lots through the LandCare program is associated with lower gun violence, higher property values, and lower levels of stress for the people who live around them.[10]

Today, greening has become well established as a way of dealing with urban vacant lots. Cities are looking at green solutions to the nagging problem of storm-sewer overflows by redirecting storm water away from the sewers and onto open land, where it can naturally filter back into the groundwater aquifer. In Detroit, John Hantz, a financial planner turned urban pioneer, has bought 1,800 lots from the city, planted them with saplings, and turned them into a tree farm.[11] In Detroit and elsewhere, true urban farms, not just glorified gardens, are starting to take root, such as the Earthworks Urban Farm run by the Capuchin Friars in Detroit, which generates 14,000 pounds of produce each year on its 2.5 acres of ground.

The most effective program to date to get vacant houses back in use and back on the tax rolls, though, has been in Baltimore. Using a legal procedure known as receivership, under which a court can take vacant property away from an owner who has persistently refused to fix it and put it back to use, the city has created a streamlined process where developers—mostly small mom-and-pop operations rather than large corporations—can get houses they can rehab, at a low price and with clean, marketable title. The city calls the program Vacants to Value. From 2010, when the city initiated the program, to the end of 2016, roughly 2,000 vacant houses have been fixed up and reoccupied, with another 1,000 in the pipeline.[12] This is quite an achievement, particularly when one realizes that the developers are spending their own money to fix up these houses, not getting subsidies from the city. But there's a catch. Actually, a couple of catches.

First, when you look at the neighborhoods where developers are rehabbing the houses, you start to see an odd pattern emerge. In some areas, as houses are fixed up, the total number of vacant houses goes down, which is what one would expect. In others, though, like Pen Lucy, as people fix up houses, the total number goes *up*. What that means, in those neighborhoods, is that despite the city's and the developers' efforts, people are still walking away from houses faster than the city can get them rehabbed. The second catch is that the program doesn't work at all in the city's most distressed neighborhoods, because developers won't spend their money fixing up houses in those areas, no matter how easy it is to get the properties. In the end, for all the city's success, the total number of vacant houses in Baltimore was about the same in 2017 as it was in 2010.

What this means is that it's not really about the houses. It's about the neighborhood. That doesn't mean that Baltimore's efforts are in vain. On the contrary, they've jump-started major change in some neighborhoods—where the numbers are going down—and kept the situation from getting worse in others, even if the numbers are going up. But the houses are only one part of the picture, and often not the most important part. And ultimately, if you fix up some houses, but the neighborhood is still going downhill, you haven't changed the things that matter most. The tough question is, how do you change or stabilize a neighborhood?

Back in the 1970s, a lot of planners and activists besides Roger Starr were also seeing their neighborhoods going downhill, and they started to look closely at what was going wrong. Rather than walk away, though, they tried to figure out what they could do about it. One of those activists was Dorothy Richardson, a homeowner on Pittsburgh's Central North Side. She was angry about what seemed to be her neighborhood's steady decline, and decided to fight back. Going from door to door in her neighborhood, and from City Hall to the downtown offices of the city's banks, she organized her neighbors, pressed homeowners to improve their homes and the city to enforce its housing codes, and pushed local banks to provide the loans homeowners needed to fix up their properties and new home-buyers needed to move into the neighborhood. Named Neighborhood Housing Services of Pittsburgh, the model she had designed by trial and error caught on. In 1978, President Carter signed legislation creating the Neighborhood Reinvestment Corporation to support similar projects nationwide. Forty years later, since renamed NeighborWorks America, the same organization is still working through 240 local member organizations to support people's efforts to rebuild their neighborhoods across the country.

Dorothy Richardson's work dramatized how much the fall of urban neighborhoods was not just a matter of supply and demand, but was affected by the bank practices known as redlining. Although by the 1970s the Home Owner's Loan Corporation was just a memory, and the FHA had put an end to open racial discrimination, redlining was still alive and well in America's banking industry. While Richardson, with a strong assist from the city, was able to get local banks to put up some money for her neighborhood, the activist who triggered change at the national level was Gale Cincotta, daughter of a Greek restaurant owner who lived in Chicago's working-class Austin neighborhood. Austin was changing, and she tried to understand why; as she wrote later:

> We were told . . . that changing neighborhoods were a natural phenomenon. But we started to see that . . . they were being racially changed on purpose—*targeted* for change. First the realtors would come in . . . and pass out leaflets, telling white people they had better get out or they would lose money. Then the banks wouldn't give mortgages, and the insurance companies wouldn't write policies.[13]

Cincotta was a high school dropout, but she was also a determined, effective organizer. From Austin, along with a band of dedicated colleagues, she expanded her work first to Chicago and then on to the national scene by creating National People's Action to replicate her Chicago work.

Her efforts ultimately led to enactment of the Home Mortgage Disclosure Act (HMDA) in 1975 and the Community Reinvestment Act (CRA) in 1977. HMDA required lenders for the first time to publicly disclose where and to whom they were making mortgages, by race and income. CRA was intended "to encourage depository institutions to help meet the credit needs of the communities in which they operate, including low- and moderate-income neighborhoods."[14] CRA and HMDA were not a fix for what was ailing the cities, but they set a clear precedent that lenders were accountable for the loans they made—and the ones they didn't—and were powerful tools for community activists.

Despite the determined efforts of people like Dorothy Richardson and Gale Cincotta, though, urban neighborhoods, including Cincotta's Austin neighborhood, were continuing to decline. In the late 1960s, a new type of organization begun to emerge to fight neighborhood decline. These organizations were known as Community Development Corporations, or CDCs. CDCs became the most sustained effort to rebuild distressed urban neighborhoods that the United States has ever seen.

Many of the underlying ideas behind CDCs can be traced back to the early-twentieth-century settlement houses like Jane Addams's Hull House in Chicago and to nineteenth-century European efforts to create healthy workingmen's housing. Robert Kennedy may have coined the term; testifying in 1966 to a congressional committee about his plans to revitalize Brooklyn's Bedford-Stuyvesant neighborhood, he called for creating "community development corporations, which would carry out the work of construction, the hiring and training of workers, the provision of services and encouragement of associated enterprises."[15] Kennedy, along with the corporate executives, elected officials, and Ford Foundation leaders he brought on board, saw these organizations mainly as engines for bringing companies and jobs to distressed ghetto areas like Bedford-Stuyvesant. That was to change, however, over the next few decades.

The idea of grassroots organizations working with residents to rebuild urban neighborhoods was welcomed in the 1970s, driven both by the widespread concern with the decline of the cities and by even-more-widespread disenchantment with the top-down urban renewal model. During the seventies, the growth of CDCs was helped along not only by a friendly Congress and the Carter Administration, but also by the growth of a national support system, not only in the form of the Neighborhood Reinvestment Corporation, but with the creation of two more of what came to be known as "intermediary" organizations: the Enterprise Foundation created by shopping-center developer turned philanthropist James Rouse, and the Local Initiatives Support Corporation (LISC), the brainchild of anti-poverty warrior turned Ford Foundation executive Mitchell Sviridoff. During the same period, socially driven lenders that later came to be known as "community development financial institutions," or CDFIs, also began to appear, forming another part of the increasingly far-flung CDC support system.

The drying up of governmental support during the eighties if anything gave still greater impetus to the nascent CDC movement. As the Reagan Administration pulled back from the cities, and public attention waned, urban activists realized that more than ever they were on their own, and increasingly they took matters into their own hands. As CDC chronicler Alexander von Hoffman puts it, "During the 1980s and 1990s, the community development movement provided the most visible signs of new life in the inner city."[16] Today, the most widely quoted figure, although dating from 2005, is that there are 4,600 community development corporations in America's cities, towns, and rural areas.

Other than making it clear that there are a lot of CDCs, this number actually doesn't mean very much. It is both all-encompassing and fuzzy. It lumps together large, powerful organizations with hundreds of employees and decades of experience alongside volunteer outfits operating out of church basements that might fix up a house or two every few years. The definition also fails to distinguish among organizations that focus on a single neighborhood, those that work in a larger but still relatively tightly defined geographic area, and those that work, as it were, "all over the map."

Indeed, many strong CDCs start out working in a single neighborhood, but eventually outgrow that area and redefine their mission, often renaming themselves at the same time. Chelsea Neighborhood Developers became The Neighborhood Developers when they moved beyond the small city of Chelsea, Massachusetts. When Reynoldstown Revitalization Corporation decided to leave the Reynoldstown neighborhood and work across the Atlanta metro area, they changed their name to Resources for Residents and Communities, keeping the same initials.

It has never been that clear where to draw the line between organizations that are rooted in a particular community, carrying out many different activities designed to improve or transform that community, and those which are basically housing developers, but with nonprofit status and a social purpose. Indeed, part of the problem is that the idea of community development itself is something of a moving target. While Roland Ferguson and William Dickens, the editors of a popular textbook on community development, define it as "asset building that improves the quality of life among residents of low- to moderate-income communities," they admit that it is often "narrowly conceived as housing and commercial development."[17] In practice, it often seems that community development has come to mean little more than "whatever it is CDCs do."[18] What they do, however, has been fraught with role conflicts from the beginning: are they community organizers, service providers, or developers, and is it possible for them to be more than one of those things?

As Senator Kennedy's remarks suggested, many CDCs, including the pioneering Bedford-Stuyvesant Restoration organization in Brooklyn, initially saw their mission as economic development, creating new businesses or drawing businesses from outside into their neighborhoods. That model proved to be highly problematic in practice. While IBM, under strong pressure from politicians and other corporate executives, agreed to put a plant in Bedford-Stuyvesant, it closed after a few years. A 2004 study found that failure rates among businesses created by CDCs ranged from 28 percent to nearly 50 percent.[19]

Given that CDCs are usually located in distressed, high-poverty communities, this is hardly surprising. Such areas rarely have the attributes that make themselves attractive business locations, and no CDC has a magic bullet at its disposal to change the underlying economic realities of the area. As *New York Times* writer Nicholas Lemann has bluntly but aptly pointed out, "The problem is that, on the whole, urban slums have never been home to many businesses except for sweatshops and minor neighborhood provisioners."[20] Indeed, although there are a few exceptions, the evidence suggests that successful retail and other businesses usually tend to follow increases in the number of houses, and particularly in the incomes of their residents, rather than the other way around.

The upshot was that by the 1990s CDCs were spending more and more of their time, energy, and money on developing housing. After Congress passed the Low-Income Housing Tax Credit (LIHTC) as part of the 1986 tax reform package, which provided a steady and at least somewhat predictable stream of money for organizations with the skills and resources to tap it, CDCs—along with for-profit developers—redirected their efforts toward building housing projects using the LIHTC, generally known as tax credit projects, in the neighborhoods where they were working.

Tax credit projects appealed to CDCs for a number of different reasons. First, given the poor quality of much of the housing in the typical low-income neighborhood, they enabled the CDC to provide housing for people in their neighborhood that was not only somewhat affordable, but, what was often more important, high-quality. Second, it allowed them to create large and highly visible projects, which made them attractive to the funders and politicians the CDC relied upon for support. Third, and often particularly important for CDCs that found it increasingly difficult to raise funds to cover their growing operating budgets, the development fees they earned from the projects often became a lifeline for the organization.

This is not meant cynically, since the CDCs involved clearly believed their work was benefiting their communities. It was, though, a shift driven strongly by financial considerations from the arduous and often unremunerative business of building a stronger community from the ground up toward a more narrow, top-down model of what it meant to be a community development corporation. As one frustrated Newark resident put it to then HUD Secretary Cisneros at a meeting I attended, referring to one of the city's most prominent CDCs, that model risked making the organization seen by the community itself as "just another [expletive deleted] landlord."[21] Meanwhile, the money to be made in the program drew in a host of for-profit developers, who competed with CDCs to build tax credit projects, often on the same sites in the same distressed neighborhoods.

It's not clear, though, how much these projects necessarily benefit the neighborhood as a whole. In some cities like Detroit or Buffalo, the rents being charged in the tax credit projects are actually higher than typical private-market rents in the same area. Since the apartments in the new projects are usually nicer than those in the often shabby older buildings around them, most of their tenants are people who move out of houses and apartments owned by private landlords in the same neighborhoods. Since few new families are moving into those neighborhoods, that means in turn that a lot of those houses and apartments end up being abandoned. The projects themselves run the gamut, as the two projects from Albany, New York, pictured in figure 8-2 show, from sensitively designed developments that fit nicely into a nineteenth-century urban streetscape to no-frills garden apartments, self-contained and fenced off from the surrounding community.

Affordable-housing projects do benefit most of the people who live in them, although not only at the risk of undermining private landlords and increasing abandonment, but also at the cost of becoming self-contained enclaves in the hearts of their neighborhoods. As Lemann points out, in 1994 Newark's New Community Corporation, one of the nation's largest CDCs, employed 120 security guards to protect its roughly 2,500 apartments, together with a cluster of social service facilities, day-care centers, and a supermarket.[22] It is also not clear that affordable-housing projects change conditions in their neighborhoods, outside their four walls.

Since the inception of the LIHTC program, which accounts for all but a handful of the affordable-housing projects built in the United States in the last twenty years, quite a few researchers have looked at its effects on neighborhoods, with thoroughly inconsistent and even conflicting findings. The only thing one can say with certainty is that there is no certainty. This is hardly surprising. Some affordable-housing developments have had positive effects on their neighborhoods, for any

Figure 8-2 Two low-income tax credit projects in Albany, New York. (Source: Google Earth)

of many different possible reasons. Those reasons, though, may have had nothing to do with their role in providing affordable housing, but in how they affected the neighborhood in other ways. Valuable as providing decent housing is, it ultimately has only a limited relationship with the multiple social factors that make a neighborhood strong or weak.

At the same time, the proliferation of CDC-driven housing developments raises another question. Since CDCs operate largely in disadvantaged, high-poverty neighborhoods, it logically follows that their projects are located in those neighborhoods. This, indeed, turns out to be true. According to University of Kansas professor Kirk McClure, probably the nation's leading expert on the housing tax credit program, only about 17 percent of projects nationally are built in high-opportunity areas—places with low crime and good access to jobs and high-performing schools.[23] Although secure, well-built projects in high-poverty areas may offer decent housing to some people who need it, it is unlikely that they will improve their economic situation, or the life prospects of the children who live there.

While some CDCs and developers argue that they have no choice about where to build their projects, because high land costs, exclusionary practices, and NIMBY ("not in my back yard") attitudes keep them from building elsewhere, recent evidence suggests that they may be mistaken. The way the LIHTC program works, each state receives an allocation of tax credits each year, and gets to set the criteria—within broad federal guidelines—to determine which developers get a share of the allocation. During the Obama Administration, federal pressure on state and local agencies to comply with fair-housing rules led many states to revise their criteria in ways designed to encourage developers to submit projects in high-opportunity areas.

A recent New Jersey study compared the location of tax credit projects approved between 2005 and 2012, and the location of those approved between 2013 and 2015 after the state adopted new guide-lines.[24] From half of the projects being located in high-poverty areas, the share dropped to 20 percent, while large numbers of post-2012 projects were located in job centers, or in areas with high-quality public schools. The LIHTC program is both highly competitive and highly lucrative for developers. In urban states like New Jersey, three or more developers compete for every project awarded. The New Jersey experience shows that when states change their ground rules in ways that force developers to find places outside high-poverty areas to get allocations worth millions of dollars to them, they can do so.

That is even more important than it might seem, because helping poor and near-poor people to move out of concentrated-poverty ghettos is often the best ticket we know to improve their quality of life and their opportunities, both for them and for their children. At its most basic level, geography powerfully affects life expectancy; a 2008 Baltimore analysis found that "in some impoverished neighborhoods, the death rates from heart disease and stroke are more than twice as high as in wealthier places just a few blocks or miles away. At the extreme, the difference in mortality rates between some neighborhoods is as wide as the disparity in life expectancy between the United States and a third-world country like Myanmar."[25]

Separate, as the Supreme Court pointed out in *Brown v. Board of Education*, is inherently unequal. This is true not only in public education. Over and above their life expectancy, the opportunities any individual has, starting with the quality of the education they receive, are linked to where they live. The quality of public services, safety, access to transit and job opportunities, availability of fresh food, and more are all linked through a powerful network of cause-and-effect relationships to the social and economic level of the community.

Starting in the 1980s, a series of programs, usually triggered by court decisions, have enabled thousands of low-income people to move from inner cities to more-affluent suburban neighborhoods, in places like Yonkers, New York, and Chicago, and across the state of New Jersey, as a result of the New Jersey Supreme Court's *Mount Laurel* ruling. The evidence is strong. Families who have moved into affordable-housing projects in low-poverty areas or used vouchers to move from high-poverty areas into private rental housing in low-poverty areas, see significant improvement in their health conditions, less welfare dependency, and better school outcomes for their children. While many ultimately move on from their first low-poverty area home or apartment, few move back to the neighborhoods from which they came.[26]

The exclusion of lower-income people from more-affluent and opportunity-rich areas of the city and region is not only a matter of health and economic opportunity. As areas revive or gentrify, and their one-time lower-income populations dwindle or disappear, that transformation is as powerful a symbolic statement of dispossession as it is a physical or economic reality. Gentrification is an implicitly political process, and the exclusion of low-income people from areas in which they once lived, whether through literal displacement or the impersonal working of the market, is a reminder of how little poor and minority communities count in local power equations.

For all of these reasons, concerted efforts to enable lower-income people to move to what have been dubbed "places [or areas] of opportunity," areas where they will gain access to more jobs, better education, and better services, and probably live longer, healthier lives, need to be part of any meaningful equity strategy in America's cities and regions. This is a regional even more than a city issue, as people have realized and pointed out for many years. Although the balance may be shifting with the revival of urban areas and the decline of some suburbs, cities are still much poorer overall than their suburban surroundings, where places of opportunity are still more likely to be found. Still, no city, particularly one in which gentrification is taking place, should get a pass on this issue.

Recent years have seen some small but significant steps in this direction. The Obama Administration's drive to enforce fair-housing rules has led a growing number of states to change the rules governing where tax credit projects are built, with more projects going into areas of opportunity and fewer in areas of concentrated poverty. A recent study by a team headed by Princeton sociologist Douglas Massey, which looked in depth at a project in suburban Mount Laurel, New Jersey, to which most of the residents had moved from distressed inner-city neighborhoods in nearby Camden, found that "moving into the Ethel Lawrence Homes brought about a significant reduction in the incidence of negative life events, lowered levels of mental distress, increased employment and earnings while decreasing welfare receipt, and generally produced a greater level of economic independence. . . ." Their children, "having a quiet place to study and attending better schools to lower levels of violence and disorder, in turn, produced higher grades."[27] As Massey concluded, neighborhoods really do matter.

A few cities are starting to use inclusionary zoning, a model in which developers of upscale housing are required—or given incentives—to set aside a percentage of their homes or apartments for low-income families as a way of enabling lower-income families to live in the city's more expensive, opportunity-rich areas. Inclusionary housing programs have long been used in upscale, politically liberal suburbs like Palo Alto or Montgomery County, Maryland, both of which enacted such programs back in the 1970s. They have gained a foothold in some cities, including San Francisco and New York as well as Washington, DC.

Washington, DC's, program, which took effect in 2009, requires that all new developments with 10 or more houses or apartments set aside 10 percent of the units for low-income families, or 8 percent in high-rise areas that are more expensive to develop. The program got off to a slow start, but over 1,100 new affordable homes are either built or in the development pipeline, and nearly 200 came on line in 2016 alone.[28] In 2014, DC passed a related law, which provided that developers building on land sold to them by the city would have to set aside 30 percent of the units, if in a public-transit-accessible area; or 20 percent elsewhere, as affordable low-income housing.

Washington, DC, is a city with a superheated housing market where the prices developers can get for their product are high enough to allow them to meet the city's conditions. Legacy cities, where prices or rents in all but a handful of pockets are far from stratospheric, need to tread more carefully. Still, Chicago has enacted an inclusionary ordinance, which applies to housing developments receiving city financial assistance, city land, or a zoning change. Baltimore, Philadelphia, and even Detroit are exploring similar steps.

Inclusionary zoning is a limited tool, though. Two hundred units a year in Washington is useful, but not a lot, to put it mildly, in a city where over 38,000 tenants are spending half or more of their income on rent. Moreover, economic realities dictate that most of the apartments that are created are not affordable to the poorest families, who need an ongoing subsidy like a voucher to escape the cost-burden treadmill. Still, even where realistically inclusionary zoning may not add that many affordable apartments, it can be an important symbolic gesture toward inclusion and equity.

Turning back to distressed urban neighborhoods, it is hard to tell what the cumulative impact of those 4,600 or so CDCs has been on the neighborhoods where they have been working, in some cases for as long as fifty years. There is no doubt that some of those neighborhoods have changed for the better, but others have gotten worse. Ironically enough, a major study published in 2005 by the highly respected Urban Institute to show how successful CDCs have been actually suggests, to me at least, a very different picture. The researchers, as they point out, "aimed to test [their model] in neighborhoods where it would be most likely to show results," cherry-picking communities with strong CDCs most likely to show increases in property values.[29] In the end, though, only two of the five communities they studied showed property values rising significantly faster than in other low-income neighborhoods in the same city. Notably, both of those neighborhoods were in cities with particularly strong economies, Denver and Portland, Oregon.

That does not mean that these (and other) CDCs did not have a positive effect in various ways on these neighborhoods. It does raise the question, though, of what that effect is and whether it changes the trajectory of the neighborhood from what it might otherwise have been—and whether it would work elsewhere. Let's look at the Denver neighborhood the Urban Institute team studied. They write, "Five Points had development assets on which to build. Proximity to downtown; attractive, if run-down, older housing stock; and a new light rail line created circumstances for an upswing in residential markets."[30]

Put differently, what they are saying is that Five Points was an area ripe for gentrification, based on precisely the factors that I discussed in chapter 5. Location, neighborhood fabric, and to top it off, a new light rail line. At the same time, though, Five Points had serious problems, including vacant houses, crime, and a troubled public housing project nearby.

The case of Five Points highlights the critical element of successful neighborhood change. Five Points had all the features for *potential* change already in place—the location, the housing stock, the light rail line. Like the lightbulb in the psychiatrist joke, it *wanted* to change. At the same time, it had negative features—the crime, the abandoned houses—that were hindering change. Looked at from an economic standpoint, potential demand existed for the older housing in Five Points, but the neighborhood's negatives were keeping that potential from turning into actual or effective demand. The CDC, by replacing blighted properties with attractive affordable housing, revitalizing the commercial strip, and building community spirit and engagement, may well have been the catalyst—along with the light rail line—that turned the neighborhood's potential into reality. Clearly, something did. Between 2000 and 2015, household incomes in Five Points more than doubled, as the neighborhood's white population went from 42 percent to 76 percent of the total.[31] Five Points gentrified. Whether this is a CDC success story or not, then, depends on how one feels about gentrification.

This is not just about Denver's Five Points. With exceedingly rare exceptions, the places that see significant upward changes to their trajectory are the ones that have the basic conditions for change in place to begin with. But not all neighborhoods with those conditions, particularly the ones that also have strong negatives like crime or abandoned properties, actually do change. What makes the difference is that somebody or something comes along to catalyze change, either by removing the impediments, as happened in Five Points, or by putting an asset in place that becomes more powerful than the impediments, like the City Garden Montessori Charter School in St. Louis's Southwest Gardens area, which has drawn well-to-do young families from across the region to buy houses in the neighborhood.

Not far away from Southwest Gardens is Fox Park, a historic area with handsome nineteenth-century houses mixed in with small apartment buildings that was dubbed "the hottest neighborhood in the St. Louis metropolitan area" for 2017 by the real estate website Redfin.[32] In the 1990s, though, Fox Park was a depressed, high-crime area. Young families were buying and fixing up row houses in nearby neighborhoods like Lafayette Square and Shaw, but not in Fox Park. According to Tom Pickel, longtime executive director of DeSales Community Development, the neighborhood CDC, "the problem was the multifamily buildings. They were either bad or vacant." Any young family that seriously might have thought about buying a row house on the same block took one look at their prospective neighbors, and kept on driving.

DeSales started to buy empty multifamily buildings. Using the tax-credit program, DeSales fixed them up. Gradually, blight started to give way to attractive, well-maintained buildings. To make sure they stayed well maintained, they set up a property management company, which today not only manages the 300 or so houses and apartments DeSales owns in Fox Park but also manages another 1,600 apartments for other owners around St. Louis. As blocks became cleaner and more attractive, home-buyers started to buy and fix up row houses. A process of change had begun.

DeSales's efforts by themselves might have been enough to permanently change Fox Park's trajectory, but we'll never know, because other things started to happen that reinforced their progress. Thanks to a successful community-based campaign to bring them to St. Louis, a KIPP charter middle school opened, filling the vacant parochial school next door to St. Francis de Sales Church in 2009. A couple of years later, a new state-of-the-art early-childhood-education center opened a few blocks away.

Fox Park today is a very different neighborhood from what it was twenty years ago. It still has rough edges and a fair number of neglected and vacant houses, but the results of people fixing up houses and beautifying their streets can be seen on almost every block (fig. 8-3). Today the neighborhood has 200 more homeowners—a well-integrated mix of white and African American families—than it did in 2000. Crime is down sharply, and the open-air drug market on the 2700 block of Accomac Street is only a memory. And even as house prices go up, DeSales's commitment to keeping the apartments it owns affordable ensures that low-income families will always be part of the Fox Park mix.

Figure 8-3 Nineteenth-century row houses in St. Louis's Fox Park neighborhood. (Source: Google Earth)

The stories of Five Points and Fox Park are encouraging, but they raise a lot of troubling questions. Could it be that the only neighborhoods that revive are the ones that are in the right place, and have the right still-intact fabric? Even more, could it be that they revive only, or mainly, because they get an influx of new, more-affluent people moving in—that is, they gentrify? And, finally, if this indeed is the case, does that mean that one writes off the neighborhoods that don't have the right features, or are in the wrong place?

The short answer to the last question must be a simple, unequivocal no. People live there. But that raises yet another question: do some neighborhoods have little or no prospect of revival in the sense of what's happening in Fox Park or Five Points, and if so, is there an alternative to revival?

The story of one Baltimore neighborhood sheds a disturbing light on these questions. In 2015, after Freddie Gray's murder led to days of protest and violence in some Baltimore neighborhoods, newspaper reporters converged on the distressed, impoverished neighborhood called Sandtown-Winchester where he lived, and they filed the usual stories. This time, however, the neighborhood had an unusual backstory.

In the late 1980s, the Enterprise Foundation's James Rouse, who had grown up just across the Chesapeake Bay, "was looking for a project that could showcase a comprehensive approach to neighborhood renewal, one that would address all of a community's needs at once."[33] Getting then-Mayor Kurt Schmoke and community leaders on board, his goal, as he told the *Sun*, was "to transform the neighborhoods in which the very poor people live in this country in a serious and constructive way."[34] Sandtown-Winchester, the struggling African American high-poverty neighborhood in West Baltimore that he and the mayor selected, was going to prove what could be done and become a model for the rest of the country.

Rouse and the city set up the Sandtown-Winchester Neighborhood Transformation (NT) to do that. Over the next decade, NT spent $130 million ($200 to $250 million in 2017 dollars) on new and improved housing, plus vast but harder to pin down amounts to improve the local schools, create job opportunities as well as job readiness and training programs, and run health care initiatives. Yet today, Sandtown-Winchester is a neighborhood, as the *Washington Post* described it at the time of Freddie Gray's death, with "block after block of boarded-up houses and too many people without hope"—and a population of 8,500, down over a quarter from what it was in 1990.[35]

What happened? In 2013, scholars Stefanie DeLuca and Peter Rosenblatt took a look at what they called "Baltimore's daring experiment in urban renewal," twenty years later. Using some of the data from their study, I created figure 8-4. It shows a startling trend line: in each case, whether with respect to unemployment rate, family incomes, or the share of adults with a college degree, Sandtown-Winchester picked up compared to the rest of the city from 1990 to 2000—while the Neighborhood Transformation was in full swing—but then fell back.

Put differently, while NT was going on, and home-buyers were moving into the new houses, and people were starting to get better jobs, things picked up a little. Sadly, Baltimore as a whole was doing poorly

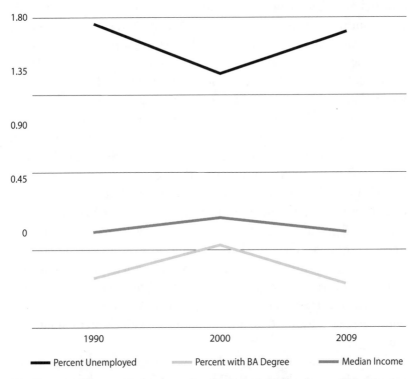

Figure 8-4 The trajectory of change in Sandtown-Winchester. (Source: data from Stefanie DeLuca and Peter Rosenblatt, "Sandtown-Winchester—Baltimore's Daring Experiment in Urban Renewal: 20 Years Later, What Are the Lessons Learned?"; analysis by author)

in the nineties, and in that light even modest improvement was meaningful. In the end, though, nothing really changed, and after the NT investments tailed off, things came back down with a thud. But why?

The most fundamental reason is that all that money, in the end, did nothing to change the neighborhood's basic reality or trajectory. Before NT, Sandtown-Winchester was a place people tried to get out of if they could, and NT didn't do anything that fundamentally changed that reality. As a result, even though we don't know for sure, it is more than likely that the people who lived there and who got better jobs and increased their income—whether as a result of the NT programs or on their own—mainly just moved out. Sandtown-Winchester was still plagued by drugs, crime, and vacant, boarded-up buildings, and that didn't change. The new houses were nice for the people who lived in them, but they were built mostly in self-contained enclaves, and they didn't change anything either for the houses or for people's lives in the rest of the neighborhood.

People in community and economic development like to talk a lot about "spillovers"—that is, the good things that are supposed to happen all around when one builds a new housing development, opens a shopping center, or, for that matter, a stadium or a convention center. The concept is sound, but the reality is complicated. Spillovers don't just happen. The underlying conditions in the area need to be right to make them happen. In recent years, a few researchers have studied the impact of different activities—demolishing derelict houses, rehabbing vacant houses, and greening vacant lots—on property values in different types of neighborhood. What they have all found is disturbing, but important. In struggling but still-vital neighborhoods, these activities often helped stabilize the market and increase the value of the houses around them. In the most distressed areas, where the values were the lowest to begin with, these activities had no effect. Sandtown-Winchester fell into the latter category.

That is the painful reality, and we need to grapple with it if we are going to think clearly about building inclusive cities. Unless a neighborhood is located close to a strong one like Fells Point or an anchor like Johns Hopkins, or unless it has nice houses, and not too many gaps between them, and preferably both, the odds of successful revitalization are vanishingly small. And, in those neighborhoods that do have location and nice housing stock, if they do revitalize, it's usually because other people, with more money, have started to move in. That's not necessarily a bad thing, but it raises questions about how much the people who lived there before actually benefit, or whether they are gradually pushed out.

What can one do, then? Three main things. First, build opportunities for the people who live in Sandtown-Winchester, Homewood, and similar places to escape poverty, a daunting but not impossible task. That is the subject of the next chapter. Second, at the same time, improve the quality of life in those neighborhoods, and make living there better, and less dangerous or traumatic, for the people who live there. And third, enable more of the people who live in those neighborhoods to move out by creating more opportunity for lower-income people to live in areas of opportunity, rather than areas of concentrated poverty.

Improving the quality of life in distressed neighborhoods is critically important as a matter of equity as well as a fundamental principle of social justice. For this reason, what many CDCs and local governments do is valuable, *whether or not it changes the economic or demographic trajectory of the area*. Improving market conditions is an important thing, but it's not the only thing. In some cases, we should be thinking less about turning neighborhoods into what they are *not*, and more about making them better versions of what they are.

As I mentioned earlier in the chapter, demolishing vacant, derelict buildings, and turning the vacant lots into attractive green areas, is an important start. Lots like the one shown in figure 8-1, located in one of Philadelphia's tougher areas, can help make areas safer and begin to change people's attitudes about the places they live.

Low-income, elderly homeowners can be given help to fix up their homes or have crews come in to add insulation and make energy-efficiency improvements, so that the owners can stay in their homes rather than be forced to move. Philadelphia has a program called Basic Systems Repair, which does just that. After funds ran out a few years ago, and the waiting list started to run into the thousands, the city council recently enacted a small increase to the city's real estate transfer tax to restore the program. The program came back to life in 2017, with $100 million in new money.[36]

A few cities, like Minneapolis, have designed programs to crack down on problem landlords, while rewarding good ones. The city maintains a database that tracks every rental property in the city on a series of measures which include fines, housing-code violations, and such matters as how often "City Solid Waste staff had to clean up a dirty collection point at a given property." Based on solid data, they adjust rental-housing fee schedules and the frequency of rental inspections; a good landlord gets her property inspected only once every eight years, while a problem landlord's building is inspected every year. A good landlord pays a fee of $70 per year for a single-family house, a problem landlord $373—these numbers based on the city's estimate of the cost of the services they have to provide.[37] Raising the bar for landlords, and making sure that every house that's offered for rent is a safe, sound, and healthy place to live, is a big thing.

Things that may seem small, like fixing sidewalks and making sure streetlights are working, are also important. In 2013, Detroit was in the middle of a streetlight crisis. As reporter J. C. Reindl wrote:

> In some neighborhoods, service is spotty and lights that may be on one day are off the next. In others, the darkness at times has persisted for months or years. […] The darkness has created a sense among some residents that leadership lost control long ago and that parts of the city have become an urban version of the Wild West. Forget about the effects on property value, some residents say. They just want peace of mind.[38]

By that point, about 40 percent of Detroit's streetlights were dark.

When Mayor Duggan was elected that same year, he vowed that he would do something about it. Early in 2014, the city and state jointly created a Detroit Public Lighting Authority, with the simple mission "to improve, modernize, and maintain the street lighting infrastructure in the City of Detroit with brighter, more-reliable, more-energy-efficient lights."[39] With the mayor keeping the pressure on, by the end of 2016, the Public Lighting Authority declared victory after spending $185 million to install 65,000 new LED lights. As resident Bryan Ferguson said at the celebration, "Now we don't have to walk in the dark anymore."[40]

Finally, the single most important thing for people who live in distressed urban neighborhoods may simply be safety—the ability to live your life without fear, for yourself and for those close to you. This is a complicated, fraught subject to which I cannot possibly do justice, but it is too important not to prompt at least a brief discussion.

The ghetto is a dangerous place. High-poverty areas have higher crime than other areas, and racially and ethnically segregated high-poverty areas have still more crime. Crime not only affects the neighborhood as a place; it affects the people who live there. As a HUD report summarized the research evidence, "The personal costs of living in a dangerous neighborhood are high. Being a victim of crime, witnessing crime, or fearing crime, in addition to the direct impact of crime . . . , can lead to stress and isolation, impair physical and mental health, and diminish school and work performance."[41] Residents of high-poverty, high-crime areas are as or more likely to show the symptoms of post-traumatic stress disorder than veterans of the wars in Iraq and Afghanistan. The combination of being poor and living in a high-poverty, high-crime area add up to a dauntingly high barrier to escaping poverty.

It is far from clear whether police practices common to many cities across the United States make matters better or worse. While for white, middle-class families in middle-class areas, the police presence tends to be modest, and is generally perceived as benign if not actually protective, it is a very different matter elsewhere. In poor, segregated neighborhoods, as Amy Lerman and Vesla Weaver write, "the infrastructure of surveillance—from police substations to squad cars to policemen descending through residents' buildings in vertical patrols—is a pervasive part of the architecture of community life. In these neighborhoods, citizens regularly encounter the police in their daily routines, through involuntary and largely unwelcome interactions."[42]

Residents of high-poverty neighborhoods, particularly African Americans, widely distrust the police. Rather than seeing them as a resource to fight the crime and violence that they fear, they are as likely to see them as a hostile occupying force. In a survey of residents in high-crime, high-poverty neighborhoods in six American cities, Nancy LaVigne and her colleagues at the Urban Institute found that only one out of three "generally support how the police act in [their] community" and that fewer than one out of four believed that "the police department holds officers accountable for wrong or inappropriate conduct in the community."[43]

Ultimately, it becomes a catch-22 for everyone. Crime *is* a problem, but, as Lerman and Weaver point out, "residents of high-policing areas report feeling less safe both because they reside in high-crime areas and because they see interactions with police as unsafe." Tensions cut both ways. Many police officers feel no more comfortable in many low-income areas than their residents feel being around the police.

Programs under the rubric of community policing, which include many different ways of building more-positive relationships between police officers and low-income community residents, have had some positive effects. Too often, though, they are seen as a "frill" rather than intrinsic to the police department's mission, and have often run aground because of budget constraints or because of conflict with the underlying police culture in the United States, which, as a Justice Department report pointed out, "encourages officers to think that their job involves going into a situation, immediately taking charge, and resolving it quickly"— if necessary, by force.[44]

Responding to that, at least a few police departments are training their officers how to de-escalate the kinds of situations that have traditionally led to violence. Camden County, New Jersey, police chief Scott Thompson says that "historically, officers have been rushing into situations because that's the training we provide, and it's been dangerous for them, and often leaving them with the only option that's left, deadly force. What we're telling officers to do is slow it down." He thinks of it as a "transition from warrior to guardian."[45] That transition is a tough one for many police departments, but essential.

No one's behavior is entirely socially and economically determined. Just the same, no one, except perhaps for a handful of saints and hermits, is completely unaffected by social and economic factors. The problems of crime and safety in distressed neighborhoods, particularly those that are largely or entirely African American, are interwoven with economic conditions and with the dynamics of race and power in the city. We will look closely at those dynamics in chapter 10, but before that, we will explore what is involved in the other critical challenge facing today's changing cities, that of lifting people out of poverty and giving them the opportunity to benefit from the revival of the cities in which they live.

Chapter 9

Jobs and Education: The Struggle to Escape the Poverty Trap

Homewood may be Pittsburgh's poorest and most neglected neighborhood. In contrast to the Hill District, immortalized in August Wilson's masterful cycle of plays, which sits prominently between downtown Pittsburgh and the University of Pittsburgh, Homewood lies in an isolated part of the city's East End well off the beaten track. As Homewood's city councilman, the Reverend Ricky Burgess, wrote in a 2015 op-ed, "Homewood is the city's poorest, least-diverse, most dangerous neighborhood, with the highest amount of violence and economic distress. Homewood also has the city's largest number of vacant, abandoned, and tax-delinquent properties. There are no grocery stores, no drugstores, no clothing stores, and no name-brand store of any kind. The terror of drugs, crime, and gun violence causes fear and despair, poisoning every resident's quality of life. It is a community in crisis."[1]

The conditions Rev. Burgess is describing are not new. Nearly forty years ago, years before most of Homewood's present residents were born, novelist John Edgar Wideman wrote about a young man in Homewood staring "into the dead storefronts." "He peeks," Wideman went on, "without stopping between the wooden slats where the glass used to be.

Like he is reading the posters, like there might be something he needed to know. . . . Like he might find out why he's twenty-five years old and never had nothing and never will. . . ."[2] Generations have grown up in Homewood, and the only thing that has changed is that each year, fewer people live there, more houses and storefronts are empty, and more of the people who do live there are poor or elderly.

What defines Homewood, though, and Baltimore's Sandtown-Winchester, and the hundreds of similar neighborhoods in older cities across the country is not the empty houses and vacant lots, or anything about their physical environment. If that were so, there would be no good reason why they have remained as they have over the decades. We know how to fix buildings. What defines them is something different. They are neighborhoods of concentrated, persistent, intergenerational poverty.

Cities, particularly industrial cities, have always had more than their share of poor people. As economist Ed Glaeser puts it, "Cities aren't full of poor people because cities make people poor, but because cities *attract* poor people with the prospect of improving their lot in life."[3] Cities have historically been places of opportunity. Most of the poor migrants who flocked to America's older cities in earlier eras did in fact improve their lot in life. A generation later, most of the children of the people who lived in the poverty-stricken ethnic ghettos that Jacob Riis or Hutchens Hapgood wrote about were prospering. Poverty wasn't pretty, but more often than not it was the starting point in a series of upward steps that created the mid-twentieth-century American middle class.

What has changed is not the presence of poverty, of which there is far less in the United States today than there was a hundred years ago, but the persistence of concentrated and intergenerational poverty. Poverty in any meaningful sense is not just about the people officially defined by the government as "below the poverty level," a measure concocted in the 1960s that fails to reflect today's reality. A single mother with two children earning $25,000 in Philadelphia today, or nearly 25 percent above the official 2017 poverty level, will spend half of her gross income to afford the median-priced two-bedroom apartment in that city. If we treat one and a half times the official poverty level as "*de facto* poverty," we find that over one-third of the residents of relatively successful legacy cities like Philadelphia and St. Louis are poor, as are half or more of the residents of more struggling cities like Detroit or Cleveland. They are disproportionately likely to live in areas of concentrated poverty, where their poverty is transmitted from generation to generation almost as predictably as the transmission of inherited genetic traits. Being poor in an American city is no longer a stepping stone to upward mobility. It is a trap from which few escape.

That trap, the sheer number of people caught in it, and its persistence and growth over time, is the flip side of the reviving American city. Unless we, as a nation and city by city, can begin to change that picture and enable more people to escape the trap, it is hard to see any alternative to our cities becoming places increasingly polarized between rich and poor. Such an outcome not only flies in the face of fairness and social justice, but if allowed to take place unchecked, may eventually undermine the revival now going on in those cities. That would be a tragedy. For American cities to revert to their hapless, seemingly hopeless, state of the 1970s will benefit no one, least of all their poor and African American communities.

Before we look at how people are trying to tackle this problem, and indeed change the picture, though, we need to ask a difficult question: why has poverty become a trap that has become so much harder to escape today?

It's a hard question to answer, because it has too many different facets to be easily grasped. Simplistic explanations, and simplistic solutions, abound. The left-wing think tank Global Research explains intergenerational poverty in straightforward but simplistic terms: "The parent . . . was unable to attain a quality education, and thus was unable to find a well-paying job and wound up in poverty. The child, still living in that same area, is also suffering from not having a quality education and the results are the same: more poverty."[4] At the other end of the spectrum, the right-wing American Action Forum touts imposing work requirements on Medicaid, arguing that it "would ensure that able-bodied Medicaid recipients are investing in themselves by engaging in work activities that inherently build skills, increase labor force attachment, and place them on a path out of poverty."[5]

Neither of these arguments hold water. Lack of quality education is a factor, but far from the dominant factor in either an individual's poverty or in the transmission of intergenerational poverty. Even more questionable, and in many respects more dangerous, is the proposition that forcing people to get jobs will enable them to move out of poverty. As has been pointed out many times, most poor people work. Nearly two out of three families living in poverty include at least one worker, and some more than one. But for low-skill workers from the inner city, jobs are not a solution. They are part of the trap.

Barbara Ehrenreich writes,

> I took jobs as a waitress, nursing-home aide, hotel housekeeper, Wal-Mart associate, and a maid with a house-cleaning service . . . the entry-level jobs most readily available to women. What I discovered is that in many ways, these jobs are a trap: They pay so little that you cannot accumulate even a couple of hundred dollars to help you make the transition to a better-paying job. They often give you no control over your work schedule, making it impossible to arrange for child care or take a second job. And in many of these jobs, even young women soon begin to experience the physical deterioration—especially knee and back problems—that can bring a painful end to their work life.[6]

The average wage of a housekeeper at a hotel or nursing home, or a home health aide, a fast-food cook at McDonalds, or a retail clerk at a Walmart or one of their competitors is about $10 per hour, or about $20,000 per year if you work at least forty hours a week, every week, year-round. Twenty thousand dollars is roughly the poverty level for a family of three, or a single mother with two children. But most poor people don't work full-time, or year-round. In Cleveland, more than one out of three working people earned less than $15,000 in 2014. The median earnings for *all* Cleveland workers, poor and non-poor, was just under $23,000 per year. In cities like Cleveland, the well-paying factory jobs of fifty years ago, which offered people with little formal education a step up into the middle class, have long since disappeared.

The barriers to escaping poverty through work for residents of urban concentrated-poverty areas go well beyond the miserable wages that are offered by most jobs that people without much formal education or specialized skills can get. Jobs are usually far from people's homes, and public transportation is inadequate, if it exists at all. Without a reliable car, which few poor people can afford, people are locked into the few jobs that are close enough to public transportation, assuming they're physically able to walk to the nearest transit stop.

For a resident of Cleveland's Central neighborhood to get to the Ahuja Medical Center, a major employer in close-in suburban Beachwood, a twenty-five-minute drive by car, it takes a fifteen- to twenty-minute walk to the nearest bus stop, two different bus rides, and another ten-minute walk to the hospital, up to an hour and a half in all if everything works right. For the same person to get to the Altenheim Senior Living facility in Strongsville, a thirty-minute drive, it will take over two hours, including over a mile of walking. It is hard to imagine any affluent commuter other than a fanatical fitness buff being willing to walk a mile to get to work, particularly in Cleveland's frigid snowy winters.

If you can get to the job, you are likely to find that you may work irregular shifts or may be given too few hours to even minimally make ends meet, like Atlanta's Dayisja Davis, who was working for Popeye's. "She thought she'd be able to work and go to school if she could find good childcare," Alana Semuels wrote in the *Atlantic*, "so she applied for CAPS, a Georgia childcare subsidy for low-income parents. She was denied because she would have been required to work twenty-five hours a week, but her fast-food hours were unpredictable and she sometimes didn't get assigned enough shifts."[7] Unpredictable hours not only mean that one never knows whether one will have enough to pay the rent at the beginning of each month, but also that any activity, from a medical appointment to a parent–teacher conference, may cause lost income, or worse, a lost job.

While poverty itself is debilitating to body and spirit, decades of research since Kenneth Clark's *Dark Ghetto* have shown how much more destructive it becomes when concentrated. Areas of concentrated poverty are not neutral in their effects on family life, job opportunity, and youth behavior, but an active, malevolent force wreaking havoc in people's lives, and undermining their efforts to forge a better life for their children. As Tom Streitz, CEO of Minneapolis's Twin Cities RISE! puts it succinctly, "poverty rewires people."

"Residence in a ghetto or barrio community," Rutgers poverty scholar Paul Jargowsky writes, "makes it harder for adults to find employment and harder for children to develop the skills to succeed. The high levels of crime, low quality of public services, and social spill-over effects imposes a tremendous burden on families that the federal poverty line alone cannot measure."[8] All the effects of poverty—the lack of jobs, the residential instability, the broken family structures, the health struggles, and the sheer stress of survival—are magnified and compounded.

Inner-city children are constantly moving from place to place and from school to school, going to often-inadequate schools, and subject to the constant peer pressure of the street. If they survive violence and escape incarceration, they rarely end up with either the formal education or so-called soft skills needed to continue to higher education, or to get and hold a stable, well-paying job. Debilitating diseases and health conditions, such as tuberculosis, diabetes, and obesity, are far more prevalent in concentrated-poverty areas. People in poverty are far more likely to be affected by crime and violence. As a report from Chicago's Heartland Institute summed up, they

> . . . experience violence committed by strangers at a rate 75 percent higher than people with high incomes, and the income disparity in the violent-crime victimization rate is even higher when the perpetrator of the crime is someone the victim knows. […] People living in poverty experience intimate-partner violence at a rate 286 percent higher than high-income people, while they experience crime committed by other family members at a rate 278 percent higher than people with high incomes and crime committed by friends/acquaintances at a rate 149 percent higher than people with high incomes.[9]

One can argue about why inner-city areas are so dangerous, but the reality is indisputable: areas of concentrated urban poverty, particularly those predominantly African American, are very dangerous places.

Children exposed to repeated violence become traumatized; as African American psychologist Erwin Randolph Parson, describes it,

> . . . from an early age, children living in the inner cities are exposed frequently to the use of drugs, guns, arson, and random violence. They witness injury, suffering, and death, and they respond to these events with fear and grief, often experiencing dramatic ruptures in their development. The list of psychological reactions is long and grim: hatred for self, profound loss of trust in the community and the world, tattered internalized moral values and ethics of caring, and a breaking down of the inner and outer sense of security and of reality.[10]

As a large-scale study from Atlanta found, "childhood trauma, adult trauma, and PTSD are highly associated with the perpetuation of interpersonal violence."[11] Dr. Kenny Ressler, leader of the Atlanta study, concluded that "the rates of PTSD we see are as high or higher than Iraq, Afghanistan, or Vietnam veterans."[12]

The effects of concentrated poverty are multigenerational. As sociologist Patrick Sharkey's research has shown, growing up in an area of highly concentrated poverty drastically increases the likelihood both that you will remain poor, and that you will never leave the area. As he points out, "It is the *cumulative* effect of living in concentrated disadvantage, over generations, that is particularly severe." Children who are the product of many generations of disadvantage "show substantially worse developmental outcomes when compared to families that live in poor neighborhoods for a single generation . . . even after we account for everything else in a family that might affect children's development."[13] Poor black children are far more likely to grow up in neighborhoods of concentrated poverty than poor white children, and as a result, more likely to remain poor as adults.

There's another piece to the puzzle, though, that goes back to the question of whether the people who live in the cities are benefiting from the economic growth that's been taking place in recent years. Until relatively recently, many people suspected that the answer to that question was no, but had a hard time proving it. In recent years, though, the US Bureau of the Census has come through with the data; mining a combination of federal and state data sources, they've built a database to which they've given the daunting name Longitudinal Employer House-hold Dynamics. More to the point, they've used this data to create a website called *On-the-Map* that shows where workers live, where they work, and how much they make, among other things, year by year from 2002 up to (as I write this) 2015.

The first thing that jumps out from this data is that, in pure numbers, there are a lot of jobs in many of America's once-industrial cities, partic-ularly the large ones. Baltimore has almost 50 percent more jobs in the city than workers who live in the city, Pittsburgh has more than twice as many jobs as workers. Second, most of the people who work in these cities don't live there. There are almost 130,000 jobs in Newark, New Jersey, but only 22,000 of them are held by people who live in the city; all the others are held by commuters.

Every day, over 106,000 people come into the city to work, and every day, over 63,000 workers leave the city for jobs in the suburbs or other nearby cities. That's typical. Every day, 204,000 people commute into Cleveland to work, and 72,000 leave the city to work in the suburbs. More city residents work in the suburbs than in the city; only 61,000 both live and work in Cleveland. The picture is even more extreme in many of the small cities and mill towns I described in chapter 7, which, with rare exceptions, are hemorrhaging jobs at a frightening clip.

From this perspective, there are three groups of workers. Workers who both live and work in the city (live in/work in); workers who live in the city and work in the suburbs (live in/work out); and workers who live in the suburbs and work in the city (live out/work in). If we look at how each of those three groups has changed since 2002, the results are startling. While the total number of *jobs* in Cleveland went up, although very slightly, over these years, the number of *city residents* holding those jobs (live in/work in) went down by 22,000, or 26 percent. In other words, there were 22,000 fewer city residents working in Cleveland in 2014 than in 2002. The number of city residents working in the sub-urbs dropped by a similar number; all in all, over only twelve years, the number of people living in Cleveland who had jobs—wherever they might work—went down by 45,000. Meanwhile, the number of people commuting into Cleveland to work went up by 25,000.

Eight out of Cleveland's 177 census tracts actually gained workers; one was the census tract that included University Circle, the others were either in downtown or the gentrifying Tremont neighborhood. By comparison, the number of people with jobs living in the neighborhoods of Glenville and Forest Hills on the city's East Side—only two miles and ten minutes by car from the Cleveland Clinic and job-rich University Circle—dropped by 2,500, or 40 percent.

Unlike Cleveland, Baltimore has been growing jobs at a respectable clip, adding 27,000 jobs from 2002 to 2015. But the same thing is happening there: fewer people who live in the city with jobs, more and more commuters. The number of people who live in Baltimore and also work in the city went down by 15,000, while the number of commuters went up by 42,000.

Not only are the ranks of commuters growing, as they take over more and more of the jobs that were once held by city residents, but they have the best jobs. They earn far more than the city residents who still work in the city, and their incomes have been growing faster. The median commuter working in Cleveland earned $50,000 in 2014, compared to just over $31,000 for city residents working in the city and $26,000 for city residents working in the suburbs. On top of this, commuters' earnings rose by an average of 40 percent from 2002 to 2015, while city residents working in the city saw their earnings go up by 22 percent, and those commuting to the suburbs by only 15 percent. Since the rate of inflation over this period was 32.5 percent, they were falling behind in real dollar earnings.

This data actually underestimates the extent of the imbalance, because the citywide data lumps together the areas where the Young Grads are moving in—downtown, Tremont, and University Circle—with the rest of the city. These are the areas where the Cleveland residents are making good money, and where the number of workers is growing. In the rest of the city, neither is true. In fact, when I compared the rate of job loss to the poverty rate by census tract in Baltimore, I found the powerful correlation visible in figure 9-1.

The economic growth taking place in the downtowns and the job clusters like University Circle, or Johns Hopkins in Baltimore, or West Philadelphia, is not spilling over into the distressed, struggling

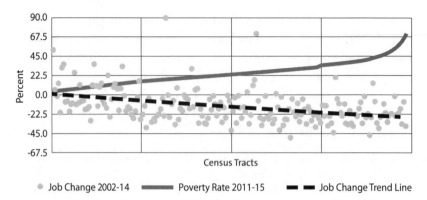

Figure 9-1 Change in number of jobs and poverty by census tract in Baltimore. (Source: US Census Bureau)

neighborhoods that surround those areas. A few years ago, when I wrote an article about this, I called it "the uncoupling of the economic city."[14] What I meant was that the economic city—that is, the city defined by its jobs and employers—is disconnecting from the people who live in the city. Instead, the economic city is coming to rely more and more on a workforce who live, in some cases, in the city's privileged neighborhoods, but more often outside the city entirely. Put bluntly, for the growing urban economy, the people who live in most of the city don't matter a whole lot. Marxist economists, who argue that the new urban revival is exploiting the poor, have it dead wrong. The revival is *ignoring* the poor.

The question is: why is this happening? Many explanations have been offered. While each seems to explain part of the situation, it's not clear they add up to a complete answer. The "spatial mismatch" hypothesis, which is the mismatch between where low-income minority households live and where the jobs have been moving, is well known. As low-income families remain stuck in the cities, due to housing costs and discrimination, the jobs have been moving to the suburbs.

That's true, up to a point, but as we've seen, not only are there still a lot of jobs in the cities, but hundreds of thousands of inner-city workers commute every day to suburban jobs. It's a bad bargain. Most of the jobs pay poorly, high transportation costs take a big bite out of what little they earn, and for many, the suburban jobs lock them into poverty rather than offering them a ticket out. But, despite everything, thousands of low-income people in every American city find their way to those jobs.

Another explanation is the jobs–education mismatch, which holds that more and more jobs require higher education or other specialized skills, which most city residents lack. Again, there's some truth to that. If we look at the jobs in the cities, we find that a lot more of the jobs are held by college graduates than the percentage of college graduates among the adults who live in the cities. Over one-third of all the jobs in Cleveland are held by college graduates, but fewer than one out of six adults living in Cleveland have a BA or higher degree.

That said, many of those jobs may not *require* a college degree; a recent study by labor economist Stephen Rose found in 2014 that one out four college graduates held jobs for which they were overqualified.[15] Part of that may be the product of a tight labor market, and part may be what some call "credential creep," which is the tendency of employers to give preference to candidates with more education, even if the job itself doesn't require those skills. Either way, the jobs–education mismatch disproportionately affects urban African Americans, who are less likely to have college degrees than whites; in Baltimore, only 14 percent of black adults had a BA or higher degree, compared to 55 percent of white adults. But, still, it only accounts for part of the picture.

The gap between inner-city residents and the job world is not just about measurable things like college degrees. The young man with a high school diploma from an inner-city school may lack the skills that even lower-skill jobs may require, such as reading and doing math at a ninth-grade level, or communicating clearly both orally and in writing. Just as important are the so-called soft skills—the person's attitudes, work ethic, and ability to relate to co-workers and customers; as one retail HR executive told researchers Phillip Moss and Chris Tilly, "I tell my personnel managers . . . if they don't smile, don't hire them."[16]

As soft skills become more important, that may work against many African Americans—not all, but particularly young men, and particularly young men from isolated, concentrated-poverty communities, where the culture of the street rewards behaviors very different from those rewarded by mainstream culture. Although there is little doubt that discrimination is a factor, it is telling that of the personnel managers interviewed by Moss and Tilly, those in businesses located in the inner city were more than *three times* as likely to have a negative view of black men's soft skills than those in businesses in the suburbs.

There's another factor, too, that may have more impact than people have tended to give it—what Northwestern professor Lauren Rivera calls "cultural matching," or the tendency of people to hire other people who look or act like them. Rivera, who studied hiring patterns in elite law, banking, and consulting firms, found that in these firms, cultural matching is built in; as one law firm partner told her, "In our new associates, we are first and foremost looking for *cultural compatibility*. Someone who . . . will *fit in*."[17]

While cultural fit is not necessarily about race (the partner Rivera quoted was black), race is likely to be a factor, particularly in non-elite settings where people making hiring decisions may not be as attuned to diversity concerns. Most people doing most hiring are likely to be white. In a famous 2004 study entitled "Are Emily and Greg More Employable than Lakisha and Jamal?" economists Marianne Bertrand and Sendhil Mullainathan found that résumés with "white" names were 50 percent more likely to be called in for interviews than those with "black" names.[18]

These points are not new, even if the particular statistics may be. Fifty years ago, the Kerner Commission painted a bleak, unsparing picture of racially segregated concentrated-poverty areas, arguing that "the culture of poverty that results from unemployment and family disorganization generates a system of ruthless, exploitative relationships within the ghetto," and singling out the high rate of unemployment and under-employment among black men as a particularly critical factor. The commission's recommendations, as relevant today as they were then, include "motivating the hard-core unemployed," removing "artificial barriers to employment and promotion," providing "quality education in ghetto schools," and "increasing efforts to eliminate *de facto* segregation."[19]

It would not be fair to say that no progress has been made since then. The poverty rate among those classified at the time as "nonwhite," or mainly African American, in 1966 was over 40 percent. Today, among African Americans it is 25 percent. That is still far too high, but is nevertheless a vast improvement. The benefits of that improvement, though, are felt more in the suburban areas where upwardly mobile black families have moved than in the central cities. The poverty rate for black residents of St. Louis and Milwaukee is 35 percent, and in Cleveland and Buffalo, over 40 percent. In this respect at least, these cities are still living in the 1960s.

For many decades, people have grappled with the question of how to create meaningful opportunities for better jobs and careers, and how to break the seemingly endless cycle of intergenerational poverty. Some of their efforts, indeed, have been successful, and many others have shown promise. At the same time, as we will see, in the absence of any effort to grapple with the larger systemic issues driving the persistence of poverty, much of the experience of the last few decades can be summed up as one step forward, one—and perhaps two—steps backward.

From a national perspective, the most successful efforts have been those that have increased peoples' incomes, like the Earned Income Tax Credit (EITC), or allowed the poor to meet their most fundamental needs. "Although it was not originally billed as an anti-poverty program," Brookings researchers Natalie Holmes and Alan Berube write, "in its forty years, the EITC has become one of the nation's most effective tools for lifting low-income workers and their families above the poverty line."[20] A 2013 Brookings study estimated that the EITC lifted 6.2 million people, half of them children, out of poverty.[21]

The EITC gives low-income working families with children a refund of their federal income tax and social security payments, with the size of the refund based on their income, marital status, and number of children. Up to a certain point, the refund goes up as the family's earnings go up, helping to offset the way some other programs reduce or eliminate benefits as a family's earnings grow. The EITC has more long-term impacts as well; as Robert Greenstein of the Center for Budget and Policy Priorities notes, "an impressive body of recent research indicates [that] starting from infancy—when higher tax credits have been linked with more prenatal care, less maternal stress, and better infant health—children who benefit from expanded tax credits do better throughout childhood and have higher odds of finishing high school and going to college."[22]

Other federal programs, such as the Supplemental Nutrition Assistance Program (SNAP), once known as Food Stamps; the Housing

Choice Voucher program, formerly known as Section 8; and Medicaid, which provides essential medical care to low-income people, do not put cash directly into people's pockets, but enable them to meet their basic needs for food, shelter, and health care. The SNAP and Medicaid programs are entitlements, meaning that if you are poor enough, you are entitled to the benefit. Vouchers are not entitlements. Indeed, according to the probably optimistic official numbers, only one out of every four eligible poor households receives any assistance to help pay the rent. Housing vouchers are like a lottery. Lots of people buy tickets but most of the contestants go home empty-handed.

If you are poor and don't win the voucher lottery, a series of things happen. First, your rent is likely to be 50 percent or more of your total income. The median rent in Pittsburgh in 2015 was $858 per month, or over $10,000 per year. That's two-thirds of the gross income of a single mother making $15,000 a year at a retail job in the suburbs. That means two things. First, to quote Matt Desmond's *Evicted* again, "If Arleen or Vanetta didn't have to dedicate 70 or 80 percent of their income to rent, they could keep their kids fed and clothed and off the streets. They could settle down in one neighborhood and enroll their kids in one school. [...] They could open a savings account or buy their children toys and books, perhaps even a home computer."[23]

Second, it means that Arleen and Vanetta, for whom making the rent each month is a constant struggle, are living on the edge. Anything can push them off the edge—a medical problem, a balky car that won't start, a late bus, reduced hours at work, a missed welfare appointment. When that happens, they can't make their rent payment and they lose their apartment. Either they are evicted through a formal legal process, or they leave beforehand, knowing they have no way out. As Desmond writes,

> even in the most desolate areas of American cities, evictions used to be rare. They used to draw crowds. [...] These days, there are sheriff squads whose full-time job is to carry out eviction and foreclosure orders. There are moving companies specializing in evictions, their crews working all day, every weekday. [...] These days, housing courts swell, forcing commissioners to settle cases in hallways or makeshift offices. [...] Low-income families have

grown used to the rumble of moving trucks, the early-morning knocks at the door, the belongings lining the curb.[24]

In Baltimore, thirty families are evicted every weekday of the year.

Things would be far worse for millions of American families without the EITC, SNAP, Medicaid, and what few vouchers are available, but these are survival, not opportunity, measures. If we raised the national minimum wage to $15, as many propose, it would improve matters for many people. It would probably be a good idea, but one can't be certain, since it is impossible to tell in advance whether the benefits to those low-income people who would see their wages go up would exceed the negative effects of what jobs might be lost outright or moved overseas. As with so many other complex policy proposals, the limited research that's been done is all over the map.

As with all sweeping policies, like NAFTA, the way costs and benefits would be distributed is likely to be uneven. More-affluent (and expensive) areas like the San Francisco Bay Area, where wages for low-skill jobs are already usually much higher than the current minimum, would probably lose fewer jobs than low-wage cities and rural areas, where as many as half of the jobs pay less than a $15 hourly wage currently. As with so many other economic policies, it is more likely to benefit the geographic winners, the strong-economy coastal areas, and further exacerbate the already vast gap between people living in those areas and the struggling areas inland. At the same time, though, a meaningfully higher minimum wage would add not only money but some measure of dignity to the people holding many of the jobs our society needs despite being unwilling to pay the people who hold those jobs a living wage.

Income supports and a social safety net are essential if millions of Americans are to be able to live in even minimal decency, with even a modicum of security from the pernicious effects of hunger, ill-heath, eviction, and homelessness. Income supports, though, should not be confused with opportunity. To paraphrase the slogan of the Oakland-based Family Independence Initiative, "They make poverty tolerable, when we can make it *escapable*."[25] Opportunity means at a minimum the ability to find and keep a job or open a business that can enable a worker to escape poverty and provide a stable, decent living for her family. That is a high bar, since forces well out of any city's control limit the extent to which many jobs today pay well enough to meet that standard. But the critical factors appear to be education and skills, including the soft skills I mentioned earlier.

The biggest single step to getting a good job and making good money in twenty-first-century America is getting a four-year college degree. On the average, the typical person with a BA or BS degree makes 72 percent more than someone with a high school diploma, up from 53 percent in 1997. This adds up to a lifetime earnings boost of roughly a million dollars, far more than the cost of getting the degree. Someone with an advanced degree, such as a law degree or a PhD, makes more than twice as much as the average high school graduate.[26] As figure 9-2 also shows, getting a two-year community college degree provides little wage boost over the high school diploma, although it does open up a wider range of job opportunities.

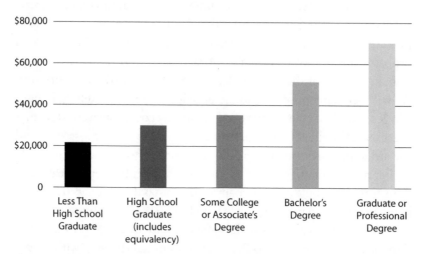

Figure 9-2 The education premium: median annual earnings by highest level of education. (Source: US Census Bureau)

As a result, it's not surprising that a lot of effort has gone into creating programs to increase the ability of inner-city youths to go to college. One well-known program, which has spawned a series of imitators, is the Kalamazoo Promise. Kalamazoo is a small city in western Michigan which has a relatively strong economic base, but suffers from considerable distress and a high poverty rate. In 2005, a group of anonymous donors announced that they would pay the tuition at any public college or university in the state of Michigan for any student graduating from the Kalamazoo public schools (KPS) who had been in the system since the ninth grade or earlier. The scholarship paid 100 percent of the cost for students who had been at KPS since first grade, down to 65 percent for those who had been in KPS only since ninth grade. It was not linked to merit or financial need, and was "first-dollar" money; that is, students did not have to max out other sources of financial aid in order to receive the Promise funds. From 2005 to 2014, the still-anonymous donors have spent $61 million on scholarships, with spending running currently at $10 to $11 million per year.

Ten years after the program started, Timothy Bartik and his colleagues at Kalamazoo's W. E. Upjohn Institute decided to find out what effect the Promise had on KPS graduates' college outcomes, by comparing KPS graduates who had been in the system from ninth grade or earlier—and were eligible for scholarships—with those who had entered the system after ninth grade, and thus were not. They found that the students receiving Promise scholarships significantly out-performed the others in three areas: the percentage going to four-year colleges, the number of credits they signed up for in the first two years, and most important, the number getting a BA or equivalent degree in six years. The increases were significant for low-income students and for African American students, although the racial gap between white and black outcomes was still wide.[27]

All of the improvement, however, for African American students was among female graduates. The program had no effect on the outcomes of male African American KPS graduates. This reflects a larger problem, the declining share of men among African American college students and graduates. In 2014, not only were 63 percent of all black students in higher education women, and 70 percent of all in graduate and professional schools women, but graduation rates for African American women were far higher than for men.[28] Many reasons have been offered for this disparity, including the ways many of the most challenging problems of inner-city life, including the effects of violence and incarceration, the absence of engaged, present fathers, and the dynamics of street culture, disproportionately affect young men; as commentator William Raspberry put it, "Inner-city conditions present a conspiracy of circumstances that almost impel young black men into trouble."[29]

The growing network of KIPP, or Knowledge Is Power Program, charter schools is an ambitious national effort to increase the number of low-income and minority students who go to college. Founded in 1995 by two alumni of the Teach for America program, in 2017 KIPP had 88,000 children and youths enrolled in 209 schools around the United States, mostly middle schools but including pre-kindergarten through high school. Ninety-five percent of their students are African American or Latino, and 88 percent are eligible for the federal free or reduced-price lunch program, meaning that their family income is no more than 1.85 times the federal poverty level. KIPP relentlessly focuses on getting their students to go to college; as they sum up their goals, "We aspire for 75 percent of our students to earn four-year degrees and all of our students to have the knowledge and skills necessary to succeed in college if they so choose."[30]

KIPP schools appear to have a strong impact on student achievement. A 2013 evaluation by the well-regarded Princeton-based research firm Mathematica found that "the average impact of KIPP on student achievement is positive, statistically significant, and educationally substantial."[31] A preliminary report on college outcomes, published by KIPP in 2011, found that "33 percent of students who completed a KIPP middle school ten or more years ago have graduated from a four-year college."[32] Given the profile of their students, these are decent results, even if they fall short of KIPP's ambitious goal.

This finding was based on the first few KIPP schools, though, and it is not clear what current data would show as the network of KIPP schools has grown all but exponentially. There seems to be some question whether KIPP can maintain its early results; even the Mathematica study found that many individual KIPP schools showed little or no student improvement. KIPP has also come under fire for its high student attrition rate.

Even more impressive results have been reported from the Match Public Charter School in Boston, a comprehensive program from pre-kindergarten through high school. Match shares many features with KIPP, including an even more determined focus on preparing its students for college. Even more than KIPP, though, it aims to be what Match High School principal Hannah Larkin calls a "high expectations, high support" school, providing at least two hours per day of individual or small-group tutoring in addition to conventional class-based instruction.[33] According to the Match website, 51 percent of the students who graduated from Match between 2004 and 2010 have since graduated from a four-year college, an impressive figure by any standard. The Match student body is largely similar to that of Boston's noncompetitive public schools, but with a much larger share of African American students than in the city's public schools.

This model gets results. As a 2016 study by team of scholars led by MIT economist Joshua Angrist that carefully controlled for student body composition concluded, "A growing body of evidence indicates that many urban charter schools have large, positive effects on the test scores of disadvantaged students. Oversubscribed charter schools in Boston increase the test scores of low-income students by a third of a standard deviation a year—enough to eliminate the black-white test score gap in a few years of attendance."[34] Independent of test scores, these charter school students were more likely to take Advanced Placement tests, did significantly better on SATs, and—if continuing to college—were significantly more likely to go to four-year rather than two-year colleges than their Boston public school peers.

Massachusetts severely caps the number of charter-school student slots, as a result of which high-performing schools like Match are forced to turn away hundreds of prospective students every year. They regulate the ones that open, and many non-performing schools have been ordered closed by state education authorities. Accountability is critical to the system; although there are some exceptions, generally charter schools that do not follow some version of the "high expectations, high support" model perform no better, and often worse, than public schools. Similarly, voucher-based school choice programs may actually, as a study of the Louisiana Scholarship Program found, "dramatically *reduce* student achievement," largely because of lack of quality control among receiving private schools.[35] Although the study did not address this, the negative impacts of low-quality options in the system, as with Detroit's troubled charter schools, are magnified for low-income families with limited information and limited resources.

Both KIPP and Match (particularly KIPP) have been widely criticized, however, for their highly structured and discipline-oriented educational approach. It is hard to sort out this issue, particularly for someone with no particular expertise in educational psychology. Although any program that follows a strict "no excuses" discipline policy is likely to appear hard-hearted and punitive from the outside, there is little question that a rigorous structure is important for mastery, as anyone who has truly mastered a musical instrument or a demanding craft knows. This may be particularly important for children from low-income, inner-city families where structure and discipline may be in short supply.

The relative success of Match or most of the KIPP schools does not necessarily translate to success for charter schools across the board. Charter schools, which have tended to locate in high-poverty, high-minority cities, are wildly uneven, as are the state laws governing them. In Detroit, where Michigan's laws allow almost anyone to open a charter school and run it with little accountability, reporter Kate Zernicke described how "the unchecked growth of charters has created a glut of schools competing for some of the nation's poorest students, enticing them to enroll with cash bonuses, laptops, raffle tickets for iPads and bicycles. [Schools] are being cannibalized, fighting so hard over students and the limited public dollars that follow them that no one thrives."[36] With no independent machinery in place to shut down poorly performing charter schools, failing schools, mostly run for profit, prey on low-income parents with few mobility options.

In Detroit, a child of well-educated, well-to-do parents, who can not only evaluate all of the options but has the resources to take advantage of the best ones wherever in the region they may be, can and probably will do well. The child of the poor single mother in the heart of the ghetto, despite all the options on paper, is no less likely to end up in a troubled, failing school than in a system in which a dysfunctional public school is the only option. Rather than foster equity, the Detroit model of school choice exacerbates inequality.

The Detroit charter school story is as much about politics and power as it is about education. Unfortunately, much of the vitriolic ongoing debate over charter schools and public schools can be described that way, with opponents pointing to charter-school support by the "non-democratic foundations of billionaires such as Bill and Melinda Gates Foundation, Broad Foundation, and the Walton Family Foundation."[37] One outspoken blogger has compared KIPP schools to World War II concentration camps,[38] while another described them as "total-compliance isolation camps that receive public dollars to support this social-control strategy that is top priority with Gates, Broad, and the Walton Klan."[39] On the other side, Betsy DeVos, Trump's secretary of education and a long-time advocate for charter schools and school choice, described public education as "a closed system, a closed industry, a closed market. It's a monopoly, a dead end."[40] Neither side likes the other much, but the rhetoric directed at charter schools by their adversaries has a particularly venomous quality. In the course of the debate, if it can be dignified by that term, the interests of children and their families can easily get lost.

Leaving aside the charter-school debate, does it really make sense to try to get everyone—or nearly everyone—to graduate from college? It's debatable whether there are as many jobs today that really need a college graduate as there already are college graduates. Aside from the ranks of overqualified baristas and Uber drivers, this leads not only to the "credential creep" I mentioned earlier, but to redefining entire occupations, like registered nurses that have historically not required a college degree, to require one. Meanwhile, that approach does not offer too much hope for the large number of adults trapped in poverty.

Over the next decade, according to the Bureau of Labor Statistics, the greatest demand for jobs—combining job growth and turnover—will come in four sectors: health care, food preparation and service, sales, and office and administrative support. Some, although far from all, don't pay too badly, while others offer at least the potential to move up in a company or a field. In all four areas, even health care, half or more of the jobs do not require a college degree. What they do require, though, in most cases is some level of specialized training, as well as a healthy measure of soft skills.

The challenge of creating opportunity for any significant number of low-income inner-city adults, however, goes well beyond providing training and inculcating soft skills. Transportation constraints keep many inner-city residents from getting access to suburban jobs, or drive them to make commutes that impose unsustainable burdens on their time and limited money. Criminal records, moreover, block an increasing number of people, disproportionately black and disproportionately male, from getting jobs.

Urban planners and policy wonks in the United States are enamored with light rail and similar fixed-route systems, which are great to look at and, like stadiums, offer politicians wonderful photo ops. They are spectacularly expensive, and they can be very useful as a transit system for high-density corridors or as a strategy to foster revival or gentrification. As a result, they may be a legitimate, albeit costly, part of the way a city tries to foster economic growth. What they do *not* do, however, is improve mobility and job access for the great majority of lower-income workers, who usually do not live along the high-intensity corridors, and whose jobs tend to be scattered all over the region.

While most workers, even among the poor, commute by car, the percentage of low-income workers who rely on buses is substantial; in Newark, where three out of four residents work outside the city, nearly half of all poor workers rely on public transportation to get to work, while in St. Louis, over a quarter of all poor workers do. For them, it's about buses, the historic poor stepsister of the public transportation industry. In most parts of the United States, buses are the only transit option for most areas. But they tend to be slow and run infrequently; the only bus line from Cleveland running eastward to the major suburban job center of Beachwood runs only once every thirty to forty-five minutes during rush hours, taking nearly an hour to cover seven miles, while large parts of highly urbanized Cuyahoga County lack even that modest bus service.

The neglect of bus service in the United States is starting to change; Daniel Vock writes in a recent issue of *Governing* magazine that "in the last few years, transit agencies in more than half a dozen major cities have totally revamped their bus routes to focus on frequent, reliable service to job centers and dense neighborhoods."[41] The question, of course, is *which* job centers, and which neighborhoods. Fast buses from reviving high-density neighborhoods to downtown may not help low-income workers. Conversely, increasing bus service in inner-city areas and to dispersed suburban job centers may not fill buses, even as it may help growing numbers of low-income workers find work with less-burdensome commutes. That means, in turn, that better bus service for low-income areas is likely to cost more money, which legislatures as well as voters have been historically reluctant to provide. This might change once autonomous or self-driving vehicles become widely available; eliminating the cost of drivers on low-ridership routes might well make them more financially feasible. The price of that, of course, is the loss of many relatively well-paying blue-collar jobs.

It might well be better for public systems to run their big, expensive, forty-plus passenger buses on major arteries and high-utilization routes, and allow small, informal systems of minibuses, vans, and car-sharing to spring up in between. Many of these already exist at the margins of the legal system. As Lisa Margonelli writes, "America's twentieth-largest bus service—hauling 120,000 riders a day—is profitable and also illegal. It's not really a bus service at all, but a willy-nilly aggregation of 350 licensed and 500 unlicensed privately owned 'dollar vans' that roam the streets of Brooklyn and Queens, picking up passengers from street corners where city buses are either missing or inconvenient."[42]

In most American cities, public transportation is a closely held monopoly. Even if the van or car is fully licensed and insured, New York and most other cities do not allow their owners to pick up riders on the street. Legalizing local, privately owned vans and car-sharing operations, and encouraging lower-income and immigrant entrepreneurs to provide those services in their neighborhoods, would almost certainly provide a more efficient, cost-effective service than bus operators could provide, while increasing the income of thousands of struggling lower-income families. A variation on this theme, which has been gaining currency, is to have government subsidize rides on Uber or Lyft for low-income commuters, either to their jobs or to the nearest public transit stop.

Finally, in many cities, particular smaller, lower-density ones, an even simpler solution exists: help low-income workers buy cars. Ways to Work, a nonprofit lender based in Milwaukee, provides low-interest, no-down-payment car loans of up to $8,000 to low-income workers, enough to buy a good-quality, reliable used car. An independent evaluation found that large numbers of their borrowers saw significant increases in their income, less reliance on welfare assistance, and improved credit scores, as a result. The same study concluded that benefits to the borrowers and to taxpayers, in terms of reduced public-assistance costs, amounted to $2.48 for every $1 invested.[43]

An even bigger problem is the effect of people's criminal records. That was far less of a problem twenty-five or thirty years ago, when far fewer people had criminal records than today, information on them was less readily available, and hiring criteria were less stringent. Today, 25 percent of non-incarcerated black men have a felony conviction on their record,[44] while the Sentencing Project notes that one out of three Americans has a criminal record.[45]

Harvard sociologist Devah Pager measured the impact of both race and a criminal record on employment in a 2001 study in Milwaukee, where she sent carefully matched white and black "testers" to apply for entry-level, unskilled jobs.[46] Jobs with legal restrictions on hiring ex-offenders were carefully excluded. At each stage, certain testers were randomly assigned a "criminal record" when applying for the job. The role of having a "criminal record" was rotated between testers to ensure that differences in results were not the result of subtle differences in the manner or appearance of the tester. She then measured how often the testers would receive either a job offer or a callback.

The results were stunning, as shown in figure 9-3. First, black testers overall were far less likely to get a callback than whites. Second, criminal records made a much bigger difference for black than for white applicants; while a criminal record reduced a white tester's chances by 50 percent, it reduced the chances of a black tester by nearly two-thirds.

People are trying hard to tackle this issue. In 2003, a group of formerly incarcerated organizers met in Oakland, California, to figure out how to combat discrimination based on past criminal history. They created an organization they called All of Us or None, which has spearheaded an amazing grassroots effort that's led to over half of the states adopting "ban the box" laws barring employers from including the question "Have you been convicted of a crime?" on initial employment and other applications. Iowa has gone a step further, enacting a special income-tax

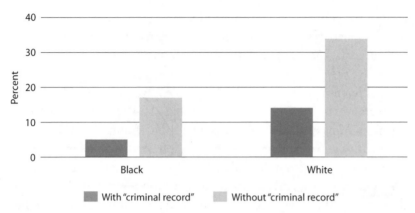

Figure 9-3 Percentage called back: How the effect of a criminal record varies for black and white job applicants. (Source: Devah Pager, "The Mark of a Criminal Record")

deduction for employers who hire ex-offenders that can be worth up to $20,000 per year.[47]

Other organizations are focusing on the immediate needs of the more than 600,000 people, largely poor, often psychologically damaged, and disproportionately black and male, who are released from prison and sent back to city streets each year. Chicago's Safer Foundation is one of the more ambitious of many organizations across the country that works with ex-offenders. Safer sees good jobs as the cornerstone of their work, but in addition to finding jobs for clients, they build in services to improve their basic educational skills and job readiness, and support them once they've been placed on the job. Safer helped 4,200 ex-offenders secure employment in 2014, with three-quarters of the people they placed still on the job after a year. Safer's efforts reduce the likelihood of going back to prison within three years from the statewide average of 47 percent down to 24 percent for all of their clients, and to 16 percent for those who have held their job for at least a year. Safer claims to have saved the state of Illinois $300 million in prison costs over the past four years, and saved the population at large untold amounts in crimes not committed.[48]

Safer's work is not inexpensive. Their operations cost $23 million a year, of which $19 million comes from government contracts and most of the rest from grants. Organizations like Safer doing similar work around the country are in a constant scramble for funds, even though it's a reasonable estimate that, when one adds up savings in prison costs, welfare costs, and the cost of the crimes not committed, programs like Safer save the public four or more dollars for every dollar they spend.

A different approach to a similar problem was followed by the program created by the One Baltimore for Jobs (1B4J) program, created by the city's Mayor's Office of Employment Development (MOED) in 2015 with a two-year demonstration grant from the US Department of Labor. Focusing on four carefully selected areas—manufacturing, health care, construction, and logistics/transportation—the city "sought to demonstrate that a workforce system could be built that fused together occupational skills training with key support services."[49]

MOED found that all the pieces were already there, but as they put it, "previously, grants for training and support services were made separately and the 'partnerships' were more of a hope than a reality." MOED entered into contracts with nineteen separate organizations to integrate their services into a single system of training, education, and support. What stands out was their focus on removing the legal barriers to their trainees getting work. MOED contracted with Maryland Legal Aid and the Maryland Volunteer Lawyers Service to work one-on-one with each participant to identify issues in their personal history that could be resolved, such as judgments, criminal convictions, or failure to pay child support, and to resolve them so that they would not prevent their obtaining a job in the field for which they were being trained.

Child support issues take on particular importance, since large numbers of inner-city men have outstanding unmet child support orders. In a telling example of a well-intended but counterproductive public policy, forty-nine of fifty states suspend or remove the driver's licenses (as well as other professional or occupational licenses) of people who fail to pay child support, thus reducing or removing entirely their ability to continue making a living, and all but guaranteeing that their child support obligations will remain unpaid. To fix this, MOED formed a partnership with the Maryland child support agency to reinstate participants' driver's licenses, and where needed, resize their child support obligations to better match their earnings.

In the first year and a half of the 1B4J program, more than 900 Baltimore residents had enrolled in training, 750 had completed training, and more than 500 had begun jobs in one of the four fields for which they had trained. Sadly, the program came to an end when the federal grant ran out at the end of 2017.

A program that looks at another aspect of the opportunity problem, and has actually convinced state government to pay them for results, is the Minneapolis-based Twin Cities RISE!, or TCR. Twin Cities RISE! goes back to some of the underlying issues behind the opportunity challenge, with a model they call Personal Empowerment. As Steven Rothschild, the former General Mills executive who founded TCR, puts it, "At RISE! we learned the need for empowerment training the hard way. In the first few years we faced a bewildering situation: too many people were dropping out during the program and even after working in the jobs we'd found for them. Something would happen—we often didn't know what—and they were gone. We were enormously frustrated." Rothschild goes on,

> We knew we were doing good work. We'd taught our participants the behaviors they needed to succeed. Show up on time, dress appropriately. Don't get into arguments. We knew they practiced these things for a while, but then they would revert back to their old behavior. [...] We came to realize that participants couldn't sustain the behaviors of accountability because fundamentally they believed, as one put it, "you're going to get screwed, no matter what you do." So if that's the case—if you think your future is hopeless and you're powerless to do anything about it—why behave like a responsible working person?[50]

The result was a model that Rothschild called Personal Empowerment, drawn from the theories of emotional intelligence and from Cognitive Behavioral Therapy, designed "to help patients address problems of dysfunctional emotions, behaviors, and cognitions."[51] As Tom Streitz, TCR's current CEO, puts it, "We not only teach somebody the hard skills to get a job, but we also teach them to value themselves and to have the confidence and belief in themselves that they know they're worthy of a great job."[52] While they don't call it that, Twin Cities RISE! is focusing on healing the trauma of life in concentrated poverty and segregation. Most of their participants (they don't call them "clients") are African American men. Four out of five are unemployed, and two-thirds have criminal histories.

TCR starts with personal empowerment, but they don't end there. They work with employers who tell them, in Streitz's words, that "these are the hard skills we need"; then they either provide the training, or work with other groups in the Twin Cities to put together training for the skills the employers are looking for. They then provide each participant with a coach who stays with him, helping him over the rough spots, for two years after they've been placed on the job. This sort of coaching, which we see in the Safer Foundation's programs and elsewhere, is doubly important. It helps the newly placed worker avoid being undone by any of the many pitfalls that inevitably arise as they try to stabilize their lives, while it gives the employer a comfort level in hiring someone from TCR, knowing that there's somebody supportive in the picture to reach out to in case of a problem.

TCR is a smaller operation than the Safer Foundation, with an annual budget running around $3.5 million. About 20 percent of that comes from an ongoing pay-for-performance contract with the state of Minnesota. The state pays for participants' training, but only after each has been placed in a job that pays at least $20,000 per year *and* $10,000 per year more than what he earned the previous year. For each participant meeting the target, the state pays TCR $9,000. TCR estimates that the State of Minnesota has received a 600 percent return on investment from its support "due to reduced government subsidies, increased tax receipts, and reduced criminal justice costs, the result of TCR graduates getting and retaining good jobs"—or, since 1997, savings of more than $35 million to Minnesota taxpayers.

To varying degrees, some of these models may make good liberals— and some who are not liberals—cringe, especially when they seem to involve poor black people and to be driven by privileged young white men and women. Whether it's the discipline-based model of the KIPP schools or the therapy-driven approach (although they would not call it that) of Twin Cities RISE!, these models all implicitly or explicitly assume that the people in they serve, whether small children, teenagers, or adult ex-offenders, are damaged in some fashion. That, in turn, is interpreted as an attack on an entire culture. As I have shown earlier, there is considerable evidence, though, that the combination of growing up or living in poverty, combined with living in an area of concentrated poverty, particularly when you add the further layer of racial discrimination pervasive in American society, is damaging, and that that damage blocks, for many different reasons, many individuals' ability to succeed in the mainstream society.

Some people, particularly those who see the American capitalist mainstream economy and society as pernicious, whether for cultural, ideological, or other reasons, would question the value of mainstream success and suggest that it isn't worth the compromises that have to be made. While one can certainly identify plenty of things wrong with that economy and the culture it reflects, the fact remains that a society has only one mainstream at a time, and indeed, that from a world perspective the American mainstream is one of the more open in terms of its acceptance, albeit within bounds, of differences. The great majority of people of all income levels and conditions of life are neither rebellious poets nor radical revolutionaries, and they want above all to be able to live a decent, productive, satisfying life. That is something difficult if not impossible to do outside the mainstream of society and the economy.

If there is one overarching lesson that emerges from this survey, it is that lifting people out of the trap of multigenerational poverty can be done, but is complicated and involves many different moving parts. The evidence is compelling that children want to learn and adults want to succeed, whatever their backgrounds. Breaking down the barriers to success, though, involves working in many different ways with many different types of people at different stages in their life's journey, from the toddler who may be unprepared to function in school, to the ex-offender who needs to rebuild his life, and the single mom desperately trying to juggle rent, transportation, children, and a physically taxing, dead-end job hours away. There is no single magic bullet.

People are starting to look at this challenge more broadly. In 2014, Mayor Greg Fisher of Louisville announced a citywide initiative he called Cradle to Career, focusing on four parallel "pillars": increasing kindergarten readiness, ensuring K–12 success, successful transition to and completion of postsecondary education, and building a qualified twenty-first-century workforce.[53] Mayor Fisher brought together four key partners, each of whom was already focusing on one of the four areas, to work together in a coordinated strategy rather than in their separate "silos," and since 2014 has hosted an annual Cradle to Career Summit in which each partner shared their successes and challenges in meeting their goals.

A more recent and more tightly focused effort has begun to emerge in Newark, New Jersey, where in the summer of 2017 Mayor Ras Baraka, along with the Newark Alliance, a business roundtable, unveiled Newark 2020, a plan to "connect 2,020 Newark residents to local work that pays a living wage by 2020," in the words of Newark Alliance CEO Kimberly McLain. Newark, with New Jersey's largest concentration of educational and medical institutions, along with some 20,000 jobs at Newark Airport and Port Newark, has the jobs, but few of them are held by local people. As part of Newark 2020, many of the city's key employers have adopted specific hiring targets to enable the city to reach its goal.

This may appear to be an ambitious target, but it may not be as ambitious as it seems. With over 20,000 unemployed adults in Newark, and with turnover alone creating an estimated 10,000 to 12,000 openings in the city each year for jobs that don't need a college degree, 2,020 in three years will hardly make a dent. At the same time, unless the city and its partners have the ability to provide a pipeline of workers who are ready to take the jobs that are being offered—with respect to attitudes, soft skills, and specific job skills—it may be a hard target to reach. To her credit, McLain recognizes at least part of this. "This is not an initiative just to connect 2,000 people to work, and then check the box," she says. "What we're trying to do is create a system . . . [so that] we will no longer need these initiatives, because we have shifted the culture and the mindset of our companies."[54]

That's important, because the world is full of impressive-looking one-shot efforts that don't lead to any real change, but questions remain, both in Newark and in Louisville. Changing the mindset of employers is critical, but so is changing the mindset not only of the workers, but of the entire system designed to help those workers overcome the barriers to stable, secure employment. That system in many places tends to be fragmented and disorganized, with many organizations working with little connection to one another, and having a depressing tendency to cherry-pick from the client pool those that can get into decent jobs with the least time and expense on the agency's part, which makes their numbers look better. An in-depth study of Newark's workforce development "landscape" done fifteen years ago found that "the lack of trust and reliability in the local workforce system seems to be a predominant factor in [local employers'] hiring decisions."[55] It is not clear so far how much progress Newark has made toward creating a system that will indeed ensure that those 2,020 jobs go to people who would not otherwise have a shot, rather than people who will find decent jobs with or without special initiatives like Newark 2020.

That, in turn, goes to the heart of the challenge for America's cities. The crisis of sustained multigenerational poverty is at the heart of the growing polarization of these cities between rich and poor, and between white and black. It is the poor or near-poor who are stuck in the poverty trap, are not benefiting from their cities' revival, and need the most help breaking out of the trap. Initiatives like Cradle to Career or Newark 2020, which on their face are agnostic about race and poverty, may benefit some of them, or only a few of them.

At the same time, it would be foolish to pretend that, over and above the cost and difficulty of such programs, there are no political obstacles to mounting efforts explicitly targeted at poor people, largely black, at a scale large enough to make a difference, particularly in today's political climate. Indeed, the entire issue of inequality in reviving older cities, as in many other aspects of twenty-first-century American society, is closely interwoven with questions of politics and power, a subject we will turn to in the next chapter.

Chapter 10

Power and Politics: Finding the Will to Change

A s the flight of people and industry from the cities was turn-ing into a tidal wave in the early 1970s, urban pundit George Sternlieb told an interviewer bluntly that "the problem of the city is a crisis of function. What actually does the city have to offer to keep people?" he speculated, and then he continued, "The answer today is: very little."[1] Ever since the tide had begun to turn against the cities after World War II, how to find a new function, rebuild their economies, and regain the prosperity they once had was the challenge that preoccu-pied public officials and the business and civic leadership of America's older cities.

The way they confronted the challenge, though, shifted sharply during the 1980s, when the so-called Reagan Revolution not only led to a dramatic decline in the flow of federal money to the cities, but, more significantly, also triggered a sea change in how people thought about the role of government; as President Reagan said as he was sworn in to his first term, "Government is not the solution to our problem; government *is* the problem." While he may have been referring directly to the federal government, his line, and the attitude it reflected, rever-berated far beyond the boundaries of Washington, DC. If government was the problem, it logically followed that if there was a solution, it would have to come from the private sector. That shift may not have changed the nature of the problem, but it changed the way people *looked at* the problem.

Public and private sectors have been interwoven, of course, throughout American history. Both nineteenth-century urban political machines and the Progressive movements that challenged them at the dawn of the twentieth century existed in a symbiotic relationship with the corporations that provided the cities with jobs and wealth. At the same time, they were not simply capitalism's handmaidens. Many Progressives saw themselves as a counterweight to the unfettered power of business; as Robin Meiksins describes Cleveland mayor Tom Johnson, who held that office from 1901 to 1909, he "represented the ideals of the Progressive movement, seeking to use government to counter the strength of big businesses and bring relief to those struggling to make ends meet."[2] Johnson built public bathhouses, forced the city's streetcar corporation to lower fares to three cents, and removed the "keep off the grass" signs from the city's parks.

Under the New Deal, cities built schools, parks, and playgrounds, fed and housed the poor and the unemployed, and put thousands to work. The New Deal years marked the beginning of an era of local government intervention that grew after the war, with urban renewal in the fifties; the Great Society, the War on Poverty, and the Model Cities program in the sixties; and still more federal programs in the early seventies for housing, health centers, home repairs, neighborhood improvement, and workforce-development programs. Looking back, these programs may have had little or no effect on the cities' downward trajectory; indeed, urban renewal programs may have done more harm than good. But many did undoubtedly improve the lives of people, helping many people find new jobs or business opportunities, although many of them probably took advantage of their new opportunities to move to the suburbs.

Most of these activities were paid for with federal money, so when those funds started to dry up in the 1980s, it was probably inevitable that the programs would shrink and, in some cases, disappear entirely. But the change was not just about numbers. If one could argue that in the sixties and seventies at least some urban mayors like New York's John Lindsay or Cleveland's Dennis Kucinich saw providing social services and ameliorating poverty as their principal responsibility, that mission now became increasingly peripheral to that of rebuilding the city's economy—or, to put it more skeptically, doing things that they hoped, often without particular reason, might help their cities regain some of their lost vitality and luster.

Powerful voices from the academic world argued strongly that cities had no alternative. In 1956, economist Charles Tiebout published a famous paper setting forth what has come to be known as the "Tiebout Model." People are mobile, Tiebout wrote, and they "vote with their feet" by picking the city or town that, as he put it, "best satisfies [their] preference pattern for public goods"; that is, they pick places to live that, from their perspective, offer the best mix of taxes, services, and other amenities. Every community is competing with other communities for the most desirable residents and businesses.[3]

In his book *City Limits*, perhaps the most influential book on urban economics of the 1980s, University of Chicago economist Paul Peterson built on Tiebout's model to offer a prescription for urban policy makers. Beginning with the proposition that "policies and programs can be said to be in the interest of cities whenever the policies or programs maintain or enhance the economic position, social prestige, or political power of the city, taken as a whole,"[4] Peterson adds that cities not only have limited powers with which to further their interests, but, as Tiebout asserted, they are constantly in competition with one another for highly mobile businesses and capital. Thus, Peterson argued that the policies that they should pursue are "limited to those few which can plausibly be shown to be conductive to the community's economic prosperity."[5] For Peterson, it was clearly necessary that cities avoid redistributional strategies that, although they may benefit the poor, worked against the city's overriding interests.

Peterson's thesis gave an economic twist to an argument made by a sociologist only a few years earlier. In what has become one of the most widely read scholarly papers ever written about American cities, University of California, Santa Barbara, professor Harvey Molotch described the city as a "growth machine." He argued that the political and economic essence of virtually any given locality, in the present American context, is growth. [...] The desire for growth provides the key operative motivation toward consensus for members of politically mobilized local elites, however split they might be on other issues, and . . . a common interest in growth is the overriding commonality among important people in a given locale. [...] Further, this growth imperative is the most important constraint upon available options for local initiative in social and economic reform.[6]

Whether or not these arguments hold water, since the 1980s cities have behaved as if they did, focusing on growth and economic development to the exclusion of almost anything else. Indeed, a lot of their behavior can be described as a sustained and sometimes desperate search for the magic bullet that would unlock their hidden economic potential. While this search has taken many forms, some more productive than others, it was perhaps most visible—and most painfully wasteful—in the spate of arena and stadium construction that swept over American cities beginning in the 1980s, culminating in the 1990s and early 2000s. According to Adam Zaretsky of the St. Louis Federal Reserve Bank, "Between 1987 and 1999, fifty-five stadiums and arenas were refurbished or built in the United States at a cost of more than $8.7 billion. [...] Of the $8.7 billion in direct costs, about 57 percent—around $5 billion—was financed with taxpayer money."[7]

Cleveland is a poster child for the stadium boom and for Harvey Molotch's "growth machine" thesis. During the nineties, the city built Jacobs (now Progressive) Field for the Indians baseball team, and Gund (now Quicken Loans) Arena for the Cavaliers basketball team in the Gateway District, and Browns (now FirstEnergy) Stadium for the Browns football team, which replaced the former Cleveland Browns, which had moved to Baltimore after the Baltimore Colts had decamped for Indianapolis, along the lakefront (fig. 10-1). The construction of these multimillion-dollar facilities was driven by a coalition of local business leaders who, in the words of researchers Kevin Delaney and Rick Eckstein, "tended to see stadium building as a way to spiff up the community's image, help corporations recruit top-flight personnel, and

Figure 10-1 What money can buy: Cleveland's baseball stadium and basketball arena. (Source: Google Earth)

(they hoped) provide some economic spin-off for their own corporations."[8] To get their way, they prevailed over substantial opposition from many local quarters, including civic and union circles.

These three stadiums, according to the League of Fans, a sports reform project founded by Ralph Nader, cost a total of $633 million, although some other sources place the figures much higher.[9] Of that, $441 million, or 70 percent, came from the public sector in the form of a complicated mix of city, county, and state taxes and revenues, including dedicated taxes on alcohol, tobacco, and parking. The city has also recently spent $30 million toward the renovation of the football stadium and is on the hook for an additional $70 million for renovations to the arena, although as of this writing that project is held up by litigation. By the time it is completed, Cleveland, Cuyahoga County, and the State of Ohio will have spent well over half a billion dollars, worth $800 million in 2017 dollars, on these three sports facilities.

While Cleveland now has three large, handsome facilities to point to as a source of civic pride, along with whatever intangible benefits it gets from such things as the presence of LeBron James, the Cavaliers' 2016 NBA title, and the Indians' 2016 American League pennant, it is hard to see that the city has gained much more. Certainly, walking around the

Gateway District, few spin-offs are visible other than the Victory Alley Sports Grille, the Brickstone Tavern, and a few parking lots. As Delaney and Eckstein sum up the stadium boom: "When urban governments finance new stadiums, they are really spending hundreds of millions of dollars to entertain suburbanites."[10]

Stadiums are the most blatant example of mindless municipal action. Each one costs hundreds of millions of dollars; they generate few spin-offs (this is particularly true of football stadiums, which are vacant all but a handful of days in the year); and they almost always take up public money that could have been spent on more-productive activities. But they are actually only a small part of the dollars being spent. States, counties, and cities spend untold billions on tax incentives for companies to move into cities, or for people to build shopping centers, office buildings, and upscale housing developments.

Some of these programs are in fact productive, but many are not. New Jersey's Grow NJ program, which since 2013 has funneled $1.2 billion dollars in tax incentives to companies willing to relocate to Camden, is a good example of the latter. There is no question that Camden needs help—it is one of the most distressed cities in America—but what the city and its people get from these vast expenditures is less clear. The state has given tax incentives to companies to move their offices and their workers from space in nearby suburbs, along with vague promises that those companies will create a modest number of additional jobs in the future.

The cost of the state incentives, taken over a ten-year period, average nearly $400,000 per job. Since almost all the jobs were already located in nearby suburbs, it's a safe bet that the same workers will simply shift their commute to their new worksite in Camden, and few new jobs will open up. The likelihood of future jobs being added is uncertain, and most will probably not end up going to Camden residents, who currently hold fewer than one out of five of the jobs in their own city, in any case.[11]

Not all tax breaks are as patently wasteful as New Jersey's. In 2000, the city of Philadelphia decided to waive all property-tax payments, a practice known as tax abatement, on the entire value of new residential developments other than the underlying land value for ten years. By 2013, over 10,000 new units and 5,000 converted or improved units had been created under the program, which was widely credited with having jump-started the housing market in and around Center City Philadelphia.[12]

In retrospect, it seems that in Philadelphia—more probably by luck than by design—the value of the tax abatement closely matched developers' "cost gap," or the difference between what it cost them to develop a project and what people were willing to pay to buy or rent the houses or apartments they built. As a result, the tax abatement suddenly made it profitable to build upscale housing in Center City, and developers flocked to the area, buying vacant office buildings and empty lots and converting them into apartments. Philadelphia can legitimately claim some credit for spurring a building boom that not only has brought thousands of mostly upscale residents into the city with their hefty buying power, but—in the long run, as the abatements expire—will add billions of dollars of real estate value to the city's tax rolls.

Two points follow from the above discussion, one minor and relatively obvious, the second more important but less obvious. The minor, obvious point is that much of what cities, counties, and states do in the name of fostering economic development is short-sighted, wasteful, and, indeed, arguably stupid. The less obvious but more substantial point is that over the past decades, whether stupid or sensible, state and local governments have been willing to spend or forgo untold billions of dollars in the pursuit of economic development, with little serious accounting of costs and benefits, of who benefits and who does not, or of other ways the same money might possibly have been used in ways that might have led to more-productive outcomes and a more equitable distribution of benefits around the city. Philadelphia is still giving new Center City projects the same generous tax abatement, even though sales prices in the area have more than doubled since 2000.

Moreover, states and cities were spending *their own* money, not, as with the few crumbs still going into lower-income neighborhoods, only what little federal money was still flowing from Washington. The rationale, of course, was that this money was leveraging private investment or enhancing the city's competitive position vis-à-vis its peers, and that it would return economic benefits to the city. Sometimes that happened, but the reality was that most decisions were made with little or no idea about whether that was true, or even plausible.

While one could argue that many of the policies of the sixties and seventies were not sensitive enough to the importance of the market in driving the cities' future, subsequent policies often moved too far in the opposite direction. Cities saw themselves as being passive subjects of market forces they barely understood. The actions they took as a result bear an uncanny resemblance to the famous Melanesian cargo cults, organized by tribesmen who believed that "that various ritualistic acts such as the building of an airplane runway [would] result in the appearance of material wealth, particularly highly desirable Western goods; that is, 'cargo,' on Western airplanes."[13] Just as the airplanes never showed up, neither do, in many cases, the benefits to urban residents. Why do cities do it, then?

A common thread runs through all of these activities. Whether or not the cities and their residents benefit, the corporate and business community does. Giving Subaru a hefty subsidy to build a new headquarters in a gated complex in Camden may or may not benefit Camden's people, but it certainly benefits Subaru's bottom line. Cleveland's stadiums may not have had much effect on the city's economic position, but from the perspective of the corporations that pushed to made them happen, they were important for what Peterson called the city's "social prestige"—or their own corporate status.

Where cities decide to put their time and energy, and above all, their money, is not only a matter of the widely shared desire for economic prosperity, but of how power is distributed in the city—that is, who pulls the strings and calls the shots. It is common to think of the mayor as the person who sets the city's direction, who moves it forward in the direction she sets, but the reality is far more complicated. For all the reams of paper written on mayoral leadership, the mayor of the American industrial city is far more constrained in her ability to define and carry out an agenda of change than might seem apparent from her visibility in the local media. Whatever levers of power a mayor can apply are constrained by a complex network of competing and sometimes overshadowing power centers.

While the precise contours of power within cities have been debated by political scientists for decades, all agree that the big decisions that go beyond the routine maintenance tasks of local government require some involvement by people outside government, what scholar Clarence Stone, founder of urban regime theory, calls a "governing coalition." As Stone writes, "the act of governance requires the cooperation of private actors and the mobilization of private resources." Stone stresses that "instead of the power to govern being something that can be captured by an electoral victory, it is something created by bringing cooperating actors together, not as equal claimants, but often as unequal contributors to a shared set of purposes."[14]

There are many players in the urban arena, but they are not equal. As the late Norwegian scholar Stein Rokkan summed it up, "Votes count, but resources decide."[15] While many different types of resources exist in the urban ecosystem that affect the governance process—technical expertise, leadership capacity, and organizational strength, to name just three—the sheer weight of material resources held by the city's major business and corporate interests tends to swamp all the others. The result is not only an urban agenda driven by economic development, but one that prioritizes the particular version of economic development that is most appealing to those interests oriented to large building projects and corporate subsidies. Stone calls them "development regimes."

There are a lot of reasons for this, beginning with the true but simplistic proposition that "money talks." Not only do mayors need the support of the local corporate, business, and financial sectors to pursue their agendas, but those sectors have the resources to promote their own agendas as well as to buy off other parts of the governing coalition. A handful of summer jobs, down-payment assistance programs, and operating grants to nonprofit community-development corporations are a small price to pay to neutralize potential opposition to the corporate agenda from the city's less well-endowed communities.

Furthermore, development strategies, which are basically about building things, whether stadiums, housing developments, or corporate offices, are both *easier* and *more visible* than fostering more fundamental economic growth or improvement. They are easier because they are clearly and narrowly defined, particularly compared to the daunting complexities of changing educational systems, integrating neighborhoods, or moving high school dropouts or ex-offenders into the workforce. They are easily defined as technical problems (how many stories, how many parking spaces) or financial ones (how much will it cost, how much can be borrowed) rather than matters involving complex human behaviors and relationships, or which demand serious consideration of ends and means, or costs and benefits. They require no more than passive acquiescence from anyone outside the small elite governmental and business circles directly involved. That acquiescence can usually be bought cheaply.

Development projects do not happen overnight, but they usually do happen within a few years. They provide direct, visible gratification to all those involved. They offer photo ops when ground is broken, when the structure is topped off, and when the ribbon is finally cut, as well as the opportunity for mayors and corporate executives to come together and watch their city's team from the luxury of the new skyboxes. These gratifications may seem trivial, but they matter.

By contrast, a governance regime that focused, in Stone's term, on "lower-class opportunity expansion," would be far more difficult to maintain and offer far less visible gratification to its members. As Stone points out, in the United States such regimes "are largely hypothetical."[16] Not only would such a regime require the close coordination and engagement of literally hundreds of different actors, from community organizations to social service providers and school districts, it would require radically different ways of thinking and working together from actors who have typically found it far more comfortable to stay within their silos, pursuing narrow organizational goals.

It would require even more radical change on the part of the corporate and business elite. While many in that elite probably see expanding opportunity for their city's low-income residents as a *desirable* goal, it is doubtful that many see it as an *important* goal, or as a priority for the expenditure of their time, energy, and resources. What *is* important to elite institutions like Key Bank in Cleveland or Johns Hopkins University in Baltimore is that the conditions for their continued successful operation be maintained, and that their massive corporate investment be secure. The best recipe for that is a development regime, coupled with such modest gestures—along with, perhaps, an effective policing system of social control—as are needed to keep the peace and keep the challenges of concentrated poverty from their doorsteps.

Ironically, an opportunity regime would probably cost much less than the typical development regime. Let's try a thought experiment. There are roughly 3,100 unemployed residents of Camden, New Jersey, between the ages of sixteen and thirty-four. Let's assume it would cost $10,000 per unemployed resident in services and support, *over and above funds already being spent on education, job training, and the like*, to enable each one to move into reasonably paid, stable employment. That adds up to $31 million dollars. Since 2013, though, the state of New Jersey has set aside $120 million each year for the next ten years in tax incentives to get companies to move into Camden, without, in all likelihood, improving the lives of even one of those 3,100 unemployed young men and women. For one-quarter of one year's tax expenditures, the state could transform the lives of thousands of city residents.

It is, of course, not just a matter of money. If the state decided to switch gears tomorrow and provide that money, it's not clear that there are people and organizations in Camden today who are fully ready to take the money and use it effectively. But that's a soluble, technical problem.

This raises a critical question. When Paul Peterson wrote *City Limits*, his intentions were not simply descriptive, but prescriptive; at the depths of the postwar urban crisis, he was laying out a series of dos and don'ts for urban areas looking to rebuild their economies and regain lost prosperity. In a nutshell, that prescription can be summed up as "focus on economic growth, make yourself attractive to highly mobile corporate capital, and avoid anything that smacks of redistribution."

Things have changed dramatically since 1981, and cities are seeing unprecedented revival. New York, Boston, and Washington, DC, have become the nation's most vibrant, dynamic centers of energy and activity. Baltimore, Philadelphia, and Pittsburgh have, in more modest fashion, seen major revival, although still mixed with continued decline and concentrated poverty. Even cities like Cleveland and Detroit, although perhaps still losing ground overall, show pockets of growing prosperity. Thus, looking back, the question arises: was Peterson right? Can one in fact associate this remarkable revival with what one might call the "Peterson Prescription" of private-sector-driven growth for economic revival—or for that matter, with any specific city government economic policies?

The short answer is no. University of Virginia law professor Richard Schragger, in his brilliant 2016 book *City Power*, writes that "the urban resurgence of the last few decades . . . does not seem to have been caused by any particular urban policies, and certainly not the ones that a competitive model of city growth and decline would favor. And yet popular efforts in economic development continue to revolve around competing for jobs. [. . .] Unsurprisingly, this approach has had little success over time." "Cities should not have a local development policy," he argues. "The urban resurgence does not provide evidence that such a policy works—indeed, that any particular policy works—whatever its parameters. Abandoning local economic-development policies is almost politically impossible for local leaders. But it is the right thing to do."[17]

I agree with Schragger's diagnosis, but not completely with his conclusion. Cities are not *only* economic entities, to be sure, but the vitality of their economy, and their export economy in particular, plays a powerful role not only in their continued ability to attract and retain a diverse population but also in their ability to expand opportunity for their lower-income residents. Cities need to walk and chew gum at the same time if they are to sustain their revival while steadily expanding the reach of revival to those sharing none of its benefits. Local economic-development policies are needed, but they have to be the right ones. They need to be policies that increase opportunity for those now largely left out, building a skilled workforce and the solid underpinnings of sustainable prosperity while creating a model of urban revival that is far more equitable and inclusive than what we are seeing in America's cities today.

I stress *local* policy, because if there's any lesson to be learned from the way power works, it is that change will only happen if the people who make local decisions want it to happen, or can be persuaded to let it happen. It is true, of course, that they operate within the constraints of national and global forces, yet in the end it is up to them, not the federal government or anyone else.

The era when the federal government could drive change, as it did with the civil rights laws of the 1960s, is long past. Even then, while the federal government could drive legal change, social and economic change was a different matter; as the late political scientist Norton Long, a clearheaded observer of the urban scene, wrote in 1977 at the high point of federal urban policy, "The federal government has generated harmfully unrealistic expectations, without recognizing its inability to fulfill them."[18] While the federal government has reduced its own expectations since then, thousands of advocates continue to believe against all evidence that it is capable of realizing their dreams.

It is not that federal action doesn't matter; on the contrary, it matters greatly. Only the federal government has the resources, for example, to provide the housing subsidies that might allow poor families to escape debilitating shelter hardship and insecurity, as it has done for food security with the SNAP program or for health care with Medicaid. The federal government can be a powerful ally to those fighting for change locally by setting standards or ground rules for local action, as the Obama Administration did by making state and local housing agencies take fair housing seriously; or it can be an equally powerful adversary, as is largely true today. It cannot, though, *be* the change. Change will not happen at the federal level; if change happens, it will happen bit by bit, city by city, metro by metro.

This may strike the reader as either dispiriting or empowering, but reflects a powerful reality. Inclusion and integration are affected by national and global economic forces, but within the limits set by those forces, inclusion and integration are driven by the choices and priorities of the local power coalitions in each city and metropolitan area. The decision to spend nearly half a billion dollars of public money to build two stadiums and an arena in Cleveland was not dictated from Washington, London, or Zurich; it was the product of powerful local players who decided not only that it was important for Cleveland to have those stadiums, but that it was important enough for them to use their power to make it happen, and who had the power to get government to use money on it that government could have used elsewhere.

The fallacy in the thinking of those who believe that massive federal programs, like that long-advocated and equally long-derided "Federal Marshall Plan for the Cities," are the solution is the belief that money equals progress. All money equals is money. It is worth reminding ourselves periodically that the closest thing this country has ever seen to a Marshall Plan for the cities, in terms of either magnitude or deliberate transformative intent, was the urban renewal program, and we know what happened there. Leaving aside direct programs of redistribution such as the Earned Income Tax Credit or an increase to the minimum wage, which translate directly into more money in the pockets of people who desperately need it, money that flows down to the cities will be used in the ways that the city's power coalition wants to use it.

When the State of New Jersey took over running the city of Camden in 2002, the legislature appropriated $175 million toward the city's economic recovery. Seven years later, as the state was giving control of the city back to its residents, *Philadelphia Inquirer* reporter Matt Katz issued a postmortem on the program. "Nearly $100 million of the $170 million spent so far went to construction projects for large institutions, like a law school and an aquarium. And much of the construction work was handled by contractors and labor unions that contribute to the authors of the takeover law, the Camden County Democrats," he found, adding that "less than 5 percent of the $175 million recovery package was spent on the things residents care about most: crime, city schools, job training, and municipal services."[19] By 2009, Camden's residents were both poorer and more likely to be unemployed than seven years before.

Any real movement in any city toward greater inclusion and equity requires moving the agenda of the city's power coalition in that direction. This is not impossible. Power coalitions pursue what their members see as their interests—and they do so sometimes strategically, but often in a more ad hoc, tactical fashion. Power coalitions are not monolithic, nor do they necessarily have coherent, clearly defined agendas. Their agendas shift, as their membership shifts, as they see their interests shifting, and as fashions in economic development and urban planning shift. The interests of today's power coalition in Pittsburgh, dominated by eds and meds players like the University of Pittsburgh Medical Center and Carnegie Mellon University and increasingly involving emerging high-technology firms and young entrepreneurs, are very different from and far more fluid than those of fifty years ago, when steelmakers like US Steel and Jones & Laughlin ruled the roost. In many cities foundations have more influence than ever before. After Mayor Duggan and billionaire Dan Gilbert, Rip Rapson, president of the Kresge Foundation, is probably the most important power player in Detroit today.

While it is important not to look at this through rose-colored glasses, it suggests at least some room for change in the system. The relationship between the cities—as people, as places, and as governments—and today's powerful institutions is very different from what it was thirty or forty years ago. Back then, urban universities like the University of Pennsylvania or Carnegie Mellon might well have seen themselves as unhappily stuck in their respective cities, hunkering down to protect their turf against the encroachment of at best indifferent, and at worst hostile forces. Today, being in those same cities has become an asset. In a remarkable reversal, suburban and small-town universities across the country are spending hundreds of millions of dollars building walkable entertainment, shopping, and residential districts designed to imbue the environs of their campuses with an "urban" aura in order to better compete for students and faculty with big-city institutions.

Institutions see their futures as interwoven with their cities in ways that go well beyond their immediate precincts. Yale has spent some $30 million since 1994 helping over 1,000 of its employees buy houses in New Haven's neighborhoods, and largely single-handedly foots the bill for the New Haven Promise, enabling over 1,000 graduates of New Haven's public schools to afford a college education. Their motives for spending this money, which is admittedly a *very* small part of their $3.3 billion annual budget, are many. There is self-interest involved, as the homeownership program helps build a more stable workforce, as well as a certain amount of noblesse oblige as the largest, wealthiest player around, but it also includes a recognition that Yale shares its destiny with a New Haven that stretches beyond the downtown and the city's elite neighborhoods.

Yale's position in New Haven is unusual, in that few cities are so totally dominated by a single institution. UPMC may be the biggest dog in Pittsburgh and Johns Hopkins the biggest in Baltimore, but in both cities they are not alone but the largest of many partners, and they cannot unilaterally set the agenda. The interests of the many coalition members in a Baltimore or Pittsburgh are likely to be different, if not outright conflicting, and all these interests must be navigated if enough support is to cohere around a serious plan for an inclusive city. The fact remains that, in a city like Baltimore or Pittsburgh, there are people one can talk to—and organizations that represent their interests—who can bring to bear significant resources that can be tapped to promote change. The picture is very different and far more problematic, in both respects, in many smaller places, where the resources are so much more limited and the potential partners far fewer.

What compounds the challenge of moving the power coalition is that the individuals and organizations who should be the logical advocates for inclusion are themselves often disorganized and working at cross-purposes. Rather than forming a cohesive movement with a clear agenda for change, those fighting poverty and trying to alleviate neighborhood distress in a typical city are more likely to be rivals controlling distinct fiefdoms, competing for resources and jealously guarding their territories. While the sum of their resources and potential influence may not compare with a Johns Hopkins or UPMC, it is not negligible, particularly when they can work in tandem with a supportive local government; it is consistently vitiated, however, by lack of cohesion and by the absence of a shared strategy or goals. That means, in turn, that local governments, community organizations, and advocates are often easily bought off with crumbs—a summer jobs program or a few city-owned houses to fix up and resell—rather than seen as credible interlocutors.

Furthermore, few strategies promoted by those who advocate for low-income communities and low-income people are transformative in any meaningful sense. Putting money into a grab bag of activities in a distressed concentrated-poverty area, as we saw in Baltimore's Sandtown-Winchester, may improve conditions for a few people for a while, but is unlikely to change the neighborhood's condition or trajectory, or alter the desperate struggle for survival most people in those neighborhoods face. For all the plethora of neighborhood plans and multiyear strategies, few organizations think past the next year, the next project, or the next state or federal grant.

What do I mean by transformative? It starts with a simple premise that I first stated in the previous chapter. Nearly all people, whether rich, poor, or middle-class, want to live satisfying, productive lives. Clearly, if you are wealthy, or even well-to-do, it comes more easily. You have far more choices in terms of how to live such a life, what to do with your time, or where to live. But if you are struggling, it most often comes down to two basic things. First, having a job that pays enough so that you can keep your head financially above water, and that potentially offers a reasonable measure of both security and psychic reward; and second, having a safe and healthy home you can afford in a decent neighborhood. Ideally, it should be in a neighborhood where poorer and more affluent people live together and share the benefits of prosperity. Even where it is not, it should be safe and offer a decent if not lavish quality of life. From the perspective of Abraham Maslow's famous hierarchy of needs, the first three are most fundamental—the physiological needs of adequate food and shelter; the safety needs of physical safety, health, and financial security; and the emotional need for belonging, in terms of family, friendships, and intimacy.[20]

Transformative strategies, then, are strategies that help the greatest number of people now living in poverty or neighborhood distress get from their present condition to where they can live satisfying, productive lives with a decent standard of living; strategies that help the greatest number of distressed places get to a point where they provide a decent environment for people to live such lives; and strategies that do so in ways that reduce the magnitude of the city's racial, economic, and geographic gaps. To paraphrase the famous saying of the ancient Jewish sage Rabbi Hillel, all the rest is commentary.[21]

How is this different from what we are doing now? Put so broadly, almost anyone doing almost anything could argue that their work fits the above description. The question that needs to be asked, however, is whether what they are doing is leading to sustained change, and whether it is taking place on a meaningful scale. What happens to the young people in the summer jobs program, or to the neighborhood after the new Low-Income Tax Credit housing project down the block opens its doors? Such questions can be asked about almost any urban initiative today. Some efforts may indeed lead to long-term change for a few people, or for a small area, but at a scale so small that their effects are lost amid the continued downward pressures exerted by the larger system. Most, though, are a sort of social Tylenol, likely to bring only transitory relief; or worse, they are wasted effort.

Transformative strategies are not simple, but, as I've suggested in earlier chapters, we know quite a bit about what they are, and how to make them work. The challenge is, first, reaching agreement around what should be done in a particular city or region; second, building a broad coalition around a finite number of transformative strategies, and the roles that each agency or organization should play; and third, gaining the broader support of the city's power coalition to make them happen.

Local efforts should never be seen as alternatives to sustained, determined efforts to change state and federal policy. Not only are many critical steps, such as increasing housing subsidies for poor renters, only possible at the federal level, but many of the ground rules that determine what can be done locally are set by the federal government and, sometimes even more so, by the states. In recent years, indeed, as cities here and there have made efforts to address local inequities by raising the minimum wage or establishing local hiring standards, Republican-dominated state legislatures have increasingly blocked their efforts, as the Missouri legislature did to St. Louis's minimum-wage law. When the rollback went into effect in August 2017, the minimum wage in the city automatically fell back from \$10/hour to the state level of \$7.70/hour. Between January 2016 and July 2017 alone, fifteen states passed laws "pre-empting" local laws dealing with minimum wage or other worker rights or benefits, as the United States Constitution allows them to do.[22]

Before moving on to the task of trying to lay out what a transformative approach to inclusion and equity might actually look like, it's important to recognize that different places offer wildly different preconditions for change. What may work in Baltimore or Pittsburgh may work less well in Youngstown, Ohio, and not at all in Aliquippa, Pennsylvania. True, Baltimore and Pittsburgh have huge problems. Along with their problems, though, both have local economies sustained by globally competitive institutions that are growing jobs at a respectable rate; an influx of educated, talented young people creating economic activity, raising property values and municipal revenues; relatively high local government capacity to manage programs and strategies; and sophisticated corporate and foundation sectors.

Finally, no matter how appropriate a strategy may be in today's conditions, it's important to remember that things change, and one can never predict exactly how and when. The biggest question mark about any strategy that focuses on jobs as a central theme is that the world of work is constantly changing, as shifting economic pressures and emerging technological advances eliminate some jobs while creating others, but not necessarily in the same places or for people with the same skills or education. This has been going on for centuries, but recent developments in automation and robotics, not to mention the vast implications of climate change, have raised it anew; as economist Sendhil Mullainathan puts it, "Prepare for change by expecting the unimagined."[23] He's right, even though *how* to imagine the unimagined is a task better suited to seers than administrators or city planners.

We will look at that question, too, in the next chapter. But the history of change reminds us to be cautious in our predictions, and to be mindful of the many uncertainties lurking behind every prescription. Uncertainty works against people with less income, fewer skills, and less formal education. More highly educated, more-affluent people are more mobile and better able to adapt to change, grafting new skill sets onto existing ones. How to create a system in which change, rather than further depressing opportunities, increases them is a daunting challenge.

In the end, though, there is no magic bullet. It still comes down to figuring out what to do, and then digging in for the slow, difficult slog to make it happen, city by city or region by region.

Chapter 11

A Path to Inclusion and Opportunity

I f I did not believe it were possible to change the seemingly inexorable trajectory of America's cities toward a future of increased segregation, polarization, and exclusion, I would not have written this
book. I believe it *is* possible, and that in some respects it may be easier
than some people may believe, but in other respects even more difficult.
Before explaining that, though, I should begin by explaining my own
thinking, and how I look at the question of change.

Everyone who writes about changing the system—and there are a lot
of us—brings a particular perspective to the question of change. Those
perspectives tend to fall along a spectrum, which can be seen as running
from incrementalist at one end to utopian at the other. The incrementalist believes that small steps and individual efforts like the first President
Bush's "thousand points of light" gradually bring about change. The utopian believes that nothing short of a fundamental reordering of society
and the economy will lead to meaningful change, and that anything
short of that is wasted effort.

Neither end of the spectrum is particularly credible. We have had
and still have many thousands of points of light, many projects and
ventures that have shown human creativity and energy at their best, and

yet the underlying patterns of inequality and segregation seem only to get worse. The points of light turn out to be fireflies, glimmering for a moment and going out.

Utopian thinking may be worse. Incrementalists for the most part do no harm. Utopians do, or would if they could. Over and above the disastrous failure rate of those utopias that have actually been tried, the utopian mindset has been well characterized by organizer and blogger Jonathan Matthew Smucker. "Why . . . bother to strategize about overcoming the particular obstacles that block our way today," he writes,

> if we believe that the accumulation of all obstacles will ultimately add up to a grand crisis that will somehow magically usher in a new era? Believing that things will "have to get worse before they get better," we may become disinterested in—perhaps even sabotaging of—efforts to improve real-life conditions in the here and now. After all, why put a band-aid on a gaping wound?[1]

I have little tolerance with the line of argument that holds that all efforts are in vain as long as the underlying economic or political system falls short of the ideal. Representative democracy and the capitalist economic system, for better or for worse, are the two conjoined frameworks that have defined the reality of American life for well over a century and are likely to do so for the next century as well, assuming Western civilization survives. Moreover, should they be replaced by anything fundamentally different, whatever that is will probably be much worse. Finally, although I share many people's belief that many things about American society need fundamental change, including the racism that remains so resistant to change, I see radical change as being at best a distant prospect. I do not believe that we should forgo the opportunities that exist to change the lives of people and their communities in important ways, even while injustice and racism may continue to exist, in the interest of a far-off and most probably illusory better society. That posture is a luxury of the affluent that the poor cannot afford.

Progress will require a different way of thinking about the challenge than either incrementalism or utopianism offers. That way of thinking is not, as some people have suggested, one of coming up with a laundry list of programs—mostly involving huge sums of money—that seem to bear some relationship, however tangential, to the challenges of inclusion and equity. True, such approaches are neither incrementalist nor utopian, in the literal sense, but they tend to share the fantasy of an all-powerful federal government, mix the valuable with the trivial, and above all, beg the question, How do we get there? These issues have far too many moving parts for anyone to be able to lay out a detailed road map, but it is important to offer at least some idea of what a plausible strategy might look like.

We need a way of thinking that is pragmatic, focused on concrete results, rather than driven by symbolism and self-expression, however powerful and deeply felt; one that accepts the reality of the existing American political and economic framework, while working to bring about change within that system, rather than pining for a socialist or anarchist utopia. Symbolism is important, but it needs to be subordinated to substance, rather than seen as an end in itself.

We need to ask two questions, and be rigorous about our answers. First, given the vast array of things we *can* do, at least in theory, which of them are most likely to do the most to foster inclusion and reduce inequity? Second, how can we pursue those activities in ways most likely to achieve our goals, and realize our vision? I think of this as a sort of focused, visionary pragmatism.

We must be visionary about our goals, but must also be realistic about what we can and cannot achieve. We can reduce poverty, but we cannot end it. We can reduce economic and racial segregation, and poverty concentration, but we cannot and should not try to make every neighborhood into a demographic and economic mirror image of every other one. We can improve distressed neighborhoods to the point where they become decent, safe places to live, but we cannot make every neighborhood into a vibrant model community. Finally, and most painfully, we may not be able to restore every distressed city, town, or neighborhood to health and vitality. That does not mean, though, that we can ignore the plight of the people in those communities.

Turning back to where I began this chapter, what do I mean that change may be both easier and more difficult than some may believe?

It is an *easier* task, because while it would cost money, it would not be as expensive as may be widely believed. We already spend hundreds of billions of dollars on education, from pre-K through college; on job training and workforce-readiness programs. We can accomplish far more with that money, if we spend it more wisely. We also waste billions on zero-sum and unproductive economic development, with little impact on overall well-being. That should end, and those dollars should be used productively. Some of the multibillion-dollar "solutions" that have been proposed, such as massive investment in public transit and high-speed rail, while they may add value to the economy as a whole, would have little or no effect on the problems of poverty and inequality. More vans and buses serving more places and running more often, although far less glamorous, would probably make more difference at a modest fraction of the cost. Some critical pieces of the solution would cost money, to be sure, but not at levels that would seriously challenge the capacity of either the economy or the federal budget. We could probably pay for most of them simply by forgoing the beggar-thy-neighbor economic incentives we currently spend billions on.

It is a *harder* task, though, because it demands something more difficult than writing a check, which is why in the end "laundry list" proposals are largely pointless. It requires changing ways of thinking, and changing the ways in which power is exercised not only in American society generally, but separately in each one of the hundreds of individual cities and regions that make up our country. We need to change federal policy, to be sure—a task that is particularly challenging at a time where the current administration seems determined to reverse even the modest steps taken by its predecessor to challenge inequality—but that is only one small part of the picture.

Trying to frame an agenda that can truly address the complex, multidimensional body of challenges that have been outlined in the preceding chapters is a daunting task. The challenge itself seems particularly slippery. It is about poverty, which is about people, but it is also about the concentration of poverty, which is about place. It is about addressing the needs of adults who are disconnected from the mainstream of the American society and economy, but it must recognize that disconnection is part of a process that began long before, in childhood, perhaps even infancy; thus any solution must tackle the needs of children as well as adults. It is, as we must remind ourselves, not just about poverty but about opportunity, which inevitably raises questions about the way in which the larger society and economy work. It is a local issue, yet so much of what can be done locally hinges on national policy and the role the federal government plays.

At the same time, in our desire to reduce poverty and inequality, we must be careful not to act in ways that may choke off the nascent revival of America's older cities. That revival is real, yet its future course remains uncertain and its continuation should not be taken for granted. A respected demographer has raised the question of whether the United States has reached what he calls "peak millennial,"[2] while the future of the American health care system and the millions of jobs it generates is heatedly contested. Unless cities like Pittsburgh and Detroit can sustain their revival—fairly solid in Pittsburgh, embryonic in Detroit—and continue to grow jobs and wealth, there will be far fewer opportunities for those who have not shared in its benefits up to now.

Thus, any serious proposal for addressing the challenge must be at least as multidimensional as the challenge itself. Following the logic of the last chapter, I will look at the question through a local lens—not only in terms of the central city by itself, but also the surrounding region— with respect first to people, and then to place, while trying to weave into that some ideas of what should happen nationally as well to bring about the change we need, not in one or two progressive outliers, but across cities and regions. While I recognize that there are many more issues that could and should be addressed, the magnitude and complexity of the full range of challenges and the solutions needed to surmount them go far beyond what I can cover in these pages. I have tried to concentrate on what I consider the two most important dimensions of social equity: first, that all people should have the opportunity to move out of poverty and earn a decent living; and second, that it is time to redeem the 1949 pledge of a "decent home and a suitable living environment for every American family."[3]

If we could bring about the change we need to see in those two areas, I believe we would see many other things change not only in our older cities, but in our society as a whole. I am not so naïve as to believe that the endemic racism in American society would disappear if one reduced the manifest economic imbalance between white and black people and the extent to which our communities are racially segregated, but there is little doubt that racism, economic inequity, and segregation all feed on one another in a host of ways large and small. While we must continue to challenge racism as such, we must also work directly to overcome economic and spatial inequity by building systems of opportunity for all.

Jobs Are Job One

If we are even remotely serious about creating opportunity for the large numbers of people who are stuck in poverty or near-poverty, we have to think in terms of jobs. Jobs, to paraphrase the old Ford slogan, are job one. There's a certain appeal to the idea of encouraging people to start businesses, which resonates with the self-image of America as a nation of entrepreneurs, but the idea is more attractive than the reality. Small-business programs are inherently limited in terms of how many people can benefit and how sustainable the businesses are, particularly in impoverished inner-city areas where people's disposable income is far too modest to sustain more than a handful of local businesses. The evidence suggests that most minority businesses generate few jobs, and that the greater part do not even provide a decent living for their owners significantly above the poverty level. While programs to encourage small-business success are important—especially if they're focused on helping viable small businesses grow rather than on supporting start-ups—such programs will never be more than a small part of the total picture.

But the jobs are there, at least in cities like Baltimore and Pittsburgh. Let's do another thought experiment. In 2015, there were roughly 30,000 unemployed people aged sixteen to sixty-four in the city of Baltimore. There were also about 325,000 jobs in the city, growing by about 2,000 per year. If jobs in Baltimore turn over at the national rate of 15 percent per year, that means that every year, between turnover and new jobs, there are 50,000 job openings in the city. One-third of the jobs in Baltimore are held by college graduates, leaving two-thirds filled by people with less formal education. What that means is that every year, 33,000 jobs *that do not require a college degree* open up in the city of Baltimore.

At one level, this comparison is not particularly meaningful. One can't simply line up the number of jobs and the number of unemployed people and draw any conclusions about how to fill those jobs. But the point here is that in Baltimore, it's less about *creating* jobs than it's about *connecting* people to them. Making those connections, though, is about far more than providing individuals with the training in the specific skills particular jobs require. What are needed are integrated workforce systems. *An integrated workforce system is one which combines skill training with all the other pieces needed to prepare an individual for sustained, successful employment and mobility, all taking place through partnerships with the firms and institutions which have the jobs to be filled.*

Such systems would operate as in figure 11-1, connecting job training to personal empowerment, education, removal of legal barriers, family support, coaching, and improved transportation access, all taking place

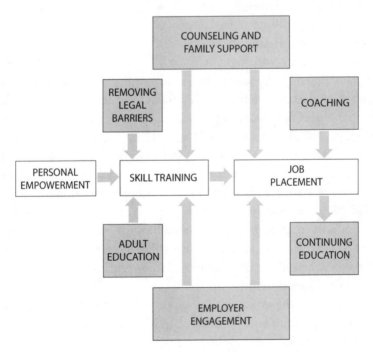

Figure 11-1 How a model integrated workforce system could work.

through close partnerships with prospective employers. All of the pieces are needed, because each one separately addresses a potential barrier or disability that can render the rest meaningless.

As important as integrating the support system into the training process is building the city's employers into the process. Ultimately, a workforce program will only succeed if it can produce workers who meet employers' needs and if the employers have high confidence that it can—and will continue to—do so. 1B4J as well as other successful programs like Twin Cities RISE! have built close relationships with employers in their communities. The more employers are engaged in designing the programs, and the more closely they will stay involved with them and the more likely they will hire their graduates on a regular, ongoing basis.

One or more organizations exist in every major city in the United States corresponding to every one of the pieces needed for an integrated workforce system, although they may need to expand their services or capability, not to mention learn how to work together as part of a team. The cost of expanding their services, as well as the cost of the management and information systems needed to keep all of the moving parts together, is surprisingly manageable. Jason Perkins-Cohen, who designed the 1B4J program in Baltimore, estimates that for each person trained and placed, it would cost only about $4,000 to $5,000 more than what people are now spending to provide those services; Tom Streitz of Twin Cities RISE! thinks it would be more, perhaps around $9,000 per person. Taking the higher number, and assuming you wanted to train and place 5,000 of Baltimore's unemployed in stable employment each year, it would cost an additional $45 million a year. That amount—which would go down sharply after a few years, once significant inroads are made into the pool of long-term unemployed workers —is quite modest, particularly in comparison to what cities and states are spending on big-ticket construction projects and economic incentives with far more limited social or economic returns.

Moreover, as the evidence of programs like Safer shows, integrated training is an investment in the future. In Maryland, the cost to keep just one prisoner incarcerated for just one year is nearly $40,000.[4] Effective jobs programs will pay for themselves many times over in terms of reduced costs in incarceration, welfare payments, and social services, not to mention the additional tax revenues coming from now-employed workers.

In 2017 dollars, the state of Maryland spent $700 million during the 1990s to subsidize construction of stadiums for the Baltimore Orioles and Baltimore Ravens. If experience elsewhere is any guide, it won't be long before the city and state are approached with proposals to upgrade, expand, or replace both facilities. A $460,000 feasibility study was approved in December 2017 for a project to expand the city's convention center and building a new arena as well as a new convention hotel, projected to cost upward of $900 million.[5] Perhaps it is time to ask whether this should be Baltimore's highest priority.

One thing, though, that is hard if not impossible to do locally is to ensure that jobs offer a decent wage and decent working conditions. For that, concerted efforts are needed at the state and federal level to increase the minimum wage and level the playing field for low-wage service workers. How badly these efforts are needed is evidenced by the extent to which, as I mentioned in the last chapter, even as local organizing efforts have led cities to raise minimum-wage levels or provide worker benefits such as paid family or sick leave, hostile state legislatures have increasingly nullified their efforts. That points out a well-known but often overlooked fact: the United States is still a federal system, and the struggle for greater equity takes place as much if not more at the state as at the federal level.

Conversely, states can enhance local efforts through incentives. Every state offers a laundry list of tax incentives for things they consider desirable. The list often includes job training and job creation. While many of these incentives are generic, and treat all jobs created or people trained equally, others, like the Iowa tax credit for hiring ex-offenders, are aimed at populations in particular need of assistance. Any effort to build an equitable jobs strategy in any city or region needs to engage state government as an important partner, and must work to focus state incentives on the people with the greatest need.

Any jobs strategy, though, starts with a basic assumption—namely, that enough jobs are there and that there's a real opportunity to move large numbers of people into the workforce. That's a fair assumption in major cities like Baltimore or Philadelphia, or even Detroit or Cleveland.

It may also be true for smaller places like Aliquippa which, even though they may not be growing jobs locally, are close enough to stronger job centers to piggyback off their opportunities. We have to be realistic, though. There are many small cities and mill towns that have too few jobs, or where the jobs are disappearing, to make opportunity a reality for all those who might want to work. I will come back to that vexing question, and the tough choices it forces on us as a society, later.

Education and Opportunity

For most adults, it makes most sense to focus directly on jobs and training, building the education they need to fill gaps in basic reading or math skills into the framework of programs designed to lead to jobs, rather than treating these educational gaps separately. Cities must also build educational systems that lead to opportunity for the children now growing up in poverty, particularly those growing up in the inner-city ghetto areas where poverty is most intensely concentrated, to enable them to escape poverty and join the nation's social and economic mainstream.

Instead, we have systems in which most of those children fall behind early in their educational careers and never recover. Inner-city schools, with rare exceptions, have become factories for the reproduction of chronic, multigenerational poverty. While it is not entirely the schools' *fault*—recognizing the debilitating effects of dysfunctional, often violent, family and neighborhood conditions—we look to the schools to somehow counterbalance those conditions or enable children to overcome them. While that is a daunting task, there is growing evidence that there are at least some things that can be done that make a difference, even under very difficult conditions.

First, a simple one. People have been studying the effects of pre-kindergarten programs since the 1960s, and the evidence is strong that well-designed, professionally staffed programs can produce lasting benefits in terms of educational attainment, adult behavior, and lifetime earnings for the low-income children who participate in those programs. Not all pre-K programs are equal, though. As the Center for Public Education points out, the research "shows the importance of low child/staff ratios, small class sizes, and teacher qualifications in the effective delivery of programs. Regardless of pre-K setting, whether at a school or community agency, teacher qualifications are essential."[6]

Comprehensive, high-quality pre-K education should be available to every child, especially children in low-income communities. As with the job-training programs described earlier, the research cited by the Center for Public Education has shown that money spent on pre-K education leads to major long-term financial benefits for society and for the economy in terms of less need for expensive special-education services, reduced crime and criminal justice costs, reduced welfare dependency, and increased lifetime earnings both for the children and their parents.

What happens after pre-K, in looking at the system of education from kindergarten through high school, is harder. It is harder not only because the educational issues are more complex, but even more because the debate is often less about the children than it is about politics and ideology, nowhere more than in the never-ending charter school controversy. Too often, it seems to boil down to a dispute between, on the one hand, mostly right-of-center proponents of the free market who see the public schools as a patronage and bureaucracy-encrusted monopoly; and, on the other, generally left-of-center advocates of public education who see it as a bastion of civil rights and grassroots democracy under attack from the right.

In many respects, both sides are both right and wrong. The idea that a free market in education is a path to opportunity for low-income children in concentrated-poverty areas is absurd and pernicious, as the Detroit experience has shown. At the same time, those advocating, in essence, that the public school systems should retain their *de facto* monopoly of children's education have a hard case to make. While the American public school system, taken as a whole, generally does a good job educating the children of educated, motivated middle-class parents, particularly those living in affluent suburban communities, it does a far worse job with the admittedly much harder job of educating the children of the poor, particularly those who live in urban areas of concentrated poverty.

For all the many dedicated teachers and administrators who work in public school systems, many school districts are not that far from the picture painted by their adversaries. They are often top-heavy with administrators, coordinators, consultants, and Lord knows what else; elected school boards, rather than being vehicles for popular democracy, are often creatures of machine politics; and entrenched unions often seem less concerned with children's interests than in their never-ending struggles over teacher compensation and prerogatives. It's not just about money, either. While some states still shortchange their urban schools, others have made major strides toward equalizing school funding. Since the 1990s, New Jersey has been providing its thirty-one "special needs" school districts with more money, child-for-child, than the state's typical suburban school district spends in total. While advocates can point to scattered examples of improvement, overall the results are widely acknowledged to be disappointing.

The evidence is growing that what one might call carefully managed, accountable competition may actually change the opportunity equation, supporting successful charter models while also supporting the improvement of public school districts. Schools like Match—and others, both charters and traditional public schools, all around the country—have shown that they can significantly reduce achievement gaps and place thousands of children from low-income families and high-poverty areas on a path to opportunity.

Still, the number of children they reach is a miniscule fraction of the number who continue to fall behind on a daily basis. If our goal as a nation is to further greater equality of opportunity and reduce poverty, there is probably nothing more important than to figure out how to replicate these successful models—both the schools themselves and the balance of flexibility and accountability in the overall system—to the point that they begin to reach not a handful of children, but millions. There are 10.6 million children in the United States between the ages of five and seventeen living in poverty, and another 6.1 million in households with earnings that put them less than 50 percent above the poverty level—altogether, more than one out of four American children. They all should have a chance to escape poverty as adults.

Tragically, instead of focusing on the children, far too much of the debate seems to be polarized between, on the one hand, the romantic vision of an idealized public school system and reflexive hostility to the tech magnates funding charter schools, and, on the other, the less romantic vision of a cutthroat free market in education, epitomized by Trump's secretary of education, Betsy DeVos, on whom a great deal of the blame for the dysfunctional Detroit system can rightly be placed. The New Jersey *Star-Ledger*, in an editorial hailing the return of Newark's public schools to local control after twenty years of a state takeover, exhorted local officials to "stop the endless political sniping over whether a school is charter, magnet, or traditional."[7] Their words are well worth heeding in many places aside from Newark.

Place and Opportunity

A host of factors come together to exacerbate inequality in the city. Poverty is debilitating, its effects are multiplied over many generations by life in areas of concentrated poverty, and those effects are multiplied in turn by racial segregation. For most people in cities, escaping poverty is not just about getting to a point where one has a decent income. Escaping poverty in cities like Detroit or St. Louis usually also means moving out, usually to one of the many suburban towns or cities which offer houses at affordable prices. That leaves two gaping holes in the equity equation: What happens to the people who cannot move to some other place that offers greater opportunity or a better quality of life? And what happens to the neighborhoods they leave behind?

Meanwhile, cities are not standing still. Some areas are reviving or gentrifying, becoming both more affluent and more expensive, while other areas, many of which were solid, stable working-class or middle-class neighborhoods until recently, are now declining, with a population that is increasingly poor, and with vacant, boarded-up houses appearing on otherwise well-tended blocks. What might be called the problem of place is not a single challenge, but a multiple one. But there's a fundamental challenge that also needs to be addressed, one that transcends questions of place and goes to basic human needs.

That challenge is the amount of money that the millions of poor and near-poor families who have not won the housing-voucher lottery must spend for even the most primitive accommodations, and the disastrous effect that has on their lives and the lives of their children in terms of instability, homelessness, and the lack of money for other basic needs.

While some may not see it as an equity issue, I see it not only as a question of opportunity but as a matter of fundamental justice. For a wealthy society like the United States to knowingly allow millions of its citizens to live in desperate hardship, *when an adequate remedy is known and is within our grasp*, strikes me as an equity issue.

In contrast to many of the other challenges where the solutions lie wholly or mostly locally, this is something that can only be addressed by the federal government. How much it costs to provide a family with a housing voucher for a year varies widely from one part of the United States to another, reflecting the variation in incomes and housing costs from one area to the next, but it averages out to about $9,000 per year. No city, and no state, can afford to provide this sort of ongoing support to more than a small fraction of the millions of households that need it. To give an idea of the scale of the need, among households with annual incomes of $35,000 or less, 9.6 million spend 50 percent or more of their gross income for rent, and an additional 2.7 million spend between 40 percent and 50 percent of their gross income for rent.

The federal government currently spends about $32 billion a year providing vouchers for 3.5 million households, with which it estimates, perhaps optimistically, that it covers one out of four eligible households.[8] A program that would provide a voucher to any eligible low-income household as a matter of right would probably cost about an additional $90 to $100 billion, or slightly more than 2 percent of the annual federal budget. It would transform the lives of a far larger share of American households. Any particular inferences aside, it is worth pointing out that home-mortgage and property-tax deductions for homeowners together cost the United States Treasury more than that, roughly $120 billion in 2017.

Rather than simply assuming that the best course is to expand the current voucher program, though, this would be a unique opportunity to step back and take stock of what we have learned about the benefits as well as the downsides of the voucher program since it was initiated over forty years ago, and also to learn from the many other models of housing assistance that have been adopted elsewhere in the world, particularly in Western European countries like the United Kingdom, France, and Germany, which provide housing benefits to all those in need. While it is unlikely that the cost in the end would be significantly less, we could probably design a program that would provide the same benefits as the Section 8 vouchers but would do more to improve the quality of the housing where low-income people live, reduce some of the negative spillovers to the housing market, and expand the ability of low-income people to move out of high-poverty ghettoes into areas of greater opportunity.

Spatial Equity

A critical equity frontier is what might be called "place opportunity" or "spatial equity," to reverse the extent to which economic classes are increasingly "sorted" geographically in the United States. That sorting, which is creating ever-greater spatial barriers between rich, middle-class, and poor in our cities, is not only a symptom of inequality, but a driver of even greater inequality in the future.

Although spatial equity is a regional issue, reflecting continued social and economic disparities between central cities and their suburbs, cities—particularly those that are seeing revival—bear a particular responsibility to foster greater spatial equity in those parts of the city that are on an upward economic trajectory or are gentrifying. That means preserving or creating opportunities for significant numbers of lower-income families to continue to live in those areas indefinitely. That will not just happen. Left to its own devices, the market will create increasingly homogenous neighborhoods, even without any overt displacement, simply through turnover and the logic of non-replacement. Ordinances to protect the interests of sitting low-income homeowners or tenants are desirable and important, but will only have a short-term effect. Cities have to make equity happen.

There are a number of ways they can do so. First, older subsidized-housing projects that are in or adjacent to reviving areas should be preserved wherever possible. This may be costly, since the owners of those projects may be eager to cash in on the area's revival by converting the projects to more expensive private-market housing. It may require a combination of regulatory pressures and financial incentives. At the same time, it is likely to be not only less expensive but far less complicated and time-consuming than trying to create the same number of units from scratch to replace them.

Maine, Massachusetts, and Maryland have passed laws that both require advance notification of an owner's intent to sell or convert their properties—in Massachusetts, for two years—and a "right of first refusal" to buy the property. In Maine, the state housing authority has the right of first refusal anytime an owner takes any action that would result "in the termination of financial assistance designed to make the rental units affordable to low-income or moderate-income people."[9] Washington, DC, has the Tenant Opportunity to Purchase Act, or TOPA, which gives the tenants the right of first refusal when the owner decides to sell the building. More states and cities need to follow their lead.

Where revival is emerging but prices are not yet astronomical, or where an area, like Five Points in Denver or Fox Park in St. Louis, is clearly showing signs of being ripe for change, cities and nonprofit organizations can take steps to create affordable housing—as DeSales did in Fox Park by buying vacant small apartment buildings and using the Low Income Tax Credit to restore them—or set aside land and buildings for future affordable-housing development, if and when the market starts to move. Cities often own land and buildings in such areas, often seized years ago for nonpayment of property taxes. They can keep them off the market as it warms up, reusing them for affordable-housing development at a pace that will not undermine the area's revival.

Cities already provide incentives like tax abatements, as in Philadelphia, to encourage private developers to build for the growing demand for upscale apartments and condos driven by Young Grads and others. Other cities beside Chicago are starting to require developers who get those incentives to provide at least a small amount of affordable housing. Cities are limited in what they can offer, but state governments could do a lot more. They could provide cities with a double benefit by adding incentives—in the form of low-interest financing, tax credits for developers, and more—contingent on providing some affordable housing. Those incentives could both help jump-start private market-rate development in many areas where it is still an iffy financial proposition, gradually adding to the affordable-housing stock and fostering integrated communities.

Ultimately, it keeps coming down to the point that if we as a nation truly want to solve these problems, we will need to provide public resources to do so. To believe that our housing crisis can be solved otherwise is self-delusion.

Quality of Life and the Poverty Ghetto

In the meantime, as important as it is to build affordable housing in places of opportunity throughout every region, and to ensure that low-income families have a place in each city's reviving neighborhoods, for the foreseeable future those options will be available for only a small percentage of the millions of families and individuals who currently live in high-poverty and declining neighborhoods. Equity demands that both attention and resources be focused on those areas. As I discussed earlier, the likelihood of most high-poverty ghetto areas reviving as long as they remain areas of concentrated poverty is slim. That does not mean they cannot be far better places to live. Instead, we need to make a concerted effort to improve the quality of life in these areas, to the extent possible enabling the families who live there to have a safe and healthy environment, both in their homes and on the street, in which to live their lives.

I've covered many of the pieces of what that would entail in chapter 9, so I will revisit them only briefly here. Creating a healthy physical environment is the starting point. That means demolishing vacant, derelict buildings and turning vacant lots into attractive green areas. Making sure that streets and sidewalks are safe and in good condition and that streetlights work, along with planting shade trees, all contribute to creating a healthy environment. Low-income homeowners should be given financial help to fix up their homes so that they have healthy and safe indoor environments and can stay in their homes rather than have to move. Proactive rental regulation, cracking down on abusive landlords, particularly those who take advantage of the generous rent ceilings under the voucher program, will improve conditions for millions of renters.

These measures cost money, to be sure, but far less than most bigticket projects. As little as $10,000 can go a long way toward making a small house livable for an elderly homeowner; $10 million can transform the lives of 1,000 such homeowners. And just $1,000 to $1,500 can transform a trash-strewn vacant lot into an attractive green space. Rental property regulation can pay for itself through licensing fees and penalties. Municipal public works departments have budgets, although never as much as they would like, for street and sidewalk repair. As important as money is, it is even more important to spend whatever money is available in a serious, coordinated fashion so that it adds up to more than the sum of its parts.

Finally, without greater public safety for people in these neighborhoods, much of this effort is likely to be for naught. As with so many other needed changes, this is not simply a matter of changing the way in which the police allocate resources and personnel, but also changing systems and ways of behavior that are deeply embedded in the distinctive, insular culture of American and particularly urban police departments. That culture, in turn, is interwoven with the power networks that underlie the policies the city chooses and the decisions it makes about policing. At the same time, the violence of the inner city is not simply a reflection of police culture, but of forces of social and behavioral instability that have emerged over generations and become embedded into the fabric of many neighborhoods.

Those need to be addressed if significant change is going to take place, and it is still unclear how. As J. D. Vance writes in his moving book *Hillbilly Elegy* of the white Appalachian community in which he was raised, "People sometimes ask whether I think there's anything we can do to 'solve' the problems of my community. I know what they're looking for: a magical public policy solution or an innovative government program. But these problems of family, faith, and culture aren't like a Rubik's Cube, and I don't think that solutions (as most understand the term) really exist."[10] In some respects, as the people who can get out continue to do so, whether from the inner city of Cleveland or the hollows of the Appalachian Mountains, these problems become increasingly intractable.

The interplay between people and place is a complicated one. It is a safe bet that few of the inner-city children who go on to graduate from college after graduating from Match or a KIPP school will come back to live in their old neighborhoods. Even if they come back to St. Louis or Boston, they'll most probably move to better neighborhoods—in the city or in its suburbs—which they can now afford thanks to their education and skills, and which reflect their new preferences and tastes. If people now living in Sandtown-Winchester or Homewood get good jobs as a result of the sorts of programs to create job opportunities that I described earlier in this chapter, most of them will also leave for greener pastures.

Whatever some ideologues or advocates might say, this is a good thing. Yes, the world contains a small number of self-sacrificing souls who devote their lives to working on behalf of their people or their community, but they are outliers. We celebrate them, but few of us want to emulate them. The purpose of an equity strategy is to give people opportunities to live lives that have meaning and value to *them*, not to some third-party arbiter, and to raise their families in safe, healthy homes and environments. If our efforts can undo the practices that have barred millions of people from those opportunities, and empower them to make their own choices and live such lives, then those are efforts well worth making.

What that means for the neighborhoods where they come from depends on a lot of things. The more the neighborhood improves while they are improving their own life chances, the more likely they are to stay or come back to the neighborhood. Whether that happens will depend in part on public policies and public actions, but probably even more on the ability of the people who live in the neighborhood to, in Jane Jacobs's words I quoted earlier, "keep sufficiently abreast of its problems so that it is not destroyed by them." J. D. Vance is right: we can't solve everything with a government program.

An important mechanism by which successful neighborhoods—whatever their racial and economic makeup—do this is known as "collective efficacy," a term coined by Harvard sociologist Bob Sampson.[11] Collective efficacy can be described as the ability of a community to establish norms and enforce them in the neighborhood through informal means of social control. This is basically what the much-abused cliché "it takes a village . . ." is about. A large body of research has found that the level of collective efficacy—as measured by tools developed by Sampson and his colleagues—is a powerful determinant of both the level of actual crime and the fear of crime in a neighborhood.

Our understanding of how collective efficacy comes about, and how it can be instilled where it does not currently exist, is far from complete. If distressed, high-poverty urban neighborhoods are to have a serious shot at a better, healthier, and more stable future, efforts to build greater neighborhood cohesion and collective efficacy need to go hand in hand with efforts to address the neighborhood's physical environment and build a better quality of life. Collective efficacy, however, is not a function of the formal organizational or institutional structure in a neighborhood; it is more osmotic, a function of the neighborhood's culture. Still, the process of building such a culture may begin with building the sort of organizational structures that bring people together. In the end, though, some neighborhoods will put the pieces together, stabilize, and perhaps in time revive. Others will not.

The Cities Left Behind

Implicitly or explicitly, most of what I've written up to now applies most directly to the larger and relatively more-successful legacy cities. Cities like Baltimore or Pittsburgh have large numbers of jobs to offer, are attracting billions of dollars in private investment, and are seeing people moving in rather than just moving out. This is not true of large numbers of smaller cities and factory towns, places that were once hubs of industry and commerce. While a few have found a path to revival, more are struggling, and many seem to have few options with which to rebuild their shattered economies.

As a nation, we must decide what we want the future of these cities to be. Our present course relegates many cities to a sort of limbo, where, despite their best efforts, they drift gradually downward, losing jobs, becoming gradually poorer, and offering progressively less hope for those who live there. Is this the only vision that we have for hundreds of small cities and towns that dot the American heartland?

That would be, in my opinion, tragic. These cities are not disposable places, roadkill on the highway of capitalist creative destruction. They are real places, with rich histories, full of real people. They have real assets. As Catherine Tumber, who chronicles the current state and prospects of small cities in her book *Small, Gritty, and Green*, writes, they "have population density and the capacity for much more. They also have land assets . . . [and they] have manufacturing infrastructure and workforce skills that can be retooled for the production of renewable technologies." She concludes that "we are on the brink of a third Industrial Revolution, and these cities are highly suited to play a central part in it."[12]

I am somewhat less optimistic than Tumber, but I share her conviction that the value is there if it can be unlocked. The question is twofold: first, is there a path to prosperity for the small cities and towns of industrial America, and second, if there is, will it benefit everyone or, as in many of the larger cities currently, just a few?

While no economic development strategy will work for long if it doesn't make economic sense, small industrial cities are highly logical places for future manufacturing in the United States, as the continued vitality of industry in cities like Kalamazoo or Grand Rapids, or smaller places like Hickory, North Carolina, suggests. Many small cities have ample land; good, affordable housing; a reservoir of skilled labor; and proximity to major markets. The Youngstown Technology Incubator, named by the University Business Incubator Index in 2014 as the "world's best business incubator associated with a university," has helped create nearly 2,000 jobs in northeastern Ohio since 2012, including many in advanced manufacturing.[13] This may not be many, true, but it's an important beginning. Meanwhile, thanks largely to the presence of Youngstown State University, downtown Youngstown has seen the first signs of revival. Ornate 1920s office buildings are being converted to apartments, and restaurants and coffee places are opening up.

Elsewhere in the city, the Youngstown Neighborhood Development Corporation has helped spur new life through its array of programs and initiatives. What YNDC does could be replicated in many other small cities similar to Youngstown, although finding people like its dynamic executive director Ian Beniston will not be easy. Danville, Virginia, has just created a citywide development corporation modeled after Youngstown's. In places like the Monongahela Valley, where no single town could potentially support such an organization, a single regional YNDC-like entity might be set up to work in five or ten different communities. This will cost some money, to be sure. But when one thinks that for around $250 million—less than the cost of a single stadium and not even a rounding error in the federal budget—we could have a national program that would support over a hundred YNDC clones around the country, it is clear that money doesn't have to be an obstacle.

There are many things that can be done to help build local economies in small industrial cities. Universities like Youngstown State or the University of Michigan–Flint can become important anchors, particularly if more housing can be built to get currently commuting students to live downtown or in nearby neighborhoods. Programs to encourage university personnel and hospital employees, as well as city police officers and firefighters, to become homeowners in the city would help. Coupled with the efforts of a YNDC-type organization, those efforts could instill new life in some of the city's neighborhoods, and increase small-business opportunities in the city.

Carefully designed incentives to entice manufacturing back to small cities or build on what's still there, where the conditions are conducive to its success, should be pursued. The Ironworks in Beloit, once the home of the Beloit Corporation, is now being resuscitated by Diane Hendriks and has thirteen separate businesses occupying a million square feet of space. There are few if any industrial behemoths that will take over an entire multimillion-square-foot factory, but there many small ones that might want some space in one. If every small city had access to funds to restore their surviving manufacturing plants, similar to what is happening in Beloit, and to create incubators like Youngstown's, the results might be amazing. The point is, it's not going to be about finding a magic bullet; rather, it's a step-by-step, bit-by-bit process of rebuilding.

There are some serious difficulties, though. First, few small cities have the capacity—financial, managerial, or technical—to put the pieces together. Without YNDC, the city of Youngstown would be hard-pressed to do even a fraction of what that organization does; in fact, the city looks to YNDC to provide services, from master planning to blight removal, that in a larger or more capable city would be provided by city government. Few cities would know how to put together a transformative economic development or neighborhood revitalization strategy, even if they had the money.

Second, it is hard to imagine any plausible strategy for bringing back more than a fraction of the jobs that existed in a Youngstown or a

Johnstown fifty years ago. In the past few years, a new state-of-the-art steel mill has been built in Youngstown on the site of one of the old ones that closed in the 1970s. The old one employed 15,000 people. The new one on its site employs 350 to create products of comparable value. Moreover, they aren't the same kind of jobs. They demand reading, writing, math, and other skills vastly beyond those required of a steelworker a hundred years ago—and far less brawn. They often require a degree from a technical school or community college.

This is not true everywhere. Many small cities and towns, particularly those whose industrial history had less to do with vast steel plants than with smaller firms making more specialized products, may be able to build healthy local economies around a manufacturing base, particularly if they can somehow overcome the pervasive prejudice among younger generations—and their teachers and mentors—that the only good jobs are the ones only available to those with college degrees. These same places, with their generally affordable housing, can offer the people who get factory jobs a first-rate quality of life.

We don't know whether there are more small places like Cedar Rapids, Iowa, where the number of manufacturing jobs has doubled since 2002 and hundreds of well-paying jobs are going begging, or more still-struggling places like Aliquippa and Johnstown out there, but the fact remains that there will still be many places, particularly in the Rust Belt heartland, where there will be too few jobs, while too many of the people who live there, struggling to get by, will never have a chance to fill them. Meanwhile, large numbers of men, who bore the brunt of the decline of blue-collar jobs over the past decade, shun jobs that open up in fields like health care, traditionally seen as woman's work. As Harvard economist Lawrence Katz argues, it's "looking for the job you used to have." "It's not a skill mismatch," he adds, "but an identity mismatch. It's not that they couldn't become a health worker, it's that they have backward views of what their identity is."[14]

Ultimately, no program can help those who cannot help themselves. This is not only about capacity, important as that is, but about a state of mind. As Richard Longworth, a clearheaded writer about the Midwest and its struggles, writes, "After a while, a town forgets how to earn a living, just as an unemployed worker loses the skills that made him employable." He quotes an analyst who works in small cities in Indiana, and who, not surprisingly, didn't want his name used. "There's a malaise here," he told Longworth. "A defeatist attitude. People have been so beat down by layoffs, they don't have the will."[15]

And then, finally, what if cities like Flint or Danville get their act together, and everything I've described above falls into place, and yet nothing changes for a lot of people—what then? There may not be enough new jobs, particularly jobs wanted by men like the one who told reporter Claire Cain Miller, "I was a welder—that's all I know how to do,"[16] and—an even bigger question mark: whether they will be able to qualify for whatever new jobs are created. Ambitious, energetic young people will still go off to college and, for the most part, not come back. The Walmart on the highway outside town is still the area's largest employer, and downtown is still dominated by government offices, social service agencies, and vacant storefronts. Things may be better, but for many people they're not good.

Often, that may be the best that one can hope for. Many of America's small legacy cities, and even more of its old mill towns, exist because of a set of conditions that existed a hundred or more years ago. Those conditions are gone, probably forever. Conditions are very different today. They may offer *some* opportunities to revive *some* cities and towns, but not all, and not back to the way that they were fifty or a hundred years ago. Some places, like the small mill towns of the Mon Valley, lack even the modest prospects of a Flint or a Youngstown. The urban transfer-payment economy, though, will make sure that they do not disappear, unlike the mining towns of the 1800s, or the ancient Roman port city of Classe.

From a public policy standpoint, the future of those places, or of the many people elsewhere that revival is unlikely to touch, poses a difficult quandary. Should our country—by which I really mean our state and federal governments—perpetuate their current posture, which is to allow these people and places to remain in a state of permanent near-poverty and frustration sustained by transfer payments, or should we intervene to create more-substantial local economies, but sustained by the public sector rather than the private market? Or should we try to hasten their demise, in the case of many of the mill towns, or their further shrinkage, in the case of small cities whose economic potential still falls short of being able to sustain their current populations?

The last approach—intervening to hasten their shrinkage or even their extinction—is most probably a nonstarter, for many reasons, but the former—bolstering their public-sector economies—is worth taking more seriously. Public intervention to create a more substantial local economy would mean, above all, creating a major publicly funded jobs and training program designed to meet the needs of these places for better home health care for the elderly and disabled, recreation programs for the children growing up in these towns, and programs to improve the physical environment of the towns and cities—rebuilding infrastructure, demolishing or restoring vacant buildings, creating parks and open spaces, planting trees and tending community farms, and more. Certainly, there is no shortage of legitimate needs that could be filled. And, albeit with some but not unreasonable effort, such a training program could give people real skills and meaningful work that mattered, rather than being a make-work program.

There's a part of me that likes the idea. But another part of me starts to raise questions. First, there's the old moral hazard issue. If such an option were readily available, why would any city or town do the hard, slow work of trying to rebuild their economy through the private sector if a far easier federally funded alternative were available? Perhaps there might be a way to design a federal program in a way that assistance would somehow be proportional to local effort, but that might turn out to be either fiendishly complicated or wildly bureaucratic, or both. Either way, it would also be very expensive.

The second question is whether one could even justify a program that was specifically limited to the nation's small industrial cities and mill towns. Indeed, one shouldn't. There are many places in the United States beyond the Midwestern Rust Belt, particularly in the rural Deep South and the Western plains, where conditions are not that different. A long-term, serious and not make-work jobs program, though, tied to persistent high unemployment and poverty, for those areas where there is no realistic way of creating enough private-sector jobs, wherever in the United States it might be, might be worth thinking about seriously. Depending on what happens to the future of work over the coming decades, this issue may become a matter of far broader national concern, touching many other people and places, than is currently the case.

Sustaining Revival

Without sustained revival, there are few prospects for expanding opportunities. While a rising tide does not lift all boats, a growing pie is needed if opportunities for some are to be increased without taking them away from others. The revival of legacy cities during the past fifteen or twenty years has opened the door for the first time to ways of thinking about social equity that are also about opportunity, rather than merely variations on a theme of shared poverty. Growth not only means that there are more resources to share, but that people and institutions are more open to sharing them with others.

The history of cities as well as the uncertainties of the present, though, teach us that we should never take revival or prosperity for granted. Not even Pittsburgh, recently heralded as a "global innovation city" and with a growing collection of glowing press clippings, can rest on its laurels.[17] Any city that truly believes that it has it made is deluding itself. There are too many question marks. Can cities count on continued growth in higher education and health care? Can they count on continued in-migration of Young Grads, or will their influx dwindle in coming years; and if it does, can cities replace them with baby boomers or immigrants? Will the Young Grads already in the cities stay there as they begin to raise families, or will they follow their parents' example and move to the suburbs? Will the federal government continue to provide the modest social safety net and support system for cities that they have provided, in some cases since the 1930s and in others since the 1960s or 1970s, or is even that pittance in doubt?

Many of the steps that cities can take to foster equity and opportunity will also strengthen the cities' revival. Building a stronger, more highly skilled local workforce is one of the most valuable things, if not *the* most valuable thing, any city can do to strengthen its local economy and enhance its competitive position nationally and globally. In their recent report heralding Pittsburgh's emerging innovation economy, the Brookings Institution raised a red flag. "At projected population levels, current labor force participation rates, and workforce skill levels," the authors write, "Pittsburgh will not be able to meet the demands of growing advanced industries."[18]

A strong IT sector requires far more than analysts with advanced degrees; as one Pittsburgh CEO told the Brookings team, "Seventy-five percent of the IT jobs in the company don't require a four-year degree."[19] The same is true of other sectors. Moreover, building a strong workforce not only helps support existing firms and helps them grow, it also attracts others, building the agglomeration economies that strong cities need.

A better quality of life, better schools, and a safer environment benefit everyone. The fact that large parts of many cities are far safer today than they were in the 1990s has certainly been a major factor in those cities' revival, but neither the safety nor the revival have spread to many other parts of those same cities. Similarly, although experts may disagree about how many Young Grads want to stay in cities as they begin to raise families, there's no doubt that some do, and that schools—as well as safety—will play a major part in their decision. The families moving to Southwest Garden and nearby neighborhoods in St. Louis in the hope of getting their kids into the City Garden charter school are not unique.

At the same time, while building the economic strength of their existing residents, cities also need to pursue other strategies that focus directly on building stronger and more-diversified local and regional economies, and continuing to draw—and retain—a diverse population. The extent to which cities as diverse as Baltimore and Dayton are economically dependent on "eds and meds" may not be a good model for future prosperity or growth. Baltimore, with institutions of global reach, appears to be in a much stronger position than Dayton, but it cannot assume that it has found a successful long-term sustainability formula.

Cities must diversify their economies if they are to continue their revival. Pittsburgh may be well on the way to a diverse, robust economy; as the Brookings report comments, the Pittsburgh area "is a powerhouse in fields like robotics, gerontology, critical care, artificial intelligence, cell and tissue engineering, neurotrauma, and software."[20] Other cities, like Philadelphia and Baltimore, are trying to leverage their medical institutions into new sectors like biotechnology, while trying to build tourism and convention business into a significant economic sector. Advanced manufacturing is another opportunity for older cities. According to Change the Equation, an organization that promotes STEM literacy in American education, Detroit, Grand Rapids, and Toledo are among the top five cities nationally in terms of growth in that sector. Cities must be realistic about their strengths and weaknesses, focusing on those areas where they have potential competitive advantages, and resisting the tendencies either to copy a successful effort in a city of different size and with very different characteristics, or to jump on the "flavor of the month" bandwagon.

In that light, economic thinking needs to be regional, not narrowly local. Growth in good jobs throughout the region benefits central cities, not least in that it increases opportunities for city residents—particularly if combined with transportation improvements—far beyond what may be possible within the central city itself. Regional growth draws new people and companies to the region; the stronger and more attractive a city is, the more likely a significant share of those new people and companies will end up in the city rather than its surrounding suburbs. Cities need actively to identify and foster those economic sectors that can become regional magnets, including specialized retail and services, restaurants, and entertainment districts. Washington Avenue in St. Louis is a regional mecca for young people, while Cleveland's Playhouse Square, which bills itself as "the country's largest performing-arts center outside of New York," draws over a million visitors per year from a vast hinterland to its theaters and other performing arts venues.[21] It is not just a local, but a regional, asset.

At the same time, cities need to be thinking far more productively about how to draw and retain populations that are more diverse—not just economically, but in terms of their household type, age, and origin as well. A few cities like Philadelphia, and organizations like Global Detroit, have begun to focus on drawing immigrants. That's important, but only one part of a larger picture. In fact, as I've traveled and talked to people in the older industrial cities, I've noticed a strange disconnect. Few cities are thinking about how to draw and retain *people*; they're thinking about how to draw *developers*, out of a sort of "if you build it, they will come" state of mind. If we can get developers to build, they believe, developers will figure out how to get the people. Not so.

Developers are important, but they are a means to an end, not an end in themselves. By focusing on them rather than the ends they want them to serve, cities risk sabotaging their own long-term interests. Developers tend to focus on what they can get financed—and hope to make money on—in the short term. They are also powerfully driven by the herd instinct; they want to build what made money for the last guy. More upscale rental apartment buildings in downtown are not necessarily a bad thing, but it is possible to overbuild even in a strong market, and they leave out a lot of the city and a lot of potential markets.

Every city should be developer-friendly, within reasonable bounds. Zoning and building codes should be predictable and reasonable, approvals need to be timely, and assistance with finding sites and navigating bureaucracies should be available. Incentives should be offered as well, but only where needed to overcome market constraints or to achieve public goals like affordable housing. At the same time, cities should not compromise on planning and design standards. The developer will be gone soon, after at most ten years or so; the building she leaves behind will still be standing to haunt the lives of the great-grandchildren of today's city planning commission members.

Few cities have seriously or systematically embraced the task of drawing and retaining diverse populations. In addition to immigrants, cities need to focus on other distinct populations. Today's Young Grads will get older. Some may stay in cities, some may not. Either way, fresh faces will be needed to fill the space that today's Young Grads will vacate. Cities need to make sure that future generations continue to flow into downtowns and nearby neighborhoods, and that the period from roughly 2000 to the present does not turn out to be a transitory blip.

Some people believe that that's all it is. As a recent *Fortune* article put it, "There's mounting evidence that millennials' love of cities was a passing fling that became a shotgun wedding thanks to the Great Recession. Millennials don't love cities any more than previous generations, the counterargument goes, they've just been stuck there longer, pining for the suburbs all the while."[22] I disagree strongly, for reasons that I've laid out earlier. Cities must be constantly on their guard, though, to keep this speculation from becoming a prophecy. Not only does that mean that housing options—and not too expensive ones—must continue to be available, but that the factors that have drawn highly skilled young people, the city's amenities and quality of life, are not compromised.

Cities should also be figuring out how to attract larger numbers of empty-nesters and aging baby boomers, a plausible source of demand for many of the expensive apartments that developers are putting up in places like downtown Philadelphia. This is not just about marketing cities, but about making downtowns and urban neighborhoods more age-friendly, from the types of services and activities that are offered to making sure that sidewalks and intersections are safe, well maintained, and well lit.

At the same time, cities need to focus on holding a larger share of young people as they get older, marry, and begin to raise families. Drawing middle- and upper-income married-couple families, to become homeowners in urban neighborhoods where they and their disposable income and stability are in short supply today, can have a dramatic impact on those neighborhoods. Cities don't have to hold *all* of them. Even a modest increase in the number that stay in the city would be significant. With a larger-than-ever pool of potential long-term residents already living in the city—residents who are already predisposed toward urban living—holding more of them should be eminently feasible.

Almost every older city has residential neighborhoods made up of attractive single-family houses that are potentially as attractive to childrearing families today as they were a hundred years ago, usually at affordable prices. Safety and schools are obviously two key factors that will determine whether they will draw people who could easily move to the suburbs. Schools, though, should not only be good schools, they should be good *neighborhood* schools—that is, schools that draw their children from the neighborhood, where parents can play a meaningful role in their children's education. Although laws or policies providing for citywide open enrollment may appear to foster equity and choice, they do so—if they do so at all—at the price of severing valuable connections of great importance to building and sustaining healthy neighborhoods. Equity can be served by reserving a substantial share of the places in schools in more-affluent neighborhoods for children whose family income makes them eligible for free or reduced-price lunches.

Cities can take other steps to make neighborhoods appealing to young families. Attractive, well-maintained, and actively used parks can be a major draw. Patterson Park in Baltimore and Tower Grove Park in St. Louis have both been major factors in making the neighborhoods around them more appealing to young families. Walkable neighborhood commercial cores are another. Elmwood Avenue in Buffalo, Butler Street in Pittsburgh's Lawrenceville neighborhood, and Ferry Street in Newark's Ironbound, with its distinctive Portuguese stores and restaurants, not only draw families to live in these neighborhoods, but are economic assets for the city.

Cities must be realistic about this. Creating wonderful urban parks like Tower Grove or vibrant, walkable shopping streets like Ferry Street from scratch is not only, at best, fiendishly expensive, but, without some degree of underlying neighborhood stability, may be effectively impossible, however much money is available. Each city should identify places where—based on existing activity, a particular amenity, or the level of social capital and collective efficacy—conditions are ripe for intervention, and then build on those conditions to turn that neighborhood into what planners call a "community of choice"—a place where families *choose* to live.

Finally, what may be most important of all is for cities to work harder to hold on to the families who already live there, particularly the working-class and middle-class African American families who have been increasingly fleeing the cities in recent years for nearby suburbs. These families want the same things that new families who might be drawn into the cities will be looking for: safe neighborhoods with decent schools, decent public services, and decent amenities.

There's another piece to this picture, though, that cities rarely think about. People want to be respected, and have their contribution to the community respected. A recurrent theme I hear, when I talk to families in urban neighborhoods in cities like Detroit, might be called the "theme of urban indifference." The families, usually homeowners, who've lived their lives in urban neighborhoods, are raising or have raised their children there, and have put up with the lean years and the struggle for survival, often feel that the city doesn't care about them, has no interest in their concerns, and is indifferent to whether they stay or leave. The sad thing is, they're probably right.

It is easy enough for overworked local officials, faced with daunting problems and the need to cultivate state governments, corporations, anchor institutions, developers, business interests, and who knows what else, to lose track of the people who are sustaining the city's vital neighborhoods, paying taxes, and contributing either through active civic engagement or simply by being a solid, respectable presence in the community. It is understandable, but a serious mistake. The more people feel they are valued, the more likely it is that they will stay and continue to contribute. That is true not only for African American middle-class families, but for everyone. It is true for young families moving into the city, as well as for families from the inner city who achieve a decent income and family stability through public-sector opportunity strategies. Cities must value *all* of their residents, whatever their race, ethnicity, and current economic condition. They cannot afford to dismiss anyone, or take anyone for granted.

Looking to the Future

As Niels Bohr, or perhaps Yogi Berra, said, prediction is difficult, especially when it's about the future.[23] This has always been true, but somehow it feels that, as we look to the future today, the uncertainties are even greater than in past times. Changing technologies will change conditions in highly unpredictable ways. According to a study by consultants PricewaterhouseCoopers, nearly 40 percent of all jobs in the United States could disappear by 2030 through automation and robotics, including half of all jobs in transportation and manufacturing.[24] Such predictions are widely disputed, as are predictions of whether and which new jobs and sectors may emerge, or whether, as some believe, a universal guaranteed income will take their place.

Almost everyone seems to believe autonomous cars, trucks, and buses will be a reality in five or at most ten years, but no one agrees on what effect they will have. Plausible scenarios can be crafted to suggest that they will enhance public transportation or eviscerate it; that they will exacerbate inequality or foster greater opportunity; and that they will reinforce the cities' central role or undermine it. Either way, they will almost certainly sharply reduce the number of blue-collar jobs; in 2016, according to the Bureau of Labor Statistics, there were over 4.5 million bus drivers, taxi drivers, and driver/sales workers and truck drivers in the United States, of whom 1.7 million were African American or Latino.[25] Many—perhaps most—of these jobs will disappear.

There are even more global uncertainties. The world, as many have pointed out, is a dangerous place. While the United States is unlikely to be invaded or seriously damaged physically by any forthcoming international upheaval, we are closely interwoven into the global economy, and we could easily suffer economically from the effects of upheaval elsewhere, not to mention from self-inflicted wounds triggered by our own irresponsible or short-sighted policies.

The effects of climate change, which today appears to be all but irreversible, are even more significant. Rising sea levels, desertification in the Southwest, increasing extreme weather events, and more are all forecast for future decades. These will all tax American society and the economy in ways that we cannot begin to predict. Perhaps, as some have predicted, these changes may actually enhance the relative attractiveness of states like Michigan and Ohio and their cities, with their cool climate and reserves of fresh water, as the Southwest dries up and the coasts flood. Again, one can speculate about it, but we really have no idea. We have no past history of such things from which we can even extrapolate. Just the same, we have to do our best to understand the implications of what may happen, and start to build our capacity to withstand the inevitable shocks that are forthcoming.

In addition to these factors, the localized factors I mentioned earlier render the future of America's older cities even more uncertain. The future of the eds and meds economy, future patterns of immigration and domestic migration, and how future American politics and public policies will affect cities, are all question marks. As we look forward, the future of individual cities is likely to lie somewhere along a continuum, with different cities falling at different points, driven not only by powerful external forces, but by how they respond to those forces. Two scenarios can try to capture the worst and best cases for the cities' future twenty or thirty years from now.

In the worst-case scenario, conditions are dire. Technology has decimated the blue-collar workforce, while economic and social change as well as technological change have reduced the dominant role of eds and meds in the economy. As the economy, buffeted by climate change and the breakdown of international trade, shrinks, all but a handful of cities are becoming once again increasingly marginalized in the national economy. As they offer fewer opportunities, and autonomous vehicles have made distance less of a concern, future generations of Young Grads no longer flock to the cities, while the aging millennial generation has largely opted for the suburbs. While the cities may not fall back to the conditions of the 1970s, most of the gains of the first decades of the new millennium have been reversed.

The cities have become even more polarized and segregated, and less resilient in the face of social and economic shocks, than they are today. As they have retrenched, the remaining upscale areas have become smaller and more concentrated, forming tightly guarded enclaves around downtowns, major universities, and medical centers, while few middle neighborhoods remain intact. Urban populations are shrinking again, as people gradually drift away from the remaining areas of concentrated, multi-generational poverty, and few move in.

As public resources shrink, fewer and fewer efforts are made to foster improvement or revival, or indeed, provide anything more than the most rudimentary public services in those areas. In the prosperous enclaves, businesses and residents tax themselves to pay for the private services that have largely replaced services cities no longer provide. Municipal government has become increasingly dysfunctional, its leaders veering between angry but futile populism and repressive elitism.

The best-case scenario is very different. As cities have diversified their economies, new jobs and businesses have replaced those lost through technological or economic change, while effective programs to build local human capital have made cities increasingly attractive locations for a wide range of emerging economic sectors. Climate change is a daunting challenge, yet far-sighted local leaders have built resilient systems that enable cities to adapt successfully to environmental, economic, and social change.

Enlightened federal policies have strengthened the social safety net, and provide a universal housing allowance. Coupled with thoughtful, inclusive urban housing strategies, housing quality is better, family stability is greater, and more neighborhoods are economically and racially integrated. While there is still poverty in the cities, people or their children routinely move out of poverty. While the poverty rate is still around the national average, it is more about people moving to the cities for opportunity than long-term, multigenerational poverty. Economic and income growth has stabilized the tax base, and allowed cities to both provide better public services and invest in their infrastructure for the future.

A welcoming city continues to be a magnet for Young Grads and immigrants, as well as to increasing numbers of older people, and its population is growing. With excellent pre-K and school options available for all, white and African American middle-class families are increasingly likely to move into or stay in the city; as more of the city's poor move out of poverty, prosperity is spreading further across the city, stabilizing the city's middle neighborhoods.

The second scenario may seem to readers to be no more than wishful thinking on my part, yet while perhaps unlikely, it is not wildly implausible. It would be hard for even the most creative and capable local leadership to achieve without some combination of enlightened national leadership and luck that keeps the national economy on a path of resilience and growth in face of the challenges of the future. Unlikely as that may seem from the vantage point of 2017, given the material and human resources the United States commands, it is far from impossible. There is nothing preordained about high poverty rates or concentrated poverty. Among major industrial nations, in fact, poverty in the United States is well above the norm. While there are reasons for that which will be hard to overcome, there is no reason that it is inevitable or unchangeable.

Moving toward Resilience

The gap between the best- and worst-case scenarios is vast. While where any city ends up falling on the continuum between the two depends in part on what happens in realms far beyond the city's control, it will also depend in part on what the city and its leaders do to build their economy, foster equity and inclusion, and build the city's resilience in face of the inevitable shocks that the coming decades will bring. While the term *resilience* may be overused, it is highly relevant to the future of America's cities, and it is about far more than the ability to adapt one's physical environment to rising sea levels, important as that is.

Resilience is the ability to bounce back. Some may think of cities like Pittsburgh and Baltimore in some respects as exemplars of resilience. Thrown by the loss of the manufacturing industry that fueled their growth, they have come roaring back to become postindustrial cities, driven by world-class medical centers and universities. Yet, are Baltimore and Pittsburgh, or for that matter Seattle, truly resilient cities, or are they simply riding a wave of economic and demographic change, fueled by the sheer dumb luck of having inherited institutions like Johns Hopkins and Carnegie Mellon or having drawn entrepreneurs like Bill Gates, Jeff Bezos, and Paul Allen?

The story of Singapore's economic resilience is fairly well known, but is worth retelling in this context. In 1965, when Singapore split off from the newly established nation of Malaysia to become an independent nation, its prospects looked far from appealing. It had no natural resources, little industry, and no domestic market, and its modest economy was dependent on its role as the entrepot for Malaysia and Indonesia, a role it had just lost. It was, in fact, little more than a sleepy port in decline from its days as a bastion of the British Empire, described by one of its early economic advisors as a "poor little market in a dark corner of Asia."[26] Indeed, Singapore in 1965 had fewer assets than most American industrial cities have today.

Within a few decades, though, it had transformed itself into a model of growth and prosperity, the smallest, and in some respect the most consistently successful, not just economically, but socially as well, of the so-called Asian Tigers. While the sometimes-authoritarian rule of Lee Kwan Yew, Singapore's founding and long-serving president, has legitimately been criticized, that should not detract from the remarkable nature of his and his nation's achievement. While his economic strategies were brilliantly opportunistic, the two critical underlying themes that drove Singapore's growth were, first, a determination to provide honest, transparent, and highly competent government based on the rule of law; and second, an intense focus on education as the means of maximizing the value of the nation's human capital. Singapore was a relatively cohesive society, which gave Lee and his colleagues considerable legitimacy, but that would have mattered little without their long-term laser-like focus on those two themes.

Singapore is not Cleveland, Pittsburgh, or Buffalo. But its lessons are relevant. Resilience will become increasingly critical in the coming decades, and the ability of cities to learn that lesson may well determine where they will fall on the continuum ten, twenty and more years from now. Building true economic and social resilience in America's legacy cities will depend not only on their specific programs and strategies, but on their ability to follow four paths:

- *Rethink municipal governance.* Governments must become more competent, better integrated internally and externally, and more responsive to the communities they serve. Competence, the willingness to build partnerships with others, and the ability to address community needs effectively are critical, but without building open, responsive government—a proposition that embodies within it transparency, outreach, and a willingness to share power with citizens—competence alone is never enough. Resilience depends on the existence of a social compact, something which today is at best weak, and at worst absent, in America's older cities. They will not be able to rebuild their social compacts and become cohesive, resilient communities unless their citizens feel they have a stake in a city government which they believe is acting in their interests.
- *Build human capital.* Creating a system by which all the city's residents—youth and adults—can gain the education, the skills, and the access to the opportunity to live economically productive, satisfying lives is the single most powerful thing that can be done to simultaneously reduce polarization and build resilience. It is the single most powerful thing a city can do to simultaneously foster equity and reduce inequality, while building a firm foundation for the long-term growth of the city's economy.
- *Build the quality of life for the many, not the few.* The quality of life in a city is not determined by stadiums and megaprojects, but by how well the city serves the people who live there, particularly those who lack the means to purchase a better quality of life beyond what the city's public services offer. Cities need to focus on the basics: making

the city safe, providing good schools and attractive parks and play-grounds, removing blight, and fostering livable neighborhoods along with a strong, dynamic downtown.

• *Think long term.* Politicians like to talk about how fixing the problems of fifty years or more will not happen overnight, but most of the time it's an excuse for failure rather than an argument for putting long-term strategies in place. Change does not merely take time, which is something of a truism, but the passage of time alone is as likely to make things worse as better. Positive change takes a *consistent, strategic* use of time. None of the ills that afflict our cities today and none of those likely to emerge in the future will be successfully addressed except through a sustained, long-term commitment to change.

I am a chastened optimist. Over the past fifty years that I have been engaged with America's cities I have seen many changes take place, some for the better, some for the worse. In many respects, today's cities are far better places than they were in the 1970s, but in other respects, they are much the same or even worse. Many plans have failed, but others have succeeded, and in the course of both failure and success, we have learned a great deal about what works and how to make change happen. There will not be a Marshall Plan for the cities, nor will any other magic wand make an appearance. Change is a long, hard slog.

I remain an optimist, because I know how many remarkable people in places like Detroit, Cleveland, and Pittsburgh, as well as Flint, Gary, and Youngstown, are at work trying to make their neighborhoods and their cities better, more inclusive, and more resilient places. I know how hard they are working, and how many long years of slogging they have devoted to this effort. It is their example that makes me believe that, despite all of the many obstacles and steps backward, our cities can become the places that we as a nation deserve.

References

Introduction

1. Mayoral campaign kick-off speech quoted in Hunter Walker, "Bill de Blasio Tells a 'Tale of Two Cities' at His Mayoral Campaign Kick-off," *Observer*, January 27, 2013, http://observer.com/2013/01/bill-de-blasio-tells-a-tale-of-two-cities-at-his-mayoral-campaign-kickoff/.

2. Robert J. Samuelson, "The 'Hollowing' of the Middle Class?" *Washington Post*, January 3, 2016, https://www.washingtonpost.com/opinions/the-hollowing-of-the-middle-class/2016/01/03/167309ea-afdc-11e5-9ab0-884d1cc4b33e_story.html?utm_term=.9a422f198b31.

3. Jacob A. Riis, *How the Other Half Lives: Studies Among the Tenements of New York* (New York: Charles Scribner's Sons, 1890; Hypertext Edition, 2006), http://depts.washington.edu/envir202/Readings/Reading01.pdf.

4. Eugene Smolensky and Robert Plotnick, *Inequality and Poverty in the United States 1900 to 1990* (Madison, WI: University of Wisconsin–Madison, Institute for Research on Poverty, 1993), https://www.irp.wisc.edu/publications/dps/pdfs/dp99893.pdf.

5. Data by Boxwood Means from PolicyMap (www.policymap.com), analysis by author.

6. Lawrence Brown, "Two Baltimores: The White L vs. the Black Butterfly," *City-Paper*, June 28, 2016, http://www.citypaper.com/bcpnews-two-baltimores-the-white-l-vs-the-black-butterfly-20160628-htmlstory.html.

7. Joel Kotkin, *The Human City: Urbanism for the Rest of Us* (Chicago: Agate B2, 2016), 116.

8. David Smith, *Third World Cities in Global Perspective: The Political Economy of Uneven Urbanization* (Boulder, CO: Westview Press, 1996), 2.

9. William Faulkner, *Requiem for a Nun* (London: Chatto & Windus, 1951), 85.

Chapter 1

1. Frances Trollope, *Domestic Manners of the Americans* (London: Whitaker, Treacher & Co, 1832), http://www.gutenberg.org/ebooks/10345.

2. Anna Brownell Jameson, *Winter Studies and Summer Rambles in Canada* (London: Saunders and Otley, 1838), https://ia600300.us.archive.org/13/items/cihm_35746/cihm_35746.pdf.

3. Eleanor Nolan Shuman, *The Trenton Story* (Trenton, NJ: McCrellish & Quigley, 1958).

4. Phillip B. Scranton, "Workshop of the World—Philadelphia," http://www.workshopoftheworld.com/overview/overview.html.

5. Quotation from Federal Writers Project, *They Built a City: 150 Years of Industrial Cincinnati* (Cincinnati, OH: *Cincinnati Post*, 1938), 4, https://archive.org/details/theybuiltcity15000federich.

6. Quotation from Scott Martelle, *Detroit: A Biography* (Chicago: Chicago Review Press 2012), 34.

7. "The Steel Business: The Lot of a Steelworker," PBS *The American Experience*, http://www.pbs.org/wgbh/amex/carnegie/sfeature/mf_steelworker.html.

8. Quoted in Jon C. Teaford, *Cities of the Heartland: The Rise and Fall of the Industrial Midwest* (Bloomington, IN: Indiana University Press, 1994), 72.

9. Teaford, *Cities of the Heartland*, 72.

10. Joseph Ferrie, "The End of American Exceptionalism? Mobility in the United States since 1850," *Journal of Economic Perspectives* 19, no. 3 (2005): 199–215.

11. Robert Beauregard, *Voices of Decline: The Postwar Fate of US Cities* (Cambridge, MA: Blackwell, 1993), 59.

12. Teaford, *Cities of the Heartland*, 179–80.

13. John T. Cumbler, *A Social History of Economic Decline: Business, Politics, and Work in Trenton* (New Brunswick, NJ: Rutgers University Press, 1989).

14. Douglas Rae, *City: Urbanism and Its End* (New Haven, CT: Yale University Press, 2003), 218.

15. Phillip Porter, quoted in James Heaphy, *Parish* (2010), http://engagedscholarship.csuohio.edu/clevmembks/7/.

16. Mark Goldman, *City on the Edge* (Amherst, NY: Prometheus Books, 2007), 101–2.

17. Quoted in Martelle, *Detroit: A Biography*, 140.

18. Martelle, *Detroit: A Biography*, 159.

19. Ray Suarez, *The Old Neighborhood: What We Lost in the Great Suburban Migration* (New York: The Free Press, 1999), 22.

20. Ibid., 3.

21. Jon C. Teaford, "Urban Renewal and Its Aftermath," *Housing Policy Debate* 11, no. 2 (2000): 443–65.

22. Martin Anderson, *The Federal Bulldozer: A Critical Analysis of Urban Renewal 1949–1962* (Cambridge, MA: MIT Press, 1964), 8. For a picture of the anger and resentment that urban renewal left behind, see Mindy Thompson Fullilove, *Root Shock: How Tearing Up City Neighborhoods Hurts America, and What We Can Do about It* (New York: One World/Ballantine Books, 2004).

23. David Jay Merkowitz, "The Segregating City: Philadelphia's Jews in the Urban Crisis 1964–1984" (PhD dissertation, University of Cincinnati, 2010), iii, https://etd.ohiolink.edu/!etd.send_file?accession=ucin1273595539&disposition=inline.

24. Quoted in Richard A. Lamanna, "Change and Diversity in American Community Life" *The Review of Politics* 34, no. 4 (1972): 26–43, 27.

25. Quoted in Lamanna, "Change and Diversity in American Community Life," 26.

26. Quoted in Beauregard, *Voices of Decline*, 201.

27. Jonathan Mahler, *Ladies and Gentlemen, The Bronx Is Burning: 1977, Baseball, Politics, and the Battle for the Soul of a City* (New York: Macmillan, 2005).

28. Teaford, *Cities of the Heartland*, 220.

29. Ibid., 223.

30. Kevin Fox Gotham, "Urban Redevelopment, Past and Present," in *Critical Perspectives on Urban Redevelopment*, vol. 6, edited by Kevin Fox Gotham (Bingley, UK: Emerald Group Publishing Limited, 2001), 13.

31. Robert H. McNulty et al., *The Return of the Livable City* (Washington, DC: Acropolis Books, 1986), 3.

32. Teaford, *Cities of the Heartland*, 229.

33. Richard Florida, *The Rise of the Creative Class* (New York: Basic Books, 2002), 217.

Chapter 2

1. See: Baltimore.org, http://baltimore.org/listings/breweriespubstaverns/maxs-taphouse.

2. See: Zillow, http://www.zillow.com/homes/for_sale/Fells-Point-Baltimore-MD/158479_rid/39.297742,-76.570716,39.269341,-76.61685_rect/14_zm/, accessed September 1, 2016.

3. "The Rising Cost of Not Going to College," Pew Research Center, http://www.pewsocialtrends.org/2014/02/11/the-rising-cost-of-not-going-to-college/.

4. Sean Reardon and Kendra Bischoff, "Growth in the Residential Segregation of Families by Income 1970–2009," USA 2010 Project, 2011, http://www.s4.brown.edu/us2010/Data/Report/report111111.pdf.

5. Shirley Bradway Laska and Daphne Spain, *Back to the City: Issues in Neighborhood Renovation* (New York: Pergamon Press, 1980), xi.

6. Terry Nichols Clark, "Introduction: Taking Entertainment Seriously," in *The City as an Entertainment Machine*, edited by Terry Nichols Clark (Lanham, MD: Lexington Books, 2011), 7.

7. "Millennials and Re-Urbanization of the City," Avison Young, http://philadelphiapjm.avisonyoung.com/millennials-and-re-urbanization-of-the-city/.

8. Ray Suarez, *The Old Neighborhood: What We Lost in the Great Suburban Migration* (New York: The Free Press, 1999), 14.

9. Quoted in Ted Hesson, "Rickshaws as a Ride to Detroit's Salvation," *Atlantic Monthly*, July 8, 2015, http://www.theatlantic.com/business/archive/2015/07/rickshaws-as-a-ride-to-detroits-salvation/426189/.

10. *Encyclopedia of Cleveland History*, http://ech.cwru.edu/Resource/Image/I02.gif.

11. John Carlisle, "The Last Days of Detroit's Chaldean Town," *Detroit Free Press*, August 2, 2015, http://www.freep.com/story/news/columnists/john-carlisle/2015/08/01/detroit-chaldean-town-last-days/30993903/.

Chapter 3

1. Quoted in Lisa Prevost, "The Yale Effect Spreads Out," *New York Times*, March 24, 2009, http://www.nytimes.com/2009/03/25/realestate/commercial/25haven.html?mcubz=1.

2. Fred Powledge, *Model City: One Town's Efforts to Rebuild Itself* (New York: Simon & Schuster, 1970), 25.

3. Douglas Rae, *City: Urbanism and Its End* (New Haven, CT: Yale University Press, 2003), 79.

4. Herbert N. Casson, *The Romance of Steel* (New York: A. S. Barnes & Co., 1907), 25.

5. Ibid., 218–19.

6. Mark Muro and Sifan Liu, "Manufacturing Sector Inflation-Adjusted Output and Employment, 1980–2015," from "Why Trump's Factory Job Promises Won't Pan Out—In One Chart," *The Avenue* / Brookings Institution, November 21, 2016, https://www.brookings.edu/blog/the-avenue/2016/11/21/why-trumps-factory-job -promises-wont-pan-out-in-one-chart/?utm_campaign=Metropolitan+Policy+Progr am&utm_source=hs_email&utm_medium=email&utm_content=38550371.

7. Enrico Moretti, *The New Geography of Jobs* (New York: Houghton Mifflin Harcourt, 2012), 26.

8. Vaclav Smil, *Made in the USA* (Cambridge, MA: MIT Press, 2013), 1.

9. Salena Zito, "The Day That Destroyed the Working Class and Sowed the Seeds of Trump," *New York Post,* September 16, 2017, https://nypost.com/2017/09/16/the -day-that-destroyed-the-working-class-and-sowed-the-seeds-for-trump/.

10. John Cumbler, *A Social History of Economic Decline: Business, Politics, and Work in Trenton* (New Brunswick, NJ: Rutgers University Press, 1989), 186–87.

11. Quoted in Bill Toland, "In Desperate 1983, There Was Nowhere for Pittsburgh's Economy to Go but Up: A Tide of Change," *Pittsburgh Post-Gazette*, December 23, 2012, http://www.post-gazette.com/business/businessnews/2012/12/23/In -desperate-1983-there-was-nowhere-for-Pittsburgh-s-economy-to-go-but-up /stories/201212230258.

12. "General Motors to Cut 70,000 Jobs; 21 Plants to Shut," *New York Times,* December 19, 1991, http://www.nytimes.com/1991/12/19/business/general-motors -to-cut-70000-jobs-21-plants-to-shut.html?pagewanted=all.

13. Tracy Neumann, *Remaking the Rust Belt: The Postindustrial Transformation of North America* (Philadelphia: University of Pennsylvania Press, 2016), 93.

14. James W. Wagner, "Multiversity or University? Pursuing Competing Goods Simultaneously," *Academic Exchange* 9, no. 4 (February/March 2007), http://www .emory.edu/ACAD_EXCHANGE/2007/febmar/wagneressay.html.

15. Clark Kerr, *The Uses of the University* (Cambridge, MA: Harvard University Press, 1963). The book was an expanded version of his 1963 Godkin Lecture at Harvard, "The Idea of a Multiversity."

16. Wagner, "Multiversity or University?"

17. Johns Hopkins University website, http://www.hopkinsmedicine.org/about /index.html.

18. National Institutes of Health website, https://report.nih.gov/award/index.cfm ?ot=&fy=2014&state=&ic=&fm=&orgid=&distr=&rfa=&om=n&pid=.

19. Aaron Aupperlee, "Developing Spinoffs Help Pitt, CMU Advance Technologies," *Pittsburgh Tribune-Journal*, September 3, 2016, http://triblive.com/news /allegheny/10994116-74/university-cmu-pitt.

20. J. R. Reed, "Up Close: A New Haven for Biotech," *Yale Daily News*, April 16, 2014, http://yaledailynews.com/blog/2014/04/16/a-new-haven-for-biotech/.

21. Cortex website, http://cortexstl.com/the-district/.

22. Bruce Katz and Julie Wagner, *The Rise of Innovation Districts: A New Geography of Innovation in America* (Washington, DC: The Brookings Institution, May 2014), 1, https://www.brookings.edu/wp-content/uploads/2016/07/InnovationDistricts1.pdf.

23. Michael Sorkin, ed., *Variations on a Theme Park: The New American City and the End of Public Space* (New York: Hill & Wang, 1992).

24. Terry Nichols Clark, "Introduction: Taking Entertainment Seriously," in *The City as an Entertainment Machine*, edited by Terry Nichols Clark (Lanham, MD: Lexington Books, 2011), 2.

25. Edward L. Glaeser, Jed Kolko, and Albert Saiz, "Consumer City," *Journal of Economic Geography* 1, no. 1 (2001): 27–50.

26. Quoted in Richard Florida, *The Rise of the Creative Class* (New York: Basic Books, 2002), 217.

27. Ibid., 224.

28. Ed Stannard, "Yale University and New Haven Team Up to Remake Broadway for Retail, Restaurants," *New Haven Register*, May 16, 2015, http://www.nh register.com/connecticut/article/Yale-University-and-New-Haven-team-up-to-re make-11357057.php.

29. Ibid.

30. Heywood T. Sanders, *Convention Center Follies: Politics, Power, and Investment in American Cities* (Philadelphia: University of Pennsylvania Press, 2014), 10.

31. Econsult Solutions, Inc., "Tourism as an Economic Engine for Greater Philadelphia: 2015 Visitation and Economic Impact Report, Prepared for Visit Philadelphia," http://files.visitphilly.com/Visit-Philly-2015-Visitation-and-Impact-Full -Report.pdf.

32. Rob Roberts, "Public Financing of Renovations at Big Hotel Is Part of One-Two KC Convention Punch," *Kansas City Business Journal*, September 28, 2016, http://www.bizjournals.com/kansascity/news/2016/09/28/public-financing-of-reno vations-at-kcs-biggest.html.

33. Nicholas J. C. Pistor, "City Struggles to Maintain $17 Million Washington Avenue Streetscape," *St. Louis Post-Dispatch*, December 5, 2015, http://www.stltoday .com/news/local/govt-and-politics/st-louis-struggles-to-maintain-million-washing ton-avenue-streetscape/article_c9ee57c4-c43d-50a8-8f88-3481f36401e9.html.

34. Glaeser et al., "Consumer City," 29.

35. Moretti, *The New Geography of Jobs*, 98.

Chapter 4

1. Charles Silberman, *Crisis in Black and White* (New York: Alfred Knopf, 1964), 4.

2. *Report of the National Advisory Commission on Civil Disorders* (Washington, DC: Government Printing Office, 1968), 1.

3. Ibid., 398.

4. "Baltimore Tries Drastic Plan of Race Segregation," *New York Times Sunday Magazine*, December 25, 1910, http://sundaymagazine.org/2010/12/baltimore-tries -drastic-plan-of-race-segregation/.

5. Quoted in "Redlined: The History of Race and Real Estate in Cleveland & Its Relationship to Health Equity Today," Kirwan Institute for the study of Race

& Ethnicity, Ohio State University, 2014 (PPT Presentation), http://kirwaninstitute
.osu.edu/wp-content/uploads/2015/02/cleveland-place-matters.pdf.

6. Douglas Linder, "The Sweet Trials: An Account," http://law2.umkc.edu/faculty
/projects/ftrials/sweet/sweetaccount.HTM.

7. Kirwan Institute, "Redlined."

8. Arnold R. Hirsch, *Making the Second Ghetto: Race and Housing in Chicago, 1940–
1960* (Cambridge, UK: Cambridge University Press, 1983), 145.

9. Scott Martelle, *Detroit: A Biography* (Chicago: Chicago Review Press, 2012),
152.

10. Steve Babson, *Working Detroit: The Making of a Union Town* (New York: Adama
Books, 1984), 157.

11. Elaine Moon, "Paradise Valley," quoted in "Detroit's Black Bottom and Paradise Valley Neighborhoods," Walter P. Reuther Library, Wayne State University,
https://reuther.wayne.edu/node/8609.

12. Mary Karmelek, "Does Lafayette Park's Landmark Status Whitewash History?" *Newsweek*, August 31, 2015, http://www.newsweek.com/does-lafayette-parks
-landmark-status-whitewash-history-367320.

13. Tim O'Neil, "A Look Back: Clearing of Mill Creek Valley Changed the Face
of the City," *St. Louis Post-Dispatch*, August 9, 2009, http://www.stltoday.com/news
/local/a-look-back-clearing-of-mill-creek-valley-changed-the/article_04738cde
-b0f8-5688-a20e-6fd86266d1ac.html.

14. Eliel Saarinen, *The City: Its Growth, Its Decay, Its Future* (New York: Rein-
hold Publishing, 1943), 143, 144; see also: Amanda Row Tillotson, "Pathologizing
Place and Race: The Rhetoric of Slum Clearance and Urban Renewal, 1930–1965,"
Agora Journal of Urban Planning and Design (2010), https://deepblue.lib.umich.edu
/handle/2027.42/120358.

15. Leah Platt Boustan, "Was Postwar Suburbanization 'White Flight'? Evidence
from the Black Migration," *Quarterly Journal of Economics* 125, no. 1 (2010): 417–43.

16. Eugene Robinson, *Disintegration: The Splintering of Black America* (New York:
Doubleday, 2010), 66.

17. Kendra Bischoff and Sean Reardon, "Residential Segregation by Income,
1970–2009," (New York: Russell Sage Foundation, 2013), 15.

18. Elon Gilad, "500 Years Later: The Mysterious Origin of the Word 'Ghetto,'"
Ha'aretz, March 29, 2016, http://www.haaretz.com/jewish/features/.premium
-1.700477. For possible origins of the word *ghetto*, see: Anatoly Lieberman, "Why
Don't We Know the Origin of the Word *Ghetto*?" Oxford Etymologist, *OUP Blog*,
March 4, 2009, http://blog.oup.com/2009/03/ghetto/.

19. Hutchins Hapgood, *The Spirit of the Ghetto* (New York: Funk & Wagnalls,
1902), 9.

20. St. Clair Drake and Horace A. Cayton, *Black Metropolis: A Study of Negro Life
in a Northern City* (New York: Harcourt Brace, 1945), 382. This discussion is also
indebted to: Mitchell Duneier, *Ghetto: The Invention of a Place, the History of an Idea*
(New York: Farrar, Strauss & Giroux, 2016).

21. Talja Blokland, "From the Outside Looking In: A 'European' Perspective on
the Ghetto," *City & Community* 7, no. 4 (December 2008): 372.

22. Justin Charity, "What Does 'Inner City' Mean, Anyway?" *The Complex*, February 1, 2016, http://www.complex.com/life/2016/02/inner-city-origin-and-proliferation-of-sloppy-political-language.

23. St. Louis population data is for area included in census tracts 1111 through 1115.

24. Joe Cortright and Dillon Mahmudi, "Lost in Place: Why the Persistence and Spread of Concentrated Poverty—Not Gentrification—Is Our Biggest Urban Challenge," *City Observatory*, December 2014, http://cityobservatory.org/lost-in-place/.

25. Randall Dodd and Paul Mills, "Outbreak: U.S. Subprime Contagion," *Finance & Development* 45, no. 2 (June 2008): 14–18, https://www.imf.org/external/pubs/ft/fandd/2008/06/pdf/dodd.pdf.

26. "The Hansen Files with Chris Hansen," *NBC News*, March 22, 2009, http://www.nbcnews.com/id/29827248/ns/dateline_nbc-the_hansen_files_with_chris_hansen/t/if-you-had-pulse-we-gave-you-loan/#.WK2gjuQzWUk.

27. Emily Badger, "The Dramatic Racial Bias of Subprime Lending During the Housing Boom," *CityLab*, August 16, 2013, http://www.citylab.com/housing/2013/08/blacks-really-were-targeted-bogus-loans-during-housing-boom/6559/.

28. Quoted in Michael Powell, "Banks Accused of Pushing Mortgage Deals on Blacks," *New York Times*, June 6, 2009, http://www.nytimes.com/2009/06/07/us/07baltimore.html.

29. Geoff Boucher, "A Politician Who Runs on Hip-Hop," *Los Angeles Times*, May 11, 2003, http://articles.latimes.com/2003/may/11/nation/na-kwame11.

30. Detroit personnel data from City of Detroit *Certified Annual Financial Reports* (CAFR), various years, compiled by author.

31. Gus Burns, "Detroit Loses 1,400 Police Officers in a Decade, Struggles to Keep Pace with Crime," *Mlive*, August 28, 2013, http://www.mlive.com/news/detroit/index.ssf/2013/08/detroit_loses_1400_police_offi.html.

32. Lauren Hood, "Escaping Like Thieves in the Night: The New Wave of Black Flight," Posted to *Michigan Now*, July 29, 2014, http://www.michigannow.org/2014/07/29/black-senior-citizen-flight/.

33. "Black Flight," *Economist*, March 31, 2011, http://www.economist.com/node/18486343, 25.

34. Akiim DeShay, quoted in Brendan Kirby, "Blacks Take Flight," *PoliZette*, May 30, 2016, http://www.lifezette.com/polizette/blacks-take-flight/.

Chapter 5

1. The phrase I have used in the title of this chapter, although not original, is simply too good not to use. "Gentrification and Its Discontents" is clearly derived from Freud & Strachey's 1930 book *Civilization and its Discontents*, with a nod to Joseph Stiglitz's 2003 volume *Globalization and its Discontents*; the first published work I have been able to find with this title is a piece by Benjamin Schwartz in the *Atlantic Monthly* in 2010. It has since been used by others, including Richard Campanella (writing about New Orleans) in 2013, and Richard Florida.

2. Chloe Detrick, "5 Reasons to Love Lawrenceville," *NEXTpittsburgh*, May 4, 2015, http://www.nextpittsburgh.com/neighborhoods/lawrenceville/things-to-do-in-lawrenceville/.

3. Census tract 902.

4. Ruth Glass, "London: Aspects of Change," reprinted in *The Gentrification Debates: A Reader*, edited by Japonica Brown-Saracino (New York: Routledge, 2013), 22.

5. J. Peter Byrne, "Two Cheers for Gentrification," *Howard Law Journal* 46, no. 3 (2003): 405.

6. Justin Davidson, "Is Gentrification All Bad?" *New York*, February 2, 2014, http://nymag.com/news/features/gentrification-2014-2/.

7. See: http://www.businessdictionary.com/definition/gentrification.html.

8. Zillow.com, http://www.zillow.com/homes/for_sale/Anacostia-Washington-DC/pmf,pf_pt/house,townhouse_type/524952_zpid/121670_rid/38.87777,-76.961804,38.8492,-77.007938_rect/14_zm/, accessed December 9, 2016.

9. Robert M. Fogelson, *Downtown: Its Rise and Fall, 1880–1950* (New Haven, CT: Yale University Press, 2001), 26.

10. Quoted in Fogelson, *Downtown*, 21.

11. Larry R. Ford, *Cities and Buildings: Skyscrapers, Skid Rows, and Suburbs* (Baltimore, MD: Johns Hopkins University Press, 1994).

12. Jon C. Teaford, "Urban Renewal and Its Aftermath," *Housing Policy Debate* 11, no. 2 (2000): 448.

13. Ibid.

14. Mitchell Schwarzer, "Downtown: A Short History of American Urban Exceptionalism," *Places Journal*, February 2016, https://doi.org/10.22269/160216.

15. Erin McCarthy, "Eleven Unexpectedly Awesome Things in St. Louis's City Museum," *Mental Floss*, November 13, 2012, http://mentalfloss.com/article/13063/11-awesomely-unexpected-things-st-louis%E2%80%99s-city-museum.

16. Bryan Christopher Zundel, *Catalyzing Urban Redevelopment on Washington Avenue*, MCRP thesis, Missouri State University, 2008.

17. Census tracts most closely approximating downtown boundaries were used for these calculations, comparing data from the 2000 census with that from the 2011–2015 American Community Survey. Census tracts in St. Louis were 1255, 1256, and 1274; in Cleveland, 1071.01, 1077.01 and 1078.02.

18. Louis Aguilar, "Putting a Price Tag on Properties Linked to Gilbert," *Detroit News*, April 28, 2016, http://www.detroitnews.com/story/business/2016/04/28/dan-gilbert-bedrock-downtown-detroit-buildings/83681698/.

19. Jackelyn Hwang and Robert J. Sampson, "Divergent Pathways of Gentrification: Racial Inequality and the Social Order of Renewal in Chicago Neighborhoods," *American Sociological Review* 79, no. 4 (2014): 726–51.

20. Todd Swanstrom, Henry S. Webber, and Molly W. Metzger, "Rebound Neighborhoods in Older Industrial Cities: The Case of St. Louis," in *Economic Mobility: Research and Ideas on Strengthening Family, Community, and the Economy*, edited by Alexandra Brown, David Buchholz, Daniel Davis, and Arturo Gonzalez (St. Louis, MO: Federal Reserve Bank of St. Louis, 2016), 340.

21. Lawrence Brown, "Two Baltimores: The White L vs. the Black Butterfly," *Citypaper*, June 28, 2016, http://www.citypaper.com/bcpnews-two-baltimores-the-white-l-vs-the-black-butterfly-20160628-htmlstory.html.

22. Kalima Rose, "Beyond Gentrification: Tools for Equitable Development," *Shelterforce* no. 117 (May/June 2001), http://www.nhi.org/online/issues/117/Rose.html.

23. "York & Fig, Part V: Flipping the Neighborhood," *Marketplace*, American Public Media, December 5, 2014, http://yorkandfig.com/#post-279.

24. Quoted in Terry Pristin, "From Abandoned Brewery to Piazza, Philly-Style," *New York Times*, November 3, 2009, http://www.nytimes.com/2009/11/04/realestate/commercial/04piazza.html.

25. Quoted in "Mayor de Blasio Signs Three New Laws Protecting Tenants from Harassment," Press Release, New York City Mayor's Office, September 3, 2015, http://www1.nyc.gov/office-of-the-mayor/news/590-15/mayor-de-blasio-signs-three-new-laws-protecting-tenants-harassment.

26. Jerome Krase and Judith N. DeSena, *Race, Class, and Gentrification in Brooklyn: A View from the Street* (Lanham, MD: Lexington Books, 2016), 32.

27. Joseph Cortright, "The Perils of Conflating Gentrification and Displacement: A Longer and Wonkier Critique of Governing's Gentrification Issue," *City Observatory*, February 2, 2015, http://cityobservatory.org/longer-governing-response/.

28. Emily Dowdall, "The Actual Value Initiative: Philadelphia's Progress on Its Property Tax Overhaul" (Philadelphia, PA: Pew Charitable Trusts, 2015).

29. Jarrett Murphy, "The Complicated Research on How Gentrification Affects the Poor," *City Limits*, November 20, 2015, http://citylimits.org/2015/11/20/the-complicated-research-on-how-gentrification-affects-the-poor/.

30. Swanstrom, Webber, and Metzger, "Rebound Neighborhoods," 342.

31. Michelle Lewis, quoted in Abigal Savitch-Lew, "Gentrification Spotlight: How Portland Is Pushing Out Its Black Residents," *Colorlines*, April 18, 2016, http://www.colorlines.com/articles/gentrification-spotlight-how-portland-pushing-out-its-black-residents.

32. Quoted in *The Guardian*, February 26, 2014, https://www.theguardian.com/cities/2014/feb/26/spike-lee-gentrification-rant-transcript.

33. Janine Bologna et al., "The Right to Stay Put: City Garden Montessori School and Neighborhood Change," George Warren Brown School of Social Work and Sam Fox School of Design and Visual Arts, Washington University in St. Louis, 2015, https://csd.wustl.edu/Publications/Documents/city-garden_final-report.pdf.

34. "Gentrification in Philadelphia's Fishtown Neighborhood Creates Tension between Original Residents and Newcomers," blog post, *Fishtown Uncovered*, October 14, 2013, https://foreverfishtown.wordpress.com/2013/10/14/tension-caused-by-gentrification-in-fishtown-is-a-choice/.

35. Jake Flanagin, "The Brooklynization of Detroit Is Going to Be Terrible for Detroiters," *Quartz*, July 15, 2015, http://qz.com/453531/the-brooklynization-of-detroit-is-going-to-be-terrible-for-detroiters/.

36. "Gentrification on Steroids: The Water Shut-Offs and You," *Movement Strategy Center* (no date), http://movementstrategy.org/gentrification-steroids-detroit-water-shut-offs/#.

Chapter 6

1. Data for Pen Lucy and Wilson Park is for census tracts 2701.01 and 901.

2. Daniel Kay Hertz, "Watch Chicago's Middle Class Disappear Before Your Very Eyes," *City Notes*, blog post, March 31, 2014, https://danielkayhertz.com/2014/03/31/middle-class/.

3. Matthew Desmond, *Evicted: Poverty and Profit in the American City* (New York: Crown Publishers, 2016), 4.

4. Foreclosure filing data provided to author by Ralph W. Voorhees Center for Civic Engagement, Rutgers University, New Brunswick, New Jersey.

5. Ellen Seidman and Bing Bai, "Where Have All the Small Loans Gone?" *Urban Institute*, blog post, April 18, 2016.

6. Quoted in "Absentee Landlords Investing in Cheap Rentals Out-of-State," *Newsweek*, October 19, 2016, http://www.newsweek.com/absentee-landlords-investing-cheap-rentals-out-state-507449.

7. Interviewed on Business Innovators Radio, June 4, 2015, http://businessinnovatorsmagazine.com/avi-cohen-trenton-real-estate-investment-expert/.

8. Quoted in Nick Carey, "Cheap Detroit Houses Scooped Up by Investors Can Be Costly for Communities, Bad News for Buyers," *Huffington Post*, July 3, 2013, http://www.huffingtonpost.com/2013/07/03/cheap-detroit-houses_n_3538213.html.

9. Data is for Census tract 1510.

10. Jane Jacobs, *The Death and Life of Great American Cities* (New York: Random House, 1961), 112.

11. Wesley G. Skogan, *Disorder and Decline: Crime and the Spiral of Decay in American Neighborhoods* (Berkeley, CA: University of California Press, 1990), 13.

12. Lauren Hood, "Gentrification in Detroit," *Honeysuckle Magazine*, September 2016, http://honeysucklemag.com/gentrification-in-detroit/.

13. Jerry Mangona, "Gentrification: Views from Both Sides of the Street," *Huffington Post*, July 10, 2012, http://www.huffingtonpost.com/jerry-mangona/gentrification-detroit_b_1662070.html.

Chapter 7

1. Kirstin Kennedy, "Aliquippa Housing Plans Show Journey of Immigrants," *Beaver County Times*, February 25, 2015, http://www.timesonline.com/progress/2015/aliquippa-housing-plans-show-journey-of-immigrants/article_8c12628e-ae3b-11e4-9978-cbb2cd1b4e8c.html.

2. Quoted in S. L. Price, "The Heart of Football Beats in Aliquippa," *Sports Illustrated*, January 26, 2011, http://carldavidson.blogspot.com/2011/01/aliquippas-harsh-realities-featured-in.html.

3. Integrated Postsecondary Education Data System, National Center for Education Statistics; salaries compiled by startclass.com; see: http://faculty-salaries.startclass.com/.

4. Higher Education Research and Development Survey, National Science Foundation, https://www.nsf.gov/statistics/srvyherd/.

5. Edward L. Glaeser, "Introduction," in *Agglomeration Economics*, edited by Edward L. Glaeser (Chicago: University of Chicago Press, 2010), 1.

6. Stuart S. Rosenthal and William C. Strange, "Small Establishments/Big Effects: Agglomeration, Industrial Organization, and Entrepreneurship" in *Agglomeration Economics*, edited by Edward L. Glaeser, 300.

7. David B. Audretsch and Maryann P. Feldman, "Knowledge Spillovers and the Geography of Innovation," in *Handbook of Regional and Urban Economics 4*, edited by J. Vernon Henderson and Jacque-Francois Thisse (Amsterdam: Elsevier, 2004), 2713–39.

8. Enrico Moretti, *The New Geography of Jobs* (New York: Houghton Mifflin Harcourt, 2012), 125.

9. Ibid., 126.

10. Ibid., 127.

11. Richard Florida, *The Rise of the Creative Class* (New York: Basic Books, 2002), 224.

12. Laura A. Reese and Minting Ye, "Policy Versus Place Luck: Achieving Local Economic Prosperity," *Economic Development Quarterly* 25, no. 3 (2011): 221–36.

13. Youngstown Neighborhood Development Corporation website, http://www .yndc.org/about.

14. Quoted in "How Rust Belt City Youngstown Plans to Overcome Decades of Decline," *PBS Newshour*, April 16, 2016, http://www.pbs.org/newshour/bb/how -rust-belt-city-youngstown-plans-to-overcome-decades-of-decline/.

15. Alexandra Stephenson, "In Weary Wisconsin Town, a Billionaire-Fueled Revival," *New York Times*, August 5, 2017.

16. J. D. Vance, "Opioid of the Masses," *Atlantic Monthly*, July 4, 2016, https:// www.theatlantic.com/politics/archive/2016/07/opioid-of-the-masses/489911/.

17. Alana Semuels, "Suburbs and the New American Poverty," *Atlantic Monthly*, January 7, 2015, https://www.theatlantic.com/business/archive/2015/01 /suburbs-and-the-new-american-poverty/384259/.

18. Elizabeth Kneebone and Alan Berube, *Confronting Suburban Poverty in America* (Washington, DC: Brookings Institution Press, 2013).

19. William H. Whyte, *The Organization Man* (New York: Simon & Schuster, 1956), 313.

20. Ibid., 314–15.

21. Advertisement found on Pinterest; see: https://www.pinterest.com/pin/279 152876876513040/.

22. John Ostenburg, "Confronting Suburban Poverty in Park Forest, Illinois," *Confronting Suburban Poverty*, blog post, February 5, 2014, http://confrontingsuburban poverty.org/2014/02/confronting-suburban-poverty-in-park-forest-illinois/.

23. Joe Mahr and Matthew Walberg, "Harvey Residents Detail Life in 'Lawless' Community," *Chicago Tribune*, December 25, 2014, http://www.chicagotribune.com /news/watchdog/ct-harvey-residents-frustrated-met-20141225-story.html.

24. Mark Glennon, "Suicidal Property Tax Rates and the Collapse of Chicago's South Suburbs," *WirePoints*, November 22, 2015, http://www.wirepoints.com/suicidal-property-tax-rates-and-the-collapse-of-chicagos-south-suburbs-wp-original/.

25. House prices and taxes, Zillow.com, https://www.zillow.com/homes/recently _sold/Park-Forest-IL/house_type/33328_rid/globalrelevanceex_sort/41.531133, -87.590561,41.423871,-87.775097_rect/12_zm/, accessed April 3, 2017.

26. Sales price data from Boxwood Means on PolicyMap, https://www.policymap .com/.

27. Reihan Salam, "How the Suburbs Got Poor—Places That Thrived in the Era of Two-Parent Families Are Struggling Today," *Slate*, September 4, 2014, http://www.slate.com/articles/news_and_politics/politics/2014/09/poverty_in_the_suburbs_places_that_thrived_in_the_era_of_two_parent_families.html.

28. Sarah Kendzior, "Down and Out in Beverly Hills, Missouri: The Tiny Town That Runs on Police Tickets," *The Guardian*, April 22, 2015, https://www.theguardian.com/us-news/2015/apr/22/beverly-hills-missouri-police-ferguson.

29. "Investigation of the Ferguson Police Department," US Department of Justice, Civil Rights Division, March 4, 2015, 3–4, https://www.justice.gov/sites/default/files/opa/press-releases/attachments/2015/03/04/ferguson_police_department_report.pdf.

30. Ben Casselman, "The Poorest Corner of Town," *FiveThirtyEight*, August 26, 2014, https://fivethirtyeight.com/features/ferguson-missouri/.

31. Michael Duncan, "Snapshot: An Ordinary Suburb, an Extraordinary Number of Foreclosures," *Bridges*, Federal Reserve Bank of St. Louis, Fall 2008, https://www.stlouisfed.org/publications/bridges/fall-2008/snapshot-an-ordinary-suburb-an-extraordinary-number-of-foreclosures.

32. Casselman, "The Poorest Corner of Town."

33. Stanton Lawrence, "How Missouri Killed the Normandy School District," *Diane Ravitch's Blog*, June 22, 2014, https://dianeravitch.net/2014/06/22/stanton-lawrence-how-missouri-killed-the-normandy-school-district/.

34. Mike Jones, quoted in Elisa Crouch, "Officials Express Shame at State of Normandy Schools," *St. Louis Post-Dispatch*, May 5, 2015, http://www.stltoday.com/news/local/officials-express-shame-at-state-of-normandy-schools/article_0966c61a-4c93-5138-9546-cb46f7b93590.html.

35. Christopher Leinberger, "The Next Slum?" *Atlantic Monthly*, March 2008, https://www.theatlantic.com/magazine/archive/2008/03/the-next-slum/306653/.

Chapter 8

1. Judy Rose, "Indian Village Mansion Was Detroit's First $1-Million Home," *Lansing State Journal*, September 16, 2014, http://www.lansingstatejournal.com/story/life/2014/09/16/indian-village-mansion-detroits-first-m-home/15748179/.

2. Roslyn Corenzwit Lieb et al., "Abandonment of Residential Property in an Urban Context," *DePaul Law Review* 23, no. 3 (Spring 1974): 1186.

3. Roger Starr, "Making New York Smaller," *New York Times Sunday Magazine*, November 14, 1976.

4. Robert W. Burchell and David Listokin, *The Adaptive Reuse Handbook* (New Brunswick, NJ: Rutgers Center for Urban Policy Research, 1981).

5. Alan Mallach, *A Decent Home: Planning, Building, and Preserving Affordable Housing* (Chicago: Planners Press, 2008), 263.

6. Detroit Land Bank Authority website, www.buildingdetroit.org.

7. Cleveland Design Collaborative website, http://www.cudc.kent.edu/projects_research/research/reimagining_cleveland.html.

8. J. Blaine Bonham Jr., Gerri Spilka, and Daryl Rastorfer, *Old Cities/Green Cities: Communities Transform Unmanaged Land*, Planning Advisory Service Report 506/507 (Chicago: American Planning Association, 2002), 110.

9. Quoted in Patrick Kerkstra, "Special Report: Vacant Land, Focused Plans," *Plan-Philly*, September 21, 2010, http://planphilly.com/articles/2010/09/21/special-report-vacant-land-focused-plans.

10. For research on vacant-lot greening effects, see, for example: Charles C. Branas et al., "A Difference-in-Differences Analysis of Health, Safety, and Greening Vacant Urban Space," *American Journal of Epidemiology* 174, no. 11 (2011): 1296–306; and Eugenia C. Garvin, Carolyn C. Cannuscio, and Charles C. Branas, "Greening Vacant Lots to Reduce Violent Crime: A Randomized Controlled Trial," *Injury Prevention* 19, no. 3 (2013): 198–203.

11. Ronnie Schreiber, "Hantz Woodlands—A Tree Grows (Actually It's More like 20,000) in Detroit," *The Truth About Cars*, August 4, 2015, http://www.thetruthabout cars.com/2015/08/tree-grows-actually-like-20000-detroit-hantz-woodlands/.

12. For a description and analysis of the Baltimore Vacants to Value program, see: Alan Mallach, "Tackling the Challenge of Blight in Baltimore: An Evaluation of Baltimore's Vacants to Value Program" (Washington, DC: Center for Community Progress, 2017).

13. Quoted in Michael Westgate with Ann Vick-Westgate, *Gale Force: Gale Cincotta, the Battles for Disclosure and Community Reinvestment* (Education and Resources Group, Inc., 2011), 26.

14. Federal Reserve System Board of Governors website, https://www.federal reserve.gov/consumerscommunities/cra_about.htm.

15. Quoted in J. Scott Kohler, "Bedford-Stuyvesant and the Rise of the Community Development Corporation," in Joel L. Fleishman, J. Scott Kohler, and Steven Schindler, *Casebook for The Foundation: A Great American Secret* (Durham, NC: Duke University Center for Strategic Philanthropy and Civil Society, 2007), 95.

16. Alexander von Hoffman, "The Past, Present, and Future of Community Development in the United States," in *Investing in What Works for America's Communities*, edited by Nancy O. Andrews and David J. Erickson (San Francisco: Federal Reserve Bank of San Francisco & Low Income Investment Fund, 2012), 35.

17. Roland F. Ferguson and William T. Dickens, "Introduction," in *Urban Problems and Community Development*, edited by Roland F. Ferguson and William T. Dickens (Washington, DC: Brookings Institution Press, 1999), 5.

18. Ibid., 1.

19. Avis Vidal, *Rebuilding Communities: A National Study of Urban Community Development Corporations* (New York: New School for Social Research, Community Development Research Center, Graduate School of Management and Urban Policy, 1992).

20. Nicholas Lemann, "The Myth of Community Development," *New York Times*, January 9, 1994, http://www.nytimes.com/1994/01/09/magazine/the-myth-of-com munity-development.html?pagewanted=all&mcubz=1.

21. The author was present at this exchange.

22. Lemann, "The Myth of Community Development."

23. Quoted in Laura Sullivan, "Affordable Housing Program Costs More, Shelters Fewer," *National Public Radio*, May 9, 2017, http://www.npr.org/2017/05/09/527046451/affordable-housing-program-costs-more-shelters-less.

24. Tim Evans, "Assessment of the New Jersey Low-Income Housing Tax Credit Program" (Trenton, NJ: New Jersey Future, 2017), http://www.njfuture.org/wp-content/uploads/2017/05/New-Jersey-Future-Assessment-of-the-NJLIHTC-program.pdf.

25. Annie Linskey, "20-Year Life Gap Separates City's Poorest, Wealthy," *Baltimore Sun*, October 16, 2008, http://articles.baltimoresun.com/2008-10-16/news/bal-te.md.ci.death16oct16_1_life-expectancy-hollins-market-neighborhoods.

26. For research on outcomes of moves, see: Micere Keels et al., "Fifteen Years Later: Can Residential Mobility Programs Provide a Long-Term Escape from Neighborhood Segregation, Crime, and Poverty?" *Demography* 42, no. 1 (February 2005); Michael P. Johnson, Helen F. Ladd, and Jens Ludwig, "The Benefits and Costs of Residential Mobility Programs for the Poor," *Housing Studies* 17, no. 1 (2002), 25–138; and Raj Chetty, Nathaniel Hendren, and Lawrence Katz, "The Effects of Exposure to Better Neighborhoods on Children: New Evidence from the Moving to Opportunity Project," *American Economic Review* 106, no. 4 (2016).

27. Douglas S. Massey et al., *Climbing Mount Laurel: The Struggle for Affordable Housing and Social Mobility in an American Suburb* (Princeton, NJ: Princeton University Press, 2013), 193.

28. Andrew Giambrone, "D.C. Affordable Housing Program Begins Seeing Results," *Washington CityPaper*, August 18, 2017, http://www.washingtoncitypaper.com/news/housing-complex/blog/20972914/dc-affordable-housing-program-begins-seeing-results.

29. George Galster et al., *The Impact of Community Development Corporations on Urban Neighborhoods* (Washington, DC: The Urban Institute, 2005), 2.

30. Ibid., 40.

31. Data for census tract 2403.

32. Sarah Fenske, "Fox Park Will Be the St. Louis Area's Hottest Neighborhood in 2017, Redfin Says," *Riverfront Times*, Janurary 20, 2017, https://www.riverfronttimes.com/newsblog/2017/01/20/fox-park-will-be-the-st-louis-areas-hottest-neighborhood-in-2017-redfin-says.

33. Quoted in Stefanie DeLuca and Peter Rosenblatt, "Sandtown-Winchester—Baltimore's Daring Experiment in Urban Renewal: 20 Years Later, What Are the Lessons Learned?" *The Abell Report* 26, no. 8 (November 2013).

34. DeLuca and Rosenblatt, "Sandtown-Winchester," quoting the *Baltimore Sun*, July 23, 1995.

35. Michael S. Rosenwald and Michael A. Fletcher, "Why Couldn't $130 Million Transform One of Baltimore's Poorest Places?" *Washington Post*, May 2, 2015, https://www.washingtonpost.com/local/why-couldnt-130-million-transform-one-of-baltimores-poorest-places/2015/05/02/0467ab06-f034-11e4-a55f-38924fca94f9_story.html?utm_term=.72b4865b5de7.

36. "Homeowners Begin Receiving Free Home Repair & Modification Assistance Authorized by City Council," Philadelphia City Council, Council News, May 18, 2017, http://phlcouncil.com/PHDC-BSRP-funding.

37. "Frequently Asked Questions: Tiering Process for Rental Licensing Inspections and Annual Renewal Billing," City of Minneapolis website, http://www

.minneapolismn.gov/www/groups/public/@regservices/documents/webcontent/wcms1p-144603.pdf.

38. J. C. Reindl, "Why Detroit's Lights Went Out," *Detroit Free Press*, November 17, 2013, https://www.usatoday.com/story/news/nation/2013/11/17/detroit-finances-dark-streetlights/3622205/.

39. Detroit Public Lighting Authority website, http://www.pladetroit.org/about-us/.

40. J. C. Reindl, "Detroit's Streetlights Go from Tragedy to Bragging Point," *Detroit Free Press*, December 15, 2016, http://www.freep.com/story/news/local/michigan/2016/12/15/detroit-streetlights-go-tragedy-bragging-point/95483846/.

41. "Neighborhoods and Violent Crime: Research Spotlight," US Department of Housing & Urban Development, *Evidence Matters*, Summer 2016, https://www.huduser.gov/portal/periodicals/em/summer16/highlight2.html.

42. Amy E. Lerman and Vesla Weaver, "Staying Out of Sight? Concentrated Policing and Local Political Action," *Annals of the American Academy of Political and Social Science* 651, no. 1 (2014): 202–19.

43. Nancy La Vigne, Jocelyn Fontaine, and Anamika Dwivedi, "How Do People in High-Crime, Low-Income Communities View the Police?" (Washington DC: Urban Institute, February 2017), 8, 10.

44. *Guide to Critical Issues in Policing*, US Department of Justice, Community Relations Service, 2016, https://www.justice.gov/crs/file/836416/download.

45. Quoted in "What Happened When Camden Started Rethinking Policing to Build Trust," *PBS Newshour*, June 30, 2017, http://www.pbs.org/newshour/bb/happened-camden-started-rethinking-policing-build-trust/.

Chapter 9

1. Rev. Ricky Burgess, "What Homewood Could Be," *Pittsburgh Post-Gazette*, September 23, 2015, http://www.post-gazette.com/opinion/2015/09/23/What-Homewood-could-be/stories/201509230017.

2. John Edgar Wideman, *Hiding Place* (New York: Houghton Mifflin, 1981), 59.

3. Edward Glaeser, *Triumph of the City* (New York: Penguin Press, 2011), 70.

4. Devon Douglas-Bowers, *Global Research* website, blog post, January 9, 2011, http://www.globalresearch.ca/intergenerational-poverty-in-america/22705.

5. Ben Gitis and Tara O'Neill Hayes, "The Value of Introducing Work Requirements to Medicaid," *American Action Forum* website, blog post, May 2, 2017, https://www.americanactionforum.org/research/value-introducing-work-requirements-medicaid/.

6. Barbara Ehrenreich, "It Is Expensive to Be Poor," *Atlantic Monthly*, January 13, 2014, https://www.theatlantic.com/business/archive/2014/01/it-is-expensive-to-be-poor/282979/.

7. Quoted in Alana Semuels, "A Different Approach to Breaking the Cycle of Poverty," *Atlantic Monthly*, December 24, 2014, https://www.theatlantic.com/business/archive/2014/12/a-different-approach-to-breaking-the-cycle-of-poverty/384029/.

8. Paul Jargowsky, *Concentration of Poverty in the New Millennium* (New York: The Century Foundation, 2013), 22.

9. Katie Buitrago, Amy Rynell, and Samantha Tuttle, *Cycle of Risk: The Intersection of Poverty, Violence, and Trauma* (Chicago: Heartland Institute, 2017), 17.

10. Erwin Parson, "Inner City Children of Trauma: Urban Violence Traumatic Stress Response Syndrome (U-VTS) and Therapists' Responses," in *Countertransference in the Treatment of PTSD,* edited by J. P. Wilson and J. D. Lindy (New York: Guilford Publications, 1994), 157.

11. Anne Gunderson, "Breaking the Cycle of Inner City Violence with PTSD Care," *Chicago Policy Review,* June 2, 2017, http://chicagopolicyreview.org/2017/06/02/breaking-the-cycle-of-inner-city-violence-with-ptsd-care/.

12. Quoted in "Inner City Violence and PTSD—A Hidden Epidemic," *Faces of PTSD* website, blog post, October 15, 2015, http://www.facesofptsd.com/civilian-ptsd-resources-blog/2015/10/15/inner-city-violence-ptsd-a-hidden-epidemic.

13. Patrick Sharkey, *Stuck in Place: Urban Neighborhoods and the End of Progress toward Racial Equality* (Chicago: University of Chicago Press, 2013), 46.

14. Alan Mallach, "The Uncoupling of the Economic City: Increasing Spatial and Economic Polarization in American Older Industrial Cities," *Urban Affairs Review* 51, no. 4 (2015): 443–73.

15. Stephen J. Rose, "Mismatch: How Many Workers with a Bachelor's Degree Are Overqualified for Their Jobs?" Washington, DC: Urban Institute, 2017, https://www.urban.org/sites/default/files/publication/87951/college_mismatch_final.pdf.

16. Phillip Moss and Chris Tilly, "'Soft Skills' and Race: An Investigation of Black Men's Employment Problems," *Work and Occupations* 23, no. 3 (August 1996): 259.

17. Lauren Rivera, "Hiring as Cultural Matching: The Case of Elite Professional Firms," *American Sociological Review* 77, no. 6 (2012): 999–1022.

18. Marianne Bertrand and Sendhil Mullainathan, "Are Emily and Greg More Employable than Lakisha and Jamal? A Field Experiment on Labor Market Discrimination," *American Economic Review* 94, no. 4 (2004): 991–1013.

19. *Report of the National Advisory Commission on Civil Disorders* (Washington, DC: Government Printing Office, 1968), 262, 416, 440, and 444.

20. Natalie Holmes and Alan Berube, "The Earned Income Tax Credit and Community Economic Stability," *Insight* (Fall 2015), http://www.gistfunders.org/documents/GCYFInSightFall2015.pdf.

21. Elizabeth Kneebone and Natalie Holmes, "Fighting Poverty at Tax Time Through the EITC," Brookings Institution website, blog post, http://www.brookings.edu/blogs/the-avenue/posts/2014/12/16-poverty-tax-eitc-kneebone-holmes.

22. Robert Greenstein, "New Research: EITC Boosts Employment; Lifts Many More Out of Poverty than Previously Thought," Center for Budget and Policy Priorities, *Off the Charts,* blog post, July 23, 2015, https://www.cbpp.org/blog/new-research-eitc-boosts-employment-lifts-many-more-out-of-poverty-than-previously-thought.

23. Matthew Desmond, *Evicted: Poverty and Profit in the American City* (New York: Crown Publishers, 2016), 295.

24. Ibid., 4–5.

25. Family Independence Initiative website, https://www.fii.org/.

26. "Usual Weekly Earnings of Wage and Salary Workers," Second Quarter 2017 and Second Quarter 1997, US Bureau of Labor Statistics, https://www.bls.gov/news.release/pdf/wkyeng.pdf, https://www.bls.gov/news.release/history/wkyeng_072297.txt.

27. Timothy J. Bartik, Brad J. Hershbein, and Marta Lachowska, *The Effects of the Kalamazoo Promise Scholarship on College Enrollment, Persistence, and Completion* (Kalamazoo, MI: W. E. Upjohn Institute, Working Paper 15-229, 2015), http://research .upjohn.org/cgi/viewcontent.cgi?article=1246&context=up_workingpapers.

28. National Center for Educational Statistics website, https://nces.ed.gov/pro grams/digest/d15/tables/dt15_306.10.asp?current=yes.

29. Quoted in "In Higher Education Black Women Are Far Outpacing Black Men," *Journal of Blacks in Higher Education* 17 (Autumn 1997): 86.

30. "The Promise of College Completion: Kipp's Early Successes and Challenges," Kipp Foundation, 2011, 8.

31. Christina Clark Tuttle et al., *KIPP Middle Schools: Impacts on Achievement and Other Outcomes: Final Report* (Princeton, NJ: Mathematica Policy Research, February 27, 2013), xiii.

32. "The Promise of College Completion," 4.

33. Quoted in David Leonhardt, "Schools That Work," *New York Times*, November 4, 2016, https://www.nytimes.com/2016/11/06/opinion/sunday/schools-that-work .html?mcubz=1.

34. Joshua D. Angrist et al., "Stand and Deliver: Effects of Boston's Charter High Schools on College Preparation, Entry, and Choice," *Journal of Labor Economics* 34, no. 2, pt. 1 (2016), 275–318.

35. Atila Abdulkadiroglu, Parag A. Pathak, and Christopher Walters, "Free to Choose: Can School Choice Reduce Student Achievement?" National Bureau of Economic Research, 2017, https://economics.mit.edu/files/12494.

36. Kate Zernicke, "A Sea of Charter Schools in Detroit Leaves Students Adrift," *New York Times*, June 28, 2016, https://www.nytimes.com/2016/06/29/us/for-detroits -children-more-school-choice-but-not-better-schools.html?mcubz=1.

37. Julian Vasquez Heilig, "10 Things to Know about the Charter School Debate," *The Progressive*, August 25, 2016, http://progressive.org/public-school-shakedown /10-things-know-charter-school-debate/.

38. Jim Horn, "KIPP Denies Access to KIPP Memphis 'Public' Schools," *Memphis Schools Matter* blog, May 5, 2014, http://memphisschoolsmatter.blogspot .com/2014/05/kipp-denies-access-to-kipp-memphis.html.

39. "Why Students Call KIPP 'Kids in Prison,'" *Schools Matter* website, blog post, March 23, 2012, http://www.schoolsmatter.info/2012/03/why-students-call-kipp -kids-in-prison.html.

40. Valerie Strauss, "To Trump's Education Pick, the U.S. Public School System Is a 'Dead End,'" *Washington Post*, December 21, 2016, https://www.washingtonpost .com/news/answer-sheet/wp/2016/12/21/to-trumps-education-pick-the-u-s-public -school-system-is-a-dead-end/?utm_term=.41583c4f896d.

41. Daniel C. Vock, "Rerouted: Big-City Bus Systems Are Finding Ways to Dig Out from Decades of Stagnation," *Governing* 30, no. 12 (September 2017): 40.

42. Lisa Margonelli, "The (Illegal) Private Bus System That Works," *Atlantic CityLab*, October 5, 2011, https://www.theatlantic.com/national/archive/2011/10 /the-illegal-private-bus-system-that-works/246166/.

43. ICF International, *2011 Evaluation of the National Ways to Work Program* (Fairfax, VA: ICF International, 2011), https://waystowork.org/docs/evaluations /2011EvalReport.pdf.

44. Binyamin Appelbaum, "Out of Trouble, but Criminal Records Keep Men Out of Work," *New York Times*, February 28, 2015, https://www.nytimes.com/2015/03/01 /business/out-of-trouble-but-criminal-records-keep-men-out-of-work.html.

45. Poverty and Opportunity Profile, The Sentencing Project website, http:// www.sentencingproject.org/wp-content/uploads/2015/11/Americans-with-Criminal Records-Poverty-and-Opportunity-Profile.pdf.

46. Devah Pager, "The Mark of a Criminal Record," *American Journal of Sociology* 108, no. 5 (March 2003): 937–75.

47. State of Iowa website, https://tax.iowa.gov/income-tax-benefit-iowa-employers -who-hire-ex-offenders.

48. See: Safer Foundation website and 2016 Annual Report at http://www.safer foundation.org and http://www.saferfoundation.org/files/documents/SFR_AR2016 .pdf.

49. Abstract June 2017, City of Baltimore, Mayor's Office of Employment Development website, http://moed.baltimorecity.gov/sites/default/files/1b4j_abstract_0617 .pdf.

50. Steven Rothschild, *The Non Nonprofit: For-Profit Thinking for Nonprofit Success* (San Francisco: Jossey-Bass, 2012), 101–2.

51. Ibid., 103.

52. Video from Twin Cities RISE! website at http://www.twincitiesrise.org/who -we-are/.

53. Greg Fisher, "Cradle to Career Is Focus of Education Efforts," *Louisville Courier-Journal*, September 20, 2015, http://www.courier-journal.com/story/opinion/2015 /09/20/cradle-career-focus-education-efforts/32564607/.

54. Kimberly McLain, "Hiring Locally Makes Good Business Sense," *Star-Ledger* (Newark, NJ), July 16, 2017, D4.

55. Robert S. Stokes, "Newark Workforce Landscape Assessment," prepared for the New Jersey Institute for Social Justice, the Newark Community Development Network, and The Enterprise Foundation, 2002, https://d3n8a8pro7vhmx.cloudfront .net/njisj/pages/164/attachments/original/1458586251/workforce.pdf?1458586251.

Chapter 10

1. George Sternlieb, "Are Cities Worth Saving?" in *The City in the Seventies*, edited by Robert K. Yin (Itasca, IL: F. E. Peacock Publishers Inc., 1972), 263.

2. Robin Meiksins, "Tom L. Johnson," Cleveland Historical, https://clevelandhis torical.org/items/show/329, accessed December 17, 2017.

3. Charles M. Tiebout, "A Pure Theory of Local Expenditures," *Journal of Political Economy* 64, no. 5 (1956): 416–24, 418.

4. Paul E. Peterson, *City Limits* (Chicago: University of Chicago Press, 1981), 20.

5. Ibid., 30.

6. Harvey Molotch, "The City as a Growth Machine: Toward a Political Economy of Place," *American Journal of Sociology* 82, no. 2 (September 1976): 309–32, 309. As of mid-2017, according to Google Scholar, this paper had been cited by 2,875 other

scholarly publications, topped, however, by more than 16,000 citations for Tiebout's article noted above.

7. Adam M. Zaretsky, "Should Cities Pay for Sports Facilities?" St. Louis Federal Reserve Bank, *The Regional Economist*, April 2001, https://www.stlouisfed.org /publications/regional-economist/april-2001/should-cities-pay-for-sports-facilities.

8. Kevin J. Delaney and Rick Eckstein, *Public Dollars, Private Stadiums* (New Brunswick, NJ: Rutgers University Press, 2003), 71.

9. "Summary of Total Cost and Public Subsidy for NFL Stadiums Constructed or Significantly Renovated Since 1990," *League of Fans* website, http://www.leagueof fans.org/mlbstadiums1990.html. Delaney and Eckstein quote a figure for the construction of the baseball stadium more than double that shown on the League of Fans summary. The League of Fans site, though, is the only one that provides data for all three stadiums.

10. Delany and Eckstein, *Public Dollars, Private Stadiums*, 198.

11. Tara Nurin, "The List: Camden Banks on Millions in Tax Subsidies to Help Fund Its Future," NJ Spotlight, October 6, 2015, http://www.njspotlight.com/stories/15/10 /05/the-list-camden-banks-on-millions-in-tax-subsidies-to-fund-its-future/.

12. Kevin C. Gillen, "Philadelphia's Ten-Year Property Tax Abatement," Business Industry Association of Philadelphia, March 2017, https://chambermaster.blob.core .windows.net/userfiles/UserFiles/chambers/9394/File/BIA-AbatementFullReport _Final.pdf.

13. See: https://en.wikipedia.org/wiki/Cargo_cult.

14. Clarence N. Stone, "Urban Regimes and the Capacity to Govern: A Political Economy Approach," *Journal of Urban Affairs* 15, no. 1 (1993): 1–28, 7, 8.

15. Quoted in Stone, "Urban Regimes," 8.

16. Ibid., 20.

17. Richard Schragger, *City Power: Urban Governance in a Global Age* (New York: Oxford University Press, 2016), 216–17.

18. Norton E. Long, "A Marshall Plan for Cities?" *The Public Interest* 46 (Winter 1977): 54.

19. Matt Katz, "Camden Rebirth: A Promise Still Unfulfilled," *Philadelphia Inquirer*, November 8, 2009, http://www.philly.com/philly/news/special_packages/inquirer /20091108_Camden_Rebirth__A.html.

20. Abraham H. Maslow, "A Theory of Human Motivation," *Psychological Review* 50, no. 4 (1943): 370–96.

21. According to the Talmud (Tractate Shabbat 31a), the first-century sage Hillel, when asked by a prospective convert to Judaism to teach him the whole Torah while he stood on one leg, replied: "That which is hateful unto you do not do to your neighbor. This is the whole of the Torah, the rest is commentary. Go forth and study." For a commentary on that saying, including evidence that it is probably apocryphal, by Rabbi Louis Jacobs, see: *My Jewish Learning* website, http://www.myjewishlearn ing.com/article/hillel/.

22. Marni von Wilpert, "City Governments Are Raising Standards for Working People—and State Legislators Are Lowering Them Back Down," Economic Policy Institute website, August 26, 2017, http://www.epi.org/publication/city-governments

-are-raising-standards-for-working-people-and-state-legislators-are-lowering
-them-back-down/.

23. Sendhil Mullainathan, "Get Ready for Technological Upheaval by Expecting the Unimagined," *New York Times*, September 2, 2017, https://www.nytimes
.com/2017/09/02/business/economy/get-ready-for-technological-upheaval-by
-expecting-the-unimagined.html.

Chapter 11

1. Jonathan Matthew Smucker, "The Danger of Fetishizing Revolution," from
Waging Non-Violence, July 1, 2014, https://wagingnonviolence.org/feature/danger
-fetishizing-revolution/.

2. Dowell Myers, "Peak Millennials: Three Reinforcing Cycles That Amplify the
Rise and Fall of Urban Concentration by Millennials," *Housing Policy Debate* 26, no.
6 (2016). Myers's analysis and conclusions have been sharply challenged by Urban
Observatory's Joe Cortright; see "Here's What's Wrong with That 'Peak Millennials' Story," *CityLab*, January 24, 2017, https://www.citylab.com/equity/2017/01/flood
-tide-not-ebb-tide-for-young-adults-in-cities/514283/.

3. This was the pledge made in the 1949 Housing Act, US Code 42, chapter 8A,
Subchapter I, §1441.

4. The per-inmate annual cost of incarceration in 2012 in Maryland was $38,383.
See: Christian Henrichson and Ruth Delaney, *The Price of Prisons: What Incarceration Costs Taxpayers* (New York: Vera Institute, 2012), https://storage.googleapis.com
/vera-web-assets/downloads/Publications/price-of-prisons-what-incarceration
-costs-taxpayers/legacy_downloads/price-of-prisons-updated-version-021914.pdf.

5. Jeff Barker, "Team Named to Study Convention Center Expansion, Possible
New Arena," *Baltimore Sun*, December 17, 2017, http://www.baltimoresun.com
/news/maryland/bs-bz-convention-center-study-20170504-story.html.

6. Eileen M. O'Brien and Chuck Dervarics, *Pre-Kindergarten: What the Research
Shows* (Alexandria, VA: Center for Public Education, 2007), http://www.centerfor
publiceducation.org/Main-Menu/Pre-kindergarten/Pre-Kindergarten/Pre-kinder
garten-What-the-research-shows.html.

7. "Now in Control, Will Newark Put Kids First?" Editorial, *Star-Ledger* (Newark, NJ), September 16, 2017, http://www.nj.com/opinion/index.ssf/2017/09/newarks
_back_in_control_of_its_schools_will_it_put.html#incart_river_index.

8. This includes what are known as "project-based" vouchers, where the voucher is
contractually tied to a particular housing unit, often in a project created through the
Low Income Tax Credit or other subsidized-housing program. If the tenant moves,
she loses her voucher, which becomes available to the next tenant. This is in contrast
to the regular "tenant-based" or "portable" voucher, which the tenant can take with
her to another unit. Roughly two-thirds of all vouchers are portable, and one-third
project-based.

9. Allison Allbee, Rebecca Johnson, and Jeffrey Lubell, *Preserving, Protecting,
and Expanding Affordable Housing: A Policy Toolkit for Public Health* (Oakland, CA:
ChangeLab Solutions, 2015), 21.

10. J. D. Vance, *Hillbilly Elegy* (New York: HarperCollins, 2016), 238.

11. For a discussion of Sampson's collective efficacy theory, see: Robert J. Sampson, "Collective Efficacy Theory: Lessons Learned and Directions for Future Inquiry," *Taking Stock: The Status of Criminological Theory* 15 (2008).

12. Catherine Tumber, *Small, Gritty, and Green* (Cambridge, MA: MIT Press, 2012), xvi.

13. Robert L. Smith, "Youngstown Business Incubator Named World's Best," *Cleveland Plain Dealer*, September 16, 2014, http://www.cleveland.com/business/index.ssf/2014/09/youngstown_business_incubator.html.

14. Quoted in Claire Cain Miller, "Why Men Don't Want Jobs Done Mostly by Women," *New York Times*, January 4, 2017, https://www.nytimes.com/2017/01/04/upshot/why-men-dont-want-the-jobs-done-mostly-by-women.html?mcubz=1.

15. Richard C. Longworth, *Caught in the Middle: America's Heartland in the Age of Globalism* (New York: Bloomsbury, 2008), 47–48.

16. Quoted in Miller, "Why Men Don't Want Jobs Done Mostly by Women."

17. Scott Andes et al., *Capturing the Next Economy: Pittsburgh's Rise as a Global Innovation City* (Washington, DC: The Brookings Institution, 2017), https://www.brookings.edu/wp-content/uploads/2017/09/pittsburgh_full.pdf.

18. Ibid., 30.

19. Ibid., 20.

20. Ibid., 6.

21. Playhouse Square website, http://www.playhousesquare.org/about-playhousesquare-main/about-playhousesquare.

22. David Z. Morris, "Why Millennials Are About to Leave Cities in Droves," *Fortune*, March 28, 2016, http://fortune.com/2016/03/28/millennials-leaving-cities/.

23. Although the saying is most often attributed to the Danish physicist, it almost certainly does not originate with him, nor with Yogi Berra; the best available evidence suggests that it is Danish, but from an earlier, anonymous source. See: https://quoteinvestigator.com/2013/10/20/no-predict/.

24. Aric Jenkins, "Robots Could Steal 40% of U.S. Jobs by 2030," *Fortune*, March 24, 2017, http://fortune.com/2017/03/24/pwc-robots-jobs-study/.

25. Bureau of Labor Statistics, Current Population Survey, https://www.bls.gov/cps/cpsaat11.pdf.

26. Quoted in Vinnie Lauria, "What Makes an Asian Tiger? Singapore's Unlikely Economic Success Lies in Its History," *Forbes Asia*, July 10, 2014, https://www.forbes.com/sites/forbesasia/2014/07/10/what-makes-an-asian-tiger-singapores-unlikely-economic-success-lies-in-its-history/#19d637366697.

About the Author

Alan Mallach is a senior fellow at the Center for Community Progress in Washington, DC. A city planner, advocate, and writer, he is nationally known for his work on housing, economic development, and urban revitalization, and has helped local governments and community organizations across the country frame creative policies and strategies to rebuild their cities and neighborhoods. A former director of housing and economic development in Trenton, New Jersey, he currently teaches in the graduate city planning program at Pratt Institute in New York City. He has spoken on housing and urban issues in the United States, Europe, Israel, and Japan, and was a visiting scholar at the University of Nevada Las Vegas for the 2010-2011 academic year. His books include *America's Urban Future: Lessons from North of the Border* (with Ray Tomalty), *A Decent Home: Planning, Building and Preserving Affordable Housing*, and *Bringing Buildings Back: From Vacant Properties to Community Assets*, which has become a resource for thousands of planners, lawyers, public officials, and community leaders dealing with problem property and revitalization issues. He holds a bachelor's degree from Yale University, and is also known as a pianist, composer, and author of books on Italian opera.

Index